On The Road

26 HITMAKERS OF THE FIFTIES & SIXTIES TELL THEIR OWN AMAZING STORIES

Dave Nicolson

MUSIC MENTOR BOOKS

York, England

For Bruno

Always On The Road.

Foreword

In this business the requests for interviews are numerous — so too are the times that your words are twisted or misquoted. What swayed me to contribute to this book was the author's clear intention to let the artists tell it like it was or how they want it to be remembered.

Looking at my fellow contributors, who represent the cream of our popular music industry from the late Fifties and early Sixties, I know that they must have responded for the same reason.

This is not one of those 'Where Are They Now?' books and it casts no opinions or judgments other than those expressed by the subjects. What many people forget is that an artist's career rarely ends after the last hit record. Most remain in the business as long as they have an audience. It is their livelihood as well as their driving force.

Many of my idols and friends are in these pages. Some of them I have had the privilege to work with, others have simply been passing back and forth for years without our paths crossing. Each one of them has made a unique contribution to the music that we all love — good old rock and roll — and I am proud to be in their company.

I read these accounts and the memories come flooding back. The joy and sadness of teenage years and careers encapsulated forever in two-and-a-half minute black vinyl jewels. Yes, there is magic for me here and for all lovers of an era and its music which remain timeless.

Bobby Vee

Contents

Contents

Introduction

Like millions of other people, music and the emotions it stirs has played a large part in my life. Having been introduced to variety theatre as a child where you could see stars from radio, screen and recording studio, going to pop concerts in adolescence and hanging around stage doors to see artists who had caught my ear and imagination on disc was a natural progression.

I had always seen the reality behind the 'glamour', but this simply intensified the fascination. We used to see the tour coach disgorge tired performers who, during long twice-nightly tours, often didn't know which town they were in. Sometimes the headliners would arrive in a separate car with their manager or family. All were human with human needs. From cheap cafes and hotel accommodation to female company arranged by the stage-door keeper and asked to stand under the lamplight so that the experienced leather-clad rocker, unseen at an upstairs dressing room window, could make his selection. We got glimpses of star lives and personalities from doormen, chauffeurs, coach drivers, hotel staff, fellow performers and of course the artists themselves.

Occasionally as a youngster I would don a display sandwich-board to sell glossy 10 x 8" photographs of the appearing acts and others outside theatres and auditoriums on concert nights. The street-sellers who employed us operated in conjunction with the artists on the show, who received a percentage of the sales. I rarely made enough for a second performance ticket, but usually earned enough to buy a photo or a show programme and sometimes got backstage when the money was handed over. It was evident then that many of the big names with big chart hits were not on big money.

I was there with a first-house ticket in Newcastle City Hall for Buddy Holly & The Crickets in 1958 when comedian/compère Des O'Connor looked at all the rows of empty seats and asked if the place was a multi-storey car park during the day! In showbusiness death at a young age has always been a great creator of legend.

Many times, we were asked to recommend places to eat. One of our number guided Buddy Holly to a local bus station café for an inexpensive meal of egg and chips. Thirty years on, one of the original Crickets, intent on buying an after-show supper, went around carefully comparing pizza prices at the city's fast food outlets. Those good ole boys sure knew the value of their hard-earned dollar and where they had come from.

For the most part they treated their public politely and patiently. Many were not much older than us, but their PR skills were well honed. Phil Everly didn't even blink when one fan introduced his young daughter and said: 'Phil, this is little Susie — the one you've got to wake up for.' A tired Bobby Vee's good humour never wavered when a whole family of fans asked him to sign some thirty or forty items that they had brought along after the show. Pat Boone never even lifted an eyebrow when he politely advised a persistent photographer to 'watch your gonads' as the chauffeur struggled to open his limousine door. Showbusiness is a tough world and these artists had to conceal their feelings and wear a public mask from a very young age.

Their polish only served to accentuate the gap between their success and our lack of it. With our cheap guitars, front-room skiffle and pop groups miming to records, big ambitions, and a diet of overnight success stories fed by the music papers and record sleevenotes, we felt the divide keenly.

On leaving school to start work, money became a little easier and I was fortunate enough to see many great acts at the height of their careers. Still, financial constraints and girlfriends made for some hard choices when two shows played within a week of each other. I never really forgave one young lady who preferred another show to that of Little Richard and Sam Cooke, as the chance to see the latter never came again.

One popular perception of rock and roll has always been that it is about having fun — for both public and performer. I knew what it felt like to sit in the audience, but wanting to know how *they* felt and saw things, and to record a colourful fragment of my own generation's social and emotional history were my motivations for conducting these interviews. Their careers and recordings have affected millions of people and, through memory and nostalgia, continue doing so.

Like any other commercial product sold to the public, artists and their talent had to be properly packaged and presented. However, you won't find much glamour within these pages; that started and ended on stage. All the rest was a very hard grind tempered with the fun of being young and getting paid for doing what you loved to do. In the company of fellow performers, lifelong friendships and memories were forged. You learned your craft from within yourself and those around you, and hopefully, sometime in your career, got a decent proportion of what was due to you.

Many of these artists were only able to have careers because of the large number of small independent record companies which existed at that time in America and allowed a wide diversity of music to be heard. It is sad to think that if they had been setting off in today's accountancy-controlled, monopolistic record industry, such great acts would probably not have been able to launch their talent. High returns on intensive investment are everything; the music no longer seems to matter.

Having been on and off the road for twenty years, my own journey is finished. The first interview with Charlie Gracie was recorded in 1981; the last one, with Freddy Cannon, took place in 2000. My agreement with all subjects is that the interviews would be faithfully reproduced. If they chose to give a version that did not accord with known facts I may have challenged it, but the last word was theirs. After all it was *their* road, and how they remembered it, not mine.

Acknowledgments

I am indebted to all the artists in this book for their interest, time and patience, and for all the pleasure that they have given and continue to give as entertainers. Special thanks to Bobby Vee for his considerable help and kindness over a number of years and for his *Foreword*. Thanks also to all the concert promoters and tour managers who facilitated interviews. Finally, my appreciation to the publisher and editor George White for his hard work, attention to detail and provision of an index, and to the other collectors and enthusiasts who kindly supplied additional illustrations.

On a personal note, I wish to record my appreciation to Steve and Christine Chick in Oxenhope, West Yorkshire for their friendship and Steve's migraine cure of full-volume blues music; my friends the Heller family of Putnam Valley, New York; the late Burne Hogarth; and the Class of '59 — even if a *Dream Lover* never came your way.

Dave Nicolson
July 2002

1

PARTY TIME
Gary 'U.S.' Bonds

His unusual stage name and string of memorable early Sixties hits including *New Orleans*, *Quarter To Three* and *School Is Out* would alone have ensured Gary 'U.S.' Bonds a place in pop history. But Fate had other plans and, thanks to a surprisingly successful collaboration with Bruce Springsteen, he resurfaced in 1981 for a second spell of chart success with *This Little Girl Is Mine*, a track off his *Dedication* album.

My real name is Gary Anderson and I was born in Jacksonville, Florida on June 6, 1949. Of course 1949! Okay, okay, seriously, it was 1939. From the age of two or three I was raised in Norfolk, Virginia and now live in New York.

My father was a professor which had nothing to do with music — he *hated* music — and my mother was a teacher who also taught music for a while, so I guess that's where I got it from. She tried to get me to do piano and I didn't want to do that because it was a wimpy thing to do in Virginia at the time... me being the leader of a gang. *[laughter]* The story that I sang in a church choir at the age of nine is untrue — I never sang in a choir.

My early musical training was basically just listening to the radio and picking up what I could from there. It was many years into my life before I realized that I enjoyed doing it — because I couldn't sing *at all* during the Fifties. I had no knowledge of how to sing or what. I sounded as bad as anybody else in the shower. But I went down to a theatre in Norfolk and I saw some acts there like Bullmoose Jackson — who you probably don't know of — and then the Flamingos came through one night and the Drifters. And then I went: 'Whoa! I think I want to do *that*.'

I got my start singing with a group, the Turks, on a street corner and Frank Guida came by and heard us. We were probably the only people he knew who sang and he asked us if we wanted to record as he was going to open a studio. About two years later, he did open the Norfolk Recording Studios and we went in, but by then most of the people who'd been in my group were in prison or in the services so I was the only one left. That's why I went in and did *New Orleans* by myself.

The Turks were formed in 1952. Actually, in the beginning it wasn't a group; it was a gang. We were pretty bad fellows and did a lot of naughty things. Then, out of boredom, we started singing and trying to copy the doo-wop material of the Drifters and the Flamingos. To start with, none of us could sing. We taught ourselves how to do it — in between fights.

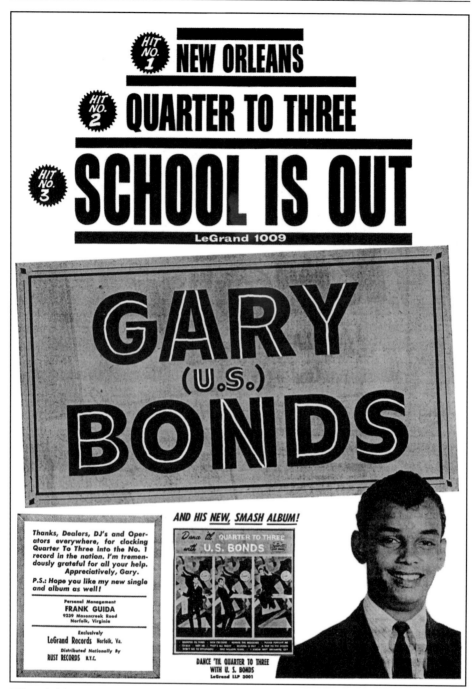

Billboard, July 1961

New Orleans wasn't really recorded in a garage as some books state, but Frank Guida's record studios were makeshift and naturally we used two-track for recording. None of us knew anything about recording or recording studios. In fact, our engineer and the original writer of New Orleans, Joe

Royster *[a friend of Frank Guida]* was a shoe salesman. He was a very, very fine gentleman and I always liked Joe, but the only thing that he knew was how to turn it on and turn it off! Everything was kind-of really screwed-up, but it all came together and we got a hit sound off it — thank God! The record was issued on Frank Guida's Legrand label.

I thought that *New Orleans* was a really good song, I really did. However, I didn't think that it was a hit because living in Virginia, which is a far cry from the music cities or capitals of the world like New York, Los Angeles and London, we didn't know that much about how to produce or do anything.

We were just working on our own, so we didn't know a hit from nothing. The backing noises on *New Orleans* were basically what anyone wanted to do, whatever they felt. We just went in and made sounds, and fortunately they were sounds that people wanted to hear. Like I say, we didn't know what we were doing — we were just doing something, not knowing that it was going to be a big thing later on in life.

Professionally, my first public performance came after that hit and was at the Howard Theatre in Washington, DC. That was a big thrill for me working with Ruth Brown, Louis Jordan, the Flamingos — I think they were on that show — and LaVern Baker. I had a ball!

I can't remember how I felt when *New Orleans* charted. Living in Virginia was a great thing to do and the record's success didn't bother me at all. I just kind-of fell into it all — no ego, no nothing. Looking back now, I find it amazing myself, but I guess at the time I was a little naïve — *very* naïve.

Frank Guida, who is my ex-manager, named me 'U.S. Bonds' which is probably one of the only things that he has done which was right! *[laughs]* Some people say that he got the idea from a government poster asking people to buy US Bonds, but I have no idea where he got the name from. He conjured it up in his mind and just tagged it. I guess it just felt good at the time. Either that, or he was trying to

LEGRAND
RECORDS

Record No.
1003
Pepe (BMI)

(KB-484)
Time: 2:44
Vocal

"NEW ORLEANS"
(Guida - Royster)

BY — U.S. BONDS

15

Billboard 1962 Who's Who In The World Of Music

induct me into the navy or army or something. I don't know what he was doing. In 1961, I became Gary 'U.S.' Bonds.

You mention *Please Forgive Me* on the other side of *New Orleans*. That was my mother's favourite. It is also the first song I ever tried to write in my life, and it's also one of my favourites. It could well be that you're right when you say that it is a cross between Tony Williams and Jackie Wilson, because at the time I was being influenced by other acts. When they said they needed another song for the flip-side of *New Orleans*, I said that I wanted to try mine and I did it. I guess that all of the influences in my career up to that point were involved in that one song.

I was singing the way I thought singers should sing, but I really didn't know. That's why I say that it took me a long time to learn how to sing, to create my own style, even though I had already created it and didn't know it. I had so many people that I was influenced by — I guess all the sounds just came together and made my own.

If I'd had the choice to record anything, it would have to be anything by Sam Cooke. Sam Cooke was my idol. He was the greatest singer ever. Otis Redding would be my next one. He was unique and a great, great artist. Unfortunately both of them are not with us today.

No, I never saw Gene Vincent in Norfolk at any time and was amazed to find out years later that he was from the same town. We did film different segments for the same film though, *Ring-A-Ding Rhythm**, in 1962. That was easy work. It was done in the States and took us about an hour to go in and record the songs, make a lot of money and leave.

The songs that I liked best weren't big sellers: records like *Get In A Groove* and *King Kong's Monkey*. Of my hits, I liked *New Orleans*, *Quarter To Three* and *School Is Out*. *School Is In* I really liked, but it didn't sell as much! I haven't picked a winner yet, but those are my favourites.

My run of hits came to an end in 1962, and from then until around 1980 *[before the association with Bruce Springsteen and the 'Dedication' album]*, we did Holiday Inns, Sheraton Hotels and a lot of cabaret stuff. Although not being in the spotlight at all, the success of my earlier records kept me working and it became my major job. I was able to work and make a really doggone good living doing that. I was very proud of it.

Looking back, I should've got rid of Frank Guida sooner! *[laughs]* On the personal side, I have a wife, we've been married twenty-three years, and I have a daughter who is twenty-two. I love them very much; they are the greatest people in my life and have been for twenty-three years. My wife keeps me all together. For my leisure, I am a golfer, a big golfer. If I'm home, I play golf. I don't care if it's zero degrees, I'm out there trying to do something.

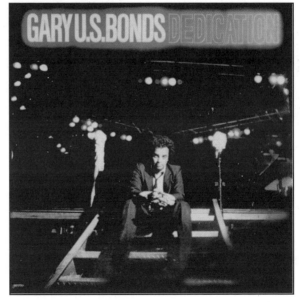

---

* UK title: *It's Trad, Dad.*

2

THE MAIN ATTRACTION
Pat Boone

Talented, well publicized and skilfully managed, Pat Boone was the acceptable face of Fifties rock and roll, and his clean-cut features are one of the enduring images of the era. His first releases — sanitized covers of original recordings by black artists — helped the new music gain acceptance within American white society, but his real forte was ballads. In the late Fifties, he enjoyed unprecedented success rivalling even Elvis Presley for a time.

It's late at night in Beverly Hills. I'm going to try and briefly answer your questions because I like the company that you are writing about and I'm happy to be in that company.

I was born Charles Eugene Boone on June 1, 1934 in Jacksonville, Florida, the great-great-great-great grandson of Daniel Boone, the frontiersman. During my mother's pregnancy, she and my father just *knew* that the baby was a girl and therefore selected the name Patricia. When a baby boy surprised them, they called me Charles Eugene, but nicknamed me 'Pat' — after their wishful thinking!

My earliest musical influence was Bing Crosby, but even before that momma taught my younger brother, Nick, who was a year younger, and me to play a little ukelele. When we were seven or eight years old, she taught us to play a few chords and sing harmony. We sang a few songs like *Sentimental Journey* to the delight of our family and relatives.

Gradually, I found that I could sing in school and whenever there was something musical to do there I would volunteer. So I would say momma first, and then we had some Bing Crosby records in the house. Early on, I decided that the quintessential pop singer was Bing Crosby and I have never changed my mind.

The earliest influences on my character were, of course, mom and daddy. Daddy was a building contractor and momma a registered nurse. There were no ministers in our immediate background, but my parents were serious Christians. They took my brother, two sisters and me to church since the time we were infants. We never missed a service: Sunday morning, Sunday School, Sunday night, Wednesday night and if there were revival meetings we were there for practically every one. Moving on to high school, my principal and Latin teacher, Mack Craig, was a significant influence.

I became a Christian when I was baptized at thirteen years of age. I

walked down the aisle at church and confessed that I believed that Jesus was the Son of God and wanted Him to be my Saviour; that I had sinned and needed his forgiveness.

And after that, I tried during my teenage years to be a good Christian and, I think, with some success — although, of course, always imperfectly. But I think by being Student Body President, President of the Junior Class and Cartoonist that, certainly from the age of thirteen onwards, I had stepped into some kind of leadership position and I have tried to live up to that.

My first amateur performance, apart from just family gatherings — and there were many of those — was at the Belle Meade Theatre's *Happiness Club*, a little stage-show on Saturday afternoons before the cartoons and the serialized dramatic things that used to run in movie theatres across America — westerns mainly, sometimes *The Lone Ranger* or *Batman*. It was at the Belle Meade Theatre, which was in a very nice suburb of Nashville, Tennessee that I auditioned somewhere around the age of twelve by singing in this amateur competition and did so a number of times after that. First prize was a banana split at the drugstore next to the theatre, and I did win it two or three times.

By the time I was in my mid-teens I wanted to be a singer, but thinking that this was an impossible dream, I planned to be a school-teacher of English and Speech during the week and a preacher on Sundays.

My family were supportive of my singing though they saw it as a hobby and did not think, I am sure, that it would ever be a career. Nor did they want it to be. With my religious background, we all believed that it was wrong to do any ballroom dancing — certainly any drinking — and therefore, what kind of experience did I possibly have to become a pop singer?

As I say, I decided in high school to be a teacher because I wanted my life to be worthwhile and meaningful. And I decided that the best way that I could do that was to stand in the crossroads of young people's lives, hopefully pointing them in the right direction. So, the teaching would simply be the means of earning a living and being in contact with young people in a role model position. I didn't care what the subject was, I just wanted to try to bend the twigs or to head kids in the right direction. Ironically, or perhaps fittingly, my singing career gave me the opportunity to do a lot of that — more than if I had been a school-teacher in only one place.

On the question of my early marriage, I don't think that anyone is ready for marriage at any age — not really ready for the responsibility. It's just something that you have to learn as you go. Shirley and I were nineteen and the only thing that made us ready was our Christian commitment and priorities. Because, when we did get married, we not only felt that we loved each other, but that we were making a covenant, an irrevocable commitment to God as well as to each other. I am quite sure that had it not been for that, then the stresses of an entertainment career and the fact that we got married so young would probably have torn us apart. But we just felt that splitting up was not an option. We had married for life and though we, of course, toyed with the idea separately — I don't think that we ever did together — it was really out of the question for us.

So we are very delighted that we stayed together. Now we are reaping, and have reaped, a lot of the many benefits of marrying young like being fit and enthusiastic so you can keep up with your kids. We had four in a hurry. When I graduated from college, we had all four kids and, of course, we sort-of grew up together. And, by the time they were married and I became a grandparent at age 42, we still had a whole lot of healthy young life in front of us.

In the early days of my recording career, for the first three or four years, Randy Wood of Dot Records chose most of my material. Eventually, I began to want a say, and have a say, in what I did, but up till then it was such an amazing dream come true and Randy did have a radar sense about what was commercial and what would sell. I am glad that he thought that I should do some standards as well as remakes of hits from the past and cover records of the present R&B things that were becoming rock and roll. So, I was delighted to let Randy choose all my material and certainly *Begin The Beguine*, *Harbor Lights*, *Stardust*, *Tenderly*... all those songs were his idea. I was very pleased to do them.

Eventually, I did have choice over recording material — though not without a struggle. *[In 1962]* I found a song called *Speedy Gonzales* in the Philippines, brought it home and was anxious to do it. Randy said: 'No, your rock and roll days are over. People want to hear movie themes from you now, they wouldn't buy you singing a rock and roll song.' I didn't agree. I argued with him for a year and finally he let me do it, and in a matter

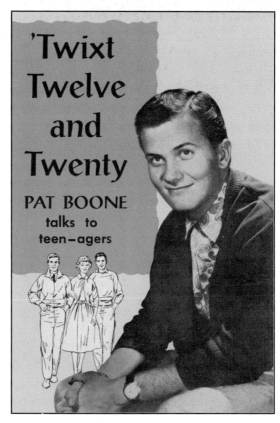

'Twixt Twelve and Twenty

PAT BOONE
talks to
teen-agers

of weeks it went right to No. 1 in virtually every country in the world that sold pop records. So, occasionally I was right.

I also brought a song back from Australia called *Tie Me Kangaroo Down Sport*. I did not convince him to let me do that until after Rolf Harris already had a worldwide smash *[1960]*. We did go in and record it, but it was too late. On another occasion, I brought a song back from England called *From Me To You* by a group called the Beatles, who were then unknown in the States.

In a way, the signing with Dot was a result of Arthur Godfrey. I was on Ted Mack's *Amateur Hour* and Arthur Godfrey's show and won them both on national television. Although nothing came from it immediately, they did of course arouse a lot of attention in Nashville and middle Tennessee where I grew up. And Randy, whose record company was located in Gallatin, a small rural town outside of Nashville, asked for us to meet when I came back from winning the Godfrey show. We shook hands over a hamburger and agreed that I would record for Dot once I had found a hit song.

Randy, of course, picked *Tutti Frutti, Ain't That A Shame*, all those early R&B songs because it was during that brief little period, of two to three years at the most, when R&B records could not get played on 95% of American radio stations, but they would play cleaned-up versions — it was called 'rock and roll' — by pop artists... and not just white artists, because Nat 'King' Cole and some other black artists also did their versions of R&B songs. But it was Randy's idea and, of course, I went along. I mean, all I wanted was to make some hit records and I hardly cared what kind of music it was.

I *did* care about lyrics. I changed lyrics sometimes, like in Little Richard's *Tutti Frutti*. I think his lyric was '*Boy you don't know what she do to me*'. I changed it to '*Pretty little Susie is the girl for me*' because I felt that his lyric was a little raunchy.

In a way, it was a clever marketing ploy to cover the records of black rock and rollers. But it was because rock and roll was starting to happen and nobody knew quite what it was. But one almost sure-fire way — or at least the highest-percentage way — of getting a rock and roll hit record was to find a R&B hit, because you knew that R&B hits could not be played on the majority of American radio stations. If you could do a cleaned-up version, then you were 75-80% on your way to having a hit record. The deejays knew it was a R&B hit and therefore were likely to play it in order to give it a chance as a pop record.

So, if you had done a good commercial job, you had a great shot, but that didn't last too long. In fairly short order — a couple of years or so — the audiences and the deejays began to demand to hear and play the originals, so the days of the cover record vanished.

I love and am grateful to Ivory Joe Hunter, the Flamingos, Little Richard and Fats Domino, and they were very grateful to me at the time: they said so openly and publicly. I have two or three tapes of interviews with Little Richard, and I went down to see Fats Domino in New Orleans at Al Hirt's place. Fats got me up on stage in front of a packed house, pointed to one of several diamond rings on his chubby fingers and said: 'You people see this diamond ring?' Then he pointed to me and said: 'This man bought me this ring with this song.' He then sat down at his piano and struck up with *Ain't That A Shame* and I sang it with him.

Fats and all the guys were saying that they knew the facts. They couldn't get played on pop stations — mainly white stations — and they were deliriously happy when a white artist or a pop artist would do a cover version of their song. Usually, they had written it and hopefully they had something to do with the publishing — although some of them got ripped-off. They knew that their songs and maybe their records were going to get exposed to a far wider audience because of it, and that's exactly what happened. So, they were grateful at the time. Occasionally now, looking back, Little Richard for example sometimes indicates that he was ripped off — not by me, but by publishers and record people. He feels that he never got paid for all that he did, and chances are that he is right.

I never bought the idea that a beat or a sound was necessarily the Devil's music. Contemporary Jesus gospel and Jesus music hadn't come into being yet and when it did I welcomed it. Back then, all I did was change the words and if I couldn't change the words, or felt I couldn't, then I wouldn't do the song. There wasn't anything intrinsically wrong with the music itself, and even though the word got around that I didn't want kids to dance to my music because I didn't dance, that really wasn't the case. I didn't care or feel it was my business whether they danced or didn't dance. I made my music to be heard and be enjoyed that way, and hoped that primarily that was the enjoyment — that kids loved to hear it.

Eventually, I got over the idea that there was anything wrong with dancing to it anyway. Of course, it was well known that I continued to be faithful and active in Church, so naturally I tried to be a good influence. I was keenly aware that kids were likely to imitate me when I was hot, so I would change the words to a Little Richard record or to some other rock and roll song. As I have said, if I couldn't change the words, then I wouldn't do the song and sometimes this meant that I lost the chance of a hit record. I remember when a song came along called *Roll With Me Henry* — 'Roll with me Henry, all night long...' — and I just felt that I couldn't change it even to *Rock With Me Henry*. Georgia Gibbs, I think, changed it to *Dance With Me Henry*. Why I didn't think of that, I don't know. If I had, I could have done it. We all knew it was going to be a big hit, and it was.

Some of my music *was* rock and roll of course, but I don't know if I'll ever make the Rock & Roll Hall Of Fame. If I do, it will be because they recognize that I was a catalyst and that, as much as Elvis perhaps, or for a little while more, I helped make rock and roll acceptable to a wide audience — even to parents — because mine seemed harmless and mine was antiseptic, a more 'sterile' kind of rock and roll. I look at it now and realize how tame it was — not that it was our intention. However, it had to be that way if it was going to be accepted by an audience that just wasn't ready for the raw, raunchy earthiness of R&B. And so, it served a purpose and did popularize rock and roll and, of course, as such *was* rock and roll, even though it was a tame version. Certainly, if the music of Ricky Nelson, Connie Francis and some of the other white artists of that day was rock and roll, so was mine. But, of course, I went on to things like movie themes, novelties, country and other kinds of music.

My own favourite recording, I think, would have to be the theme music from *Exodus* because I wrote the words and I think it is one of the most thrilling melodies to be written in pop music. I also like a song on the back of *Moody River* called *A Thousand Years*. I think it, too, is a powerful pop song emotionally and musically. But nobody ever heard it because it was on the back of a No. 1 smash hit. *A Thousand Years* was written by Red West who was of course the stunt-man, double, bodyguard friend of Elvis. He got the song to me. Why Elvis never did it I don't know, but I loved it.

Of course, *Love Letters In The Sand* and *April Love* I love because they were major, major records in my career. *April Love* has become my theme song and it was written for me by Sammy Fain and Paul Francis Webster. But just for pure singing enjoyment and musical quality, I like *Exodus* and *A Thousand Years*.

I would like to have recorded the

song *Moon River*, but Andy Williams did. I had the song first and Randy Wood and I decided that it was just too bland. It wasn't a love song and probably wouldn't be a big hit was our judgment. I've kicked myself about that a long time.

My own favourite artists were Bing Crosby, Perry Como, Nat 'King' Cole and, of course, Frank Sinatra.

You ask me about Bobby Darin — Walden Robert Cassotto. I have a lot of recollections of Bobby, more than I have time to tell you. At first, I was put off by his cockiness and the fact that he wanted to be a legend by the time he was thirty. And by the fact that he was very obviously imitating Frank

Sinatra. But gradually, I had to admire not only his audacity but his talent and his ability to accomplish what he set out to do. At first, I didn't think that he was a particularly good singer: I just didn't like the sound of his voice, which had a sort of thin, nasal quality. But I had to come to admire — like I did with Paul Anka — his ability to take what seemed to be a meagre vocal talent and stretch it, enlarge it and expand on it until it really became significant. Bobby proved himself when he did *Mack The Knife* — one of the great pop records of all time, *Beyond The Sea [La Mer]* and later, when he changed his sound 180° and did *If I Were A Carpenter*. I had to really tip my hat to him because he was inventive, audacious and talented.

Bobby was smart because he wrote and published a lot of his own music. So I was happy to know him and enjoyed the mental and verbal sparring that we did. And I'll tell you one quick story about him. I hosted a show for Coca-Cola in which I was supposed to be the Grand Old Man of the 'younger generation'. We had Bobby, Paul Anka, Frankie Avalon, Edd Byrnes, Annette, Connie Stevens. I think we also had Connie Francis and I forget who else on this big Coca-Cola special. Paul Anka was really upset because Bobby was so hip and sharp, and all the girl dancers and other people on the show got a kick out of his fast repartee. He was making jokes and poking fun at Paul and some of the others in the company. I had quick retorts, could hold my own, and would joust with him and enjoy it. But Paul, who came from Canada, was a little younger and he just wasn't used to that. He came to see me privately and said: 'Help me think of something to say to get back at Bobby.' and I said: 'Okay, I'll help you.'

There was a singer who was making a career of imitating Frank Sinatra on the West Coast; his name was Duke Hazlett. He wore a snap-brim hat,

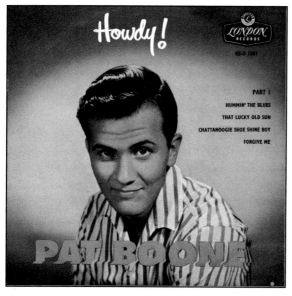

threw a trench-coat over his shoulder and sang all of Frank's songs. Duke did a lounge act and was known in showbusiness, so Bobby knew who he was, as did most of the folks on our show. So, I put Paul up to this, and the next time Bobby was holding court, making funny and being witty in front of everybody, Paul waited till there was a suitable moment and he interjected: 'Hey Bobby, you know I've been trying to think who it is that you remind me of.' Well, of course, Bobby wanted to remind everybody of Frank Sinatra so he said to Paul Anka: 'Who is it I remind you of?' and Paul said: 'Duke Hazlett!' Well, he got a big laugh from all the showbiz folks, but it made Bobby so mad that from then on he *really* gave Paul a hard time. Paul Anka very much regretted having gotten into any kind of verbal contest with Bobby.

It was a tremendous shock when Bobby Darin died. I don't think that many people knew — I didn't — that he had a congenital heart problem, and when he died at an early age it really was a genuine shock. He made a very big impact and I think he achieved his goal. I think he *did* become something of a legend in pop music by the time he was thirty.

The magazine hype between Elvis and myself didn't bother me. We both knew that it was good for our careers. And I must say that, though we were on a par for three or four years, in 1957 the *New Musical Express*, *Cash Box* and *Billboard* all voted me the No. 1 Male Singer of the Year after Elvis had been No. 1 in 1956 and again in 1958, '59 and so on. This manufactured rivalry helped both of us.

Soon after, in 1958–59, I began to feel that Elvis had certainly become the undisputed king of rock and roll and, since most of pop music for a while was rock and roll, I felt that he was on top.

That was okay with me. I'd never expected to be anywhere. He and I were friends anyway and, as our rented homes in Bel Air were very close to each other, we'd meet, laugh and kid each other about a lot of that hype. Elvis and I knew that we both had a lot of the same fans, and eventually I figured out the reason: it was because we appealed to different things in a lot of the same people. He was the rebel and the non-conformist, breaking the rules and winning; I was the conformist, playing by the rules and winning. And, of course, there is in most people the desire to be able to do that on their own: they are always fascinated by the guy who can break the rules and get away with it. One time, Elvis was asked if he was ever going to get married and have kids like Pat Boone and his famous answer at the time was: 'Why should I buy a cow when I can get milk through the fence?' And he gave it that lop-sided leer of his which fitted his image. However, when we met in each other's houses, particularly when he came to ours, it was very obvious that he was envious and there was a yearning that both Shirley and I would see when our kids jumped up on his lap. They didn't know who Elvis Presley The King of Rock and Roll was — he was just a friend of daddy and mommy's — but they liked him and he loved them. We could tell that he was aching to have this kind of thing himself. Eventually, when he did have, it didn't work out. And so, I was rarely ever envious of Elvis in any way.

Regarding my film career, yes, I agree *Yellow Canary* was good. It was written by Rod Serling and got great reviews both in the *New York Times* and the London *Times*. Unfortunately, the studio did very little — if anything — to promote it, so it never did a whole lot. The movie roles dried up and I dried up on them because my personal image was just completely out of synchronization with what they were doing. I couldn't conscientiously do most of the roles that were offered to me because more and more they wanted me to play against type, or to utilize my public image in a salacious or sensational way. They wanted me to play a good guy who went bad — a minister or family man who jumped into bed and had an affair with somebody and whose life was wrecked. They wanted to use me because I did symbolize something and they wanted to twist that and turn it into something else. I couldn't do it, and we went our separate ways. In spite of all that, I still think I may make a movie or two eventually because I did finally become an actor.

There is not a whole lot that I would have done differently. I certainly couldn't change or compromise my convictions, and I've had a wonderful career, so I'm grateful for all of that. I'd like to have had a son, but I tried as hard as I knew how when that was going on, so I don't guess that I could change that. Certainly, I wouldn't have missed having any of my daughters.

I *would* have accepted an invitation from a top TV direction/production team, Smith-Hemion, here in the States. I thought that I shouldn't do that at the time. I wish now that I had because I think that I would have settled into a long, easy, happy career on television. As it is, I have done specials and tried to do a series or two on my own which have lasted a brief time, and I think I may have missed an opportunity that was offered to me. I would have exerted my influence a little more to do more beautiful songs with Gordon Jenkins and Nelson Riddle and people that I could have recorded with at the time, in order to build up a stronger catalogue of really enduring music.

I think a lot of my music has been very commercial and contemporary, which served a purpose at the time but, to my ear and sensibilities at least, doesn't sound so great today except for the 'pretty' music like *Friendly Persuasion* and maybe *Love Letters In The Sand* and *April Love.* The early rock and roll and novelty records are okay for a time-capsule hearing, but not for enjoyable and career-building material. I think that Johnny Mathis, even Tony Bennett, certainly Frank Sinatra, have been geniuses in that way: in doing really tasteful stuff that bears repetition years later.

You ask me why I have never played Las Vegas casino lounges. Well, I have never wanted to appear in a lounge. The whole environment of it is just uncomfortable for me and I don't think that the people who go to lounges would necessarily want to hear me. However, I've certainly appeared in the main show-rooms in Las Vegas and held records at the Sahara and, for a little while, at the Sands and the Flamingo. The main rooms were fine as long as I could do my own show and they didn't tell me what I could or couldn't sing. I realized that I was performing for family people and that was okay. Even though the setting was never comfortable for me, I usually rented a house and had my family with me. In the daytime, we swam, played golf and had a ball. At night, I went over to the casino, did my two shows, went home and went to bed.

When it comes to touring, I have appeared in Playboy hotels and will appear most anywhere if the people who are putting on the shows will let me sing my songs in my way. Rarely, if ever, has anybody tried to restrict or inhibit my performance. I've even appeared at racetracks once or twice when people tried to key entertainment with the big crowds that come to the tracks. However, the sound, stages and so forth were really sub-standard. It was an environment I didn't really like.

Looking forward, I am going to continue to do some contemporary gospel and some traditional gospel. I think I'm going to do some good crossover country music. I may have to go in and produce it myself because right now the mind-set of the record business is that if you've had a major career and haven't had a hit for a while, it's over. Folks tend not to want to continue to let you get up at bat. I understand that line of thinking from the business and marketing side of things. However, I feel for people like Perry Como, Engelbert Humperdinck, Andy Williams, Connie Francis and many other terrific artists who don't have any recording contracts now, but who still perform as well or better than they ever did. I think in some ways they now have more to offer.

So, I am planning to start — and have already been in negotiations with several big, big business entities — an international label. It's called Gold Label but it's more like a senior tour, to make a golf analogy, of the seasoned pros who may not want to compete, and may not be *able* to compete, commercially with the likes of much younger performers like Madonna and Michael Jackson and certainly not with the big rock groups and so on, yet have big followings around the world. And so, we've got a concert, TV marketing and recording concept that I am putting together and I expect to be in the middle of it, but it will be a tremendous delight for me to be able to offer opportunities to other performers who I know are better than I am. Certainly, artists like Perry Como, Ella Fitzgerald and Andy Williams are treasures and they can still sing beautifully and *ought* to be singing. Therefore, if I can be instrumental in that way, then I'm going to be.

Personally, I still want to make my influence — such as it may be — felt in the lives of other people, not necessarily kids anymore, but anybody that cares what I do or think. I want to exert good, positive, moral and Christian influence while I can, because in the long run that is all that really matters — everything else is so temporal and transitory as to be almost irrelevant and unreal.

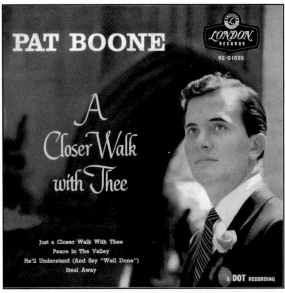

Jesus is still in charge of my life — least I *want* Him to be, and I *ask* Him to be. I suppose we all take the reins ourselves, whether we know it or not, and head off in a direction that may seem right or desirable — when maybe He is not heading us in that direction. However, since we are creatures of free will, He will allow us to do it.

Long ago, I was asked how much of my time I gave to Christian activity. I thought about it for a minute and said: 'A hundred percent.' I could tell that my reply startled the writer and so went on to say that, because I tried to be a hundred percent Christian, that meant that everything I did was a Christian activity because it was a Christian doing it. That doesn't mean that Jesus himself is always happy with what I do, but I try not to make him unhappy. I've long since learned, because He gave me my career miraculously, that I'm where He wants me to be.

I think He wants Christians in every honourable walk of life. We would make a terrible mistake to abandon any major interest in life — certainly entertainment — to non-Christian, hedonistic, non-believing, immoral or amoral people. It would be a shame. And, of course, I think that there are serious-thinking, highly-motivated and even Christian people in showbusiness. Certainly David Putnam *[Chariots of Fire]* and members of the group U2 are outspoken Christians, as well as some of the other groups who are very successful.

I don't think that you have to, or should, check or abandon your principles when you go into a recording studio or on stage, television or appear in movies. I think if God wants to use you in that arena — and if you want Him to — that He can and will give you success to some level and you don't have to compromise your beliefs. This has happened to me too many times and I do firmly believe that there is a Judgment Day, there is a God to please or displease. Furthermore, whether I am an entertainer or not, I owe my eternal destiny to Jesus who paid a fearful price for me and therefore, since He saved my life, it is His and He should be able to call the shots. Yet I know that He wants me to have fun and be successful along the way — so yep, I try to let Him drive.

3

BOOM! BOOM!
Freddy Cannon

Often called 'the last of the real rockers', Freddy Cannon exploded onto the scene in 1959 with *Tallahassee Lassie* and never looked back, clocking up a further twenty-one chart successes including *Way Down Yonder In New Orleans*, *The Urge* and *Palisades Park*. His gritty sound and rasping vocals may have been out of keeping with contemporary trends but the honesty of his music shone through, ensuring him of a place in rock and roll's front rank.

Yes, it's Freddy with a 'y', no 'ie' — I don't know why they do that. I was born Frederick Picariello on December 4, 1940 in Lynn, Massachusetts. My parents were Annette and Fred, and my sister, Mary Lou. Father's professional name was 'Freddy Carmen'. He played trumpet and was bandleader of Freddy Carmen & His Orchestra. Mother's occupation was mother and housewife.

I graduated at Lynn English High School. It was like a trade school so I was doing machine-shop and stuff like that. I really can't tell you what occupation I would have followed had I not gone into showbusiness. I haven't given it a thought: I wouldn't know anything else but this now.

As for any musical education, there was nothing formal in the way of schooling: I just picked up the guitar. At school, I played a little piano but didn't like it. With the guitar, I started to write songs. Nobody really showed me anything, but I'd meet people and they'd show me a few chords, and that's how I really started to learn.

There was always music in the house — all the time. My musical influences weren't the big band singers. When I was growing up, my dad played most of the big band stuff, but being a teenager you don't like what your parents like. So, I liked something different: I liked the rhythm & blues black music. My favourites were Chuck Berry, Little Richard, Little Anthony, Bo Diddley — gee, there are a lot of them. Big Joe Turner, to me, was the ultimate blues singer.

My singing started when I was twelve or thirteen years old. Our family had a little vacation cottage up in Georgetown, Massachusetts and I used to play at a small hall there with a couple of little friends. One kid would bang on the drums and I'd play kind-of guitar. We would play country music, as I liked Hank Williams and stuff like that: that's the way it really started. My family always encouraged me, and my first amateur public performance was in this little hall in Georgetown.

After this, my first group was called 'The Spindrifts' and we did doo-wop. *[In 1958]* we had a record out on Hot Records — a little local label — called *Cha Cha Doo*. I wrote it and it sold about 5,000 copies in Boston and all around Massachusetts. ABC-Paramount picked it up *[for national distribution]* and then dropped it, so nothing happened anywhere else.

In 1957–58 I fronted my own band, Freddy Carmen & The Hurricanes, and we played a lot of Chuck Berry and stuff like that. Carlos Perfido was the drummer, but I can't remember the names of the other guys. A couple of them have passed away now, but Carlos is still alive. He was a really close friend. I asked him to go with me, but he declined. He never wanted to go. He could have been with me today, I would have loved to have him. When they signed me, they signed me only, but I could have brought the band, only they didn't want to go. I also played guitar on one of the records by the G-Clefs: it was called *Ka-Ding-Dong*.

I was discovered by Boston deejay Jack McDermott, but keep him out of it, cross him out, don't even mention him.

Let's go right to Arnie Ginsburg at this juncture. This guy that I don't want to talk about gave a song, *Rock'n'Roll Baby* — written by my mother and myself — to Arnie, and he's the one who gave the song to Bob Crewe. And, in that team of Bob Crewe and Frank Slay — his partner at the time — Bob Crewe was really the key and the genius behind the music. He was a brilliant producer and writer. Anyway, they changed the title to *Tallahassee Lassie*.

Crewe and Slay knew Dick Clark and used to bring songs to his house, and they brought *Tallahassee Lassie* to him. As the story goes — I'm still in Boston and found this out later on — they took that demo with about ten other demos to his home. Somewhere in the middle of the bottom of the pile was me with *Tallahassee Lassie* without 'bum-bum-bum-bum' the drums in it like that.

They played it for him, and the owner of Swan Records, Bernie Bennick, who was also there with them said: 'This is a *ridiculous* saying.'

Dick asked: 'Who's this kid?' and Bob and Frank told him that I was the kid from Boston that they'd just found with a song. Dick told them: 'If you would put a kind-of drum beat in here with breaks, then it sounds like a record to me.' And he played it again and told them the same thing.

Back in the studio, Bob Crewe went in there and got a mallet on a big bass drum and started banging it on the microphone, and that's how *Tallahassee Lassie* came into being. It was all there, it just needed something to make it more exciting, you know. And I got credit for writing the song regardless of the name change from *Rock'n'Roll Baby* to *Tallahassee Lassie* by Slay and Crewe.

So, I came to sign for Swan Records through Bob Crewe. Dick

Billboard, October 1961

Clark was a part-owner of Swan Records. He was involved in payola but he wasn't thick, he knew how to get around it. He has openly talked about it now, because he is free of everything and doesn't care any more.

I must admit that, without Dick Clark and me doing his show, *American Bandstand*, I probably wouldn't have happened nationally. He was so important to people with records back then, and still is to some extent. Dick really did me justice by helping me and using me on his show, even though it also worked in his favour.

Disc jockeys on Boston radio stations came up with the 'Boom Boom' tag. I was a local boy and they were giving me a lot of nicknames. The record company — Bernie Bennick at Swan — chose the name Cannon. I was happy with that. It didn't bother me and it is an easy name to remember.

When *Tallahassee Lassie* started to be played on the radio, I was at home in Boston. I was a local boy and Arnie Ginsburg — who I mentioned earlier — was a disc jockey on the local station. He played the record maybe ten times in a row, as up to then they'd never had anybody who'd really hit it. He was playing me and saying: 'This is the greatest!' As a result, the phones were ringing and they were getting requests for my record. What a *great* feeling, you know.

At the time, I was working for a little old paint company and I would drive a small truck and deliver paint to different stores. This company — whose

name I can't remember now — was, like, a distributor and that is what I was doing when I heard my record played on the truck radio. I went *crazy*, I couldn't believe it.

I'm trying to remember where the heck I was when *Tallahassee Lassie* went into the charts when those feelings of excitement were even greater. In the UK, the record was covered, but in the States it jumped with a bullet from nowhere right into the fifties. It was climbing like crazy and was different from any record that was out. This was *real* rock and roll, and there weren't any real rock and roll records out there. Yep, I gave up my job right away: that was it!

Yes, there was pressure to find a follow-up after *Tallahassee Lassie.* Bernie Bennick and I were looking, and Bob Crewe came up with this record called *Okefenokee*, which was in the charts about the forties or high thirties in the US. I don't know what it did here in the UK.

Then he told me that I had to have a third hit record. If I got that third record, Bernie said that I would stick around — and he was right.

Bernie found *Way Down Yonder In New Orleans*: he'd seen Al Jolson singing it, and that's how that came about. I didn't like it, I was against the song. I thought: 'Too old, my dad's playing that, it ain't gonna happen'. He told me that they were going to do it with a rock and roll beat with a big trumpet, and it *exploded* in England — they loved it here. It was also a big hit in the US.

You say that I was touring in package shows successfully but had no major hits from 1960 until *Palisades Park* in 1962. Well, I disagree: what about *The Urge* and *Transistor Sister*? These records made a little noise over here in the UK I think! Right? See, you forgot! Out of the *Explosive* album, *California Here I Come* was being played; *Chattanooga Shoe Shine Boy* was being played. See those records? They charted!

Palisades Park was written by Chuck Barris, a friend of Bob Crewe and Bernie Bennick. Chuck sent the song over to Bernie, who'd told him that they were looking for uptempo material for me and had asked to hear it. Having started out as a staff producer for ABC Television, Chuck went on to have three or four big quiz shows. He only wrote this one song, *Palisades Park*, that's all I ever knew. It was one song, a great song: in the States it was a smash — it was *big*. If I don't sing that song in America, they throw stuff at me. They *want* it. In the US, people generally just *love* that song. Over here in the UK, it didn't go that high: they couldn't relate to it. There's probably not too many amusement parks over here, that's what it is.

How about one of my other hits you haven't mentioned, *Buzz Buzz A Diddle-It*? I do that on stage. Matchbox — the rockabilly group — covered that

and had a big hit here in the UK with it; it got to No. 8 or something like that*.

All my records I would like to have been like *Tallahassee Lassie* because that's the kind of stuff I love. I love Chuck Berry, I love Bo Diddley. I am a real rocker and those are dance records. Jerry Lee Lewis, Little Richard, these people are the real people, the roots. Everybody here in England — the big acts — always talk about these same people anyway, but when I talk about them I was *there*! I went to see Chuck Berry in 1956 at the Boston Gardens before I was even starting or doing anything great. I did the G-Clefs record, but nobody knew who I was. When I saw him on that stage, I thought that's for me... that's the guy. He was great.

You ask me if the 'Boom Boom' Cannon categorized me as a rocker so that I couldn't really switch to record ballads like *Venus* and *Take Good Care Of My Baby,* etc. To be honest with you, I wouldn't *want* to do those. I was put in a category, but I never wanted to be — what would they call them — not 'pretty boys'... what's their name... idols. I never thought that I was that, but they always classified me as that. I am a rock and roll singer: that's what I was and that's what I wanted to be.

I don't get this 'idol' thing, you know. Bobby Vee is one of these idols; Brian Hyland is an idol; Johnny Tillotson is an idol. I don't feel as if I'm an idol, but everytime it turns around in stories, it always seems that Freddy Cannon was an idol. I don't want to be an idol. I just want to be a good rock and roll singer and be remembered for that, see?

Which record of any artist would I like to have recorded? Well, it couldn't be a ballad as I don't do them! I would have loved — and I might still try it just for my own satisfaction — to do a collection of Chuck Berry songs. I just think that he has got the greatest rock and roll dance records ever made and, as I said earlier, the roots of this music is him without a question. Don't get me wrong, Elvis made great records, everybody... but this guy had *thirty* smash records that he wrote that were

---

* Actually No. 22.

the great records *of all time*. They stand up every day, you hear them all the time. In America, they play them to death. You hear Little Richard and you hear Fats Domino, but this guy wrote his songs and sang his songs. He doesn't need a plug from me, I'm just telling you that the respect is there.

It's nearer forty years since I toured here in the UK. My first tour here was in late 1959 with Eddie Cochran. When Eddie died, I was there in London ready to get in that taxi cab with my dad. I think I did about ten dates with him and Gene Vincent: I replaced somebody. Joe Brown backed me, but I can't remember the venues, it's all so vague. I do remember that my dad and Eddie Cochran were very good friends on that tour. We were in our room waiting to go to the airport when he got killed. Very sad.

Of my second tour of the UK in 1960 with Conway Twitty and Johnny Preston, I really don't have any particular memories. I was glad to have a the chance to work with Conway as he's gone now. And then to see him cross over to country where he had a lot of hits was *amazing*. He always wanted to sing country and never wanted to be a rock and roll singer. I don't know if anyone remembers seeing him on stage, but he wasn't really rock and roll. He just stood there with his guitar and sang: he wasn't an entertainer, but for country music he was perfect.

In 1962, my third visit, I toured with Del Shannon and Buzz Clifford, having replaced Dion for the end of the tour. Del and I were good friends and we used to hang around and go the movies. He's gone now, too. Very sad. He was a nice guy, but always a little depressed. I didn't know what was on his mind, and he was going through a lot of different things.

I have no memories at all of any of my other tours including those marathon US tours — it's so far back — but I did get something out of them: it was like a school and you learnt how to be better on the stage. If the acts that toured then and still tour didn't learn anything by doing these tours by going on the stage night after night, then what did they get out of it? It's just like anything: you learn your craft, and the more you do it the better you get. There are a lot of acts who have great records, but they are not that good live. With some shows — like the Nader ones — where you have a very short spot, it's hard to get anything out of them, and I don't particularly care to do those kind of shows.

There were no rivalries on tour: everybody gets on with everybody in this business. Blacks get on with whites — the racial thing happened when we were starting out, but all the people on the buses and tours we did were all good friends. I knew all the black acts: they like me and my family, and I liked them. Even to this day, my wife and my kids are all friends with Bo Diddley, Little Anthony & The Imperials... these people are friends of ours and they are really nice people. You will always find good and bad in any race.

I've been everywhere except the Far East: all the European countries and Australia. For me, to do that at a young age, that's a thrill. People wait a lifetime trying to take a vacation to go somewhere and they never go. Here am I, with my wife — or my father back then when he was alive — doing all these things. Now I'm doing it and getting paid! *[laughter]* It's wonderful, it really is.

Apart from the manager I don't want to talk about, I don't remember if I always got paid by promoters and record companies. I doubt it. If I did, I would jump in and tell you right away. There was a lot of underhanded things going on back then, you know, not like it is today.

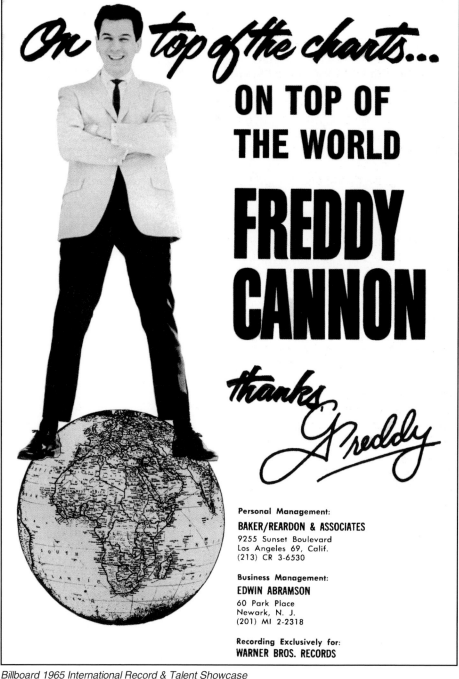

Billboard 1965 International Record & Talent Showcase

How much did I get paid back then for headlining a UK tour? Probably $500 a night or less — cheap! With all these hits, it was nothing. You did it because you wanted to come and be accepted by the kids over here. The kids didn't know. It wasn't great; it wasn't even good.

With *Palisades Park* I didn't even get paid. Nothing! I got a nice ring — which I can't find — and a beautiful $150 sweater, and that was it. *Palisades Park* was a *giant* record in the States and that's what I got: I got nothing. I always owed the record company money. I always owed the manager money. I always owed the accountant money. I always owed everybody money. Nobody owed me nothing. Look, I'm not mad: hey, I'm still going and half of those people don't have anything going. I don't have to dwell on it, but you asked me the questions and I'm telling you.

Yes, my move from Swan Records to Warner Brothers was about money, that's true. *[laughs]* After Boston, I lived in Philadelphia for a couple of year, then moved to California where I still live now. By going over to that Warner Brothers' label, I made pretty good money and moved house with my wife and kids. My mom, my sister, everybody, moved out to California following us.

I got paid nothing at Swan. I was too young and didn't know anything about this business to take any action. This is why I don't talk about the managers that you asked me about. They would steal the gold teeth right out of your head. That's the way it went on back there.

I had no input on my recordings. When I first started I had a little say about *Tallahassee Lassie*, but after that they just wouldn't listen to me any more. Not that they were *wrong*, but they weren't right *all the time* and I wanted to do something else. Just before I went to Warner Brothers in early 1963, I had a little control with a record called *Patty Baby*. It wasn't a big hit, but it was a big upstate New York record. The record cost $35 to make and sold 80,000 copies! Me, a writer, and Bobby Comstock, we did the record all by ourselves with no Frank Slay, no Bob Crewe, no nobody. It made money and Swan couldn't believe it. They would never give me any chance to do what I wanted to do. When I went to Warners, they signed me to another producer — what can I tell you!

Frank Slay was responsible for me recording *Abigail Beecher* at Warner Brothers: how he got in there I don't know. It wasn't named after anyone, just a fictitious name.

Of course, the British Invasion affected my career: it affected everybody's. Whoever said it didn't would be lying. They did great records — I'm not holding that against them at all. They were doing good things here, they really were. At the beginning of the music they were covering everybody, then they found their own little spot. The Beatles started, and the Rolling Stones and all these people. I gotta give them credit: this is why they became big. They did good things, they wrote good songs — you can't dispute that. Give credit where credit is due: they would not have been big if they weren't good.

There's good and bad in everything, that's how I feel. But, yes, they did hurt us because they just came over with great songs and radio started to play them one after another. We still worked, but we couldn't have a hit because the Beatles in America had the top ten records. They *owned* the charts!

You're right about the coincidence of the Beatles having their second US No. 1 record, *She Loves You*, on my label, Swan. Not a lot of people are aware of that. Brian Epstein had met Bernie Bennick and sold Swan the master of *She Loves You*. It didn't do anything on its first release in 1963, but when Swan re-activated it at the beginning of 1964, it became their second No. 1 and replaced *I Want To Hold Your Hand* at the top.

ACTION
ACTION
ACTION
ACTION
ACTION
ACTION
Where there is

FREDDY CANNON

There is

ACTION
RECORD SALES

ACTION
PERSONAL APPEARANCES

ACTION
TELEVISION

ACTION
RADIO

ACTION
SALES

ACTION
ACTION
ACTION

Personal Management
Don Reardon Assoc. Inc.
1633 Westwood Blvd.
Los Angeles, Calif.

Billboard 1966
International Record &
Talent Showcase

I had a hit — *Action* — in 1965 and was then twenty-six years old. I was married at Tallahassee, but nobody knew that either in the States or anywhere. We hid that then, but I am still with my same wife, Jeanette, who I love. She is coming over to join me on November 19th *[2000]* and it will be our 35th wedding anniversary. Wow, see how long we've been married? We were young; Jeanette was fifteen years old, a little child. We have two boys and a girl and two of them are married, how do you like that?

I am a religious man, but I'm not a good one. My wife is very good. We're Catholics, you know, we're Italian. I go to church, but I haven't been at all here in England. When she comes over to join me, she'll find a church and

Billboard, July 1961

we'll go. She's always praying for me so that I stay healthy. I never had any problems with drink or drugs, but I smoked cigarettes like crazy back then. Not any more, but I did.

I continued working in showbusiness up until 1969, then I stopped and did record promotion for Buddha Records in the States until 1970. In 1971, I did a Richard Nader show with Chuck Berry in Boston Gardens. Then it started up again and other people started to call me: back in action again! Since then, I have worked right through; so only those two years without it.

My last hit record was *Let's Put The Fun Back In Rock N Roll*, in 1981. It was a great song. I didn't write it: Freddie Milano of the Belmonts found this song and came to me in Providence, Rhode Island. He turned up at a show I was doing and said: 'We've got a song for you, you must hear it! We want you to sing it and we'll sing background. We think it's a hit.' When I heard the song, it *was* great and I said: 'All right, let's do it!' So, we went into the studio and did it.

Nostalgia shows don't bother me, or performing my hits over and over again. I *would* be bothered if they packaged me with acts that don't fit my style or don't work right. Now, Bobby Vee and Brian Hyland, they fit: the guys can do an uptempo rock thing and it sounds great, they do a good job. But sometimes they put me with Frankie Avalon and Fabian and I don't belong, I don't fit. The glove doesn't fit right. So sometimes they've done that and, as I'm not crazy about doing it, I try to keep away.

Keeping your material fresh is hard to do, but if you've got a good band it helps. The Vees on this UK tour are great. If I had to rate them, of all the bands I've worked with, they are first band: that's how good they are — right 'up there'.

I'm doing records now, but I'm not cutting them for myself: I'm writing a lot of songs for other artists and giving them to people to put them around. When I'm home that's what I like to do. I liked the old ways of making a record but I also like the new technology and have my own studio. When I started out, it was easier for artists to make their way and have a hit, because there were many small labels and power in the industry wasn't as concentrated.

It has often been said that some of the businessmen who run today's record industry wouldn't even know what a hit song should sound like. Their ears don't say 'music': they're business people who want to make a lot of money. That's great, I don't begrudge them: I'd probably do the same. But don't make the money and try to say 'This is good' and 'This is no good' when you don't even know yourself: *that's* what's bad about it.

In the old days it was great: they had a little label and they'd run out there and test the record. Top Rank was great over here. If they got a record out, they'd go right after it. Frank Chalmers, that was the guy, my *hero* over here in the UK. He was the head of Top Rank promotion, sales and everything else. When I came over here, he was the first guy I met and he was a wonderful man. I don't think that he is alive any more. His son emailed me one day and told me that his dad would have been proud to hear me talking about him.

Outside of music, I like to write songs. The family has a beach house in California near the ocean which I just bought this last year. We have barbecues and just enjoy ourselves. It's nice.

Looking back, I wish that I knew what I know now back then, but I wouldn't change anything: the way things happen are the way that they are supposed to happen, the way that they made the records and the way they were hits and whatever. I would have tried to avoid some of the people that I haven't wanted to mention in this interview. If they were out of the picture perhaps things might have been different, I don't really know. I can't really give you a straight answer on that one.

For the future, it has got to be my songwriting. I've got a couple of terrific songs, really good ones, and they're out there now with a couple of big people, but I don't want to mention their names or anything. I have one dream left in this business and I'm gonna tell you about this dream, you'll be one of the first ones to know this. My dream — my wife smiles when I say it to her — is to walk down the aisle at the Grammies and get a Grammy for songwriting. That's all I want. I don't want another hit record for me, but for somebody else for whom I wrote it: and if that ever happens... *wooooooh*, that would be the greatest thing!

My sincere good wishes for Christmas and the New Year to all my friends in Great Britain

FREDDIE CANNON

New Musical Express 1961 Annual

4

THE CHIRPING CRICKETS
Jerry Allison, Sonny Curtis & Joe B. Mauldin

The Crickets are chiefly renowned for being Buddy Holly's backing group, though they also enjoyed a recording career in their own right after his death in February 1959.

Jerry Allison — one of the original line-up and a veteran of recording sessions with the likes of Eddie Cochran, the Everly Brothers and Johnny Burnette — is highly regarded as one of rock and roll's most innovative and influential drummers. He is also one of the youngest (co-)writers of a No. 1 hit, *That'll Be The Day*.

We are real busy. I gotta do sound checks and stuff. We've got a new record out. We're interested in promoting our new record, so if you can mention the record in your book that would be all right. Okay, tell me what you wanna know.

My real name is Jerry Ivan Allison and I was born on August 31, 1939 in Hill County, Texas. My dad worked for the highway department and my mom was a schoolteacher; I have one brother. Country music is what we mainly hear on the radio back in Texas, and I'm sure my first musical experience was singing in church. I remember songs like *Goodnight Irene*, *Mockin' Bird Hill*, and *Buttons And Bows* from the old Bob Hope movie. Mom played the piano and my dad played the harmonica. My folks gave me piano lessons starting about four or five years old, and I took these on and off until I moved away from home when I was seventeen. I took up the drums as I was interested in playing in the school band, and I just liked the drums.

I'm sure my first amateur performance was with the school band in the fifth grade. I think I realized that music was what I wanted to do while I was sacking groceries in a grocery store when I was thirteen or fourteen. A fellow named Cal Wayne came by and asked if I played drums. I said yeah, I played drums in school and had a set of drums, and he said that would be fine. As a result, I played one night at a club and made five dollars — we played for about three hours. I was making 40 cents an hour sacking groceries, so I knew right then that was better money than sacking groceries, and that's when I decided to do it professionally. That was back when I was still in Lubbock High School, and I did almost a semester at college before Buddy and I got a tour together. I was taking advertising art and architecture classes.

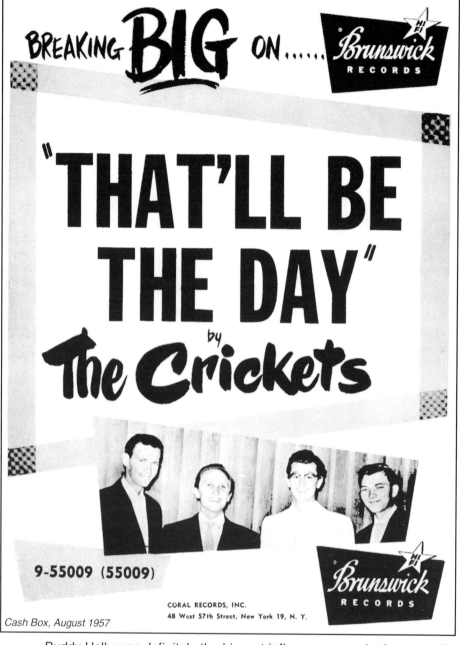

BREAKING **BIG** ON..... *Brunswick* RECORDS

"THAT'LL BE THE DAY" by The Crickets

9-55009 (55009)

Brunswick RECORDS

CORAL RECORDS, INC.
48 West 57th Street, New York 19, N. Y.

Cash Box, August 1957

Buddy Holly was definitely the biggest influence on me both personally and professionally because he and I went to high school together, were good friends and started playing rock and roll together.

We came to write *That'll Be The Day* because there was a movie called *The Seachers* that John Wayne was in and he said: 'That'll be the day!' about five times in the movie. We then started saying: 'That'll be the day!' when fooling around, kidding ourselves that one day we'd have a hit record. A couple of days later, right in that time period, I don't know exactly when, Buddy and I were rehearsing, or practising, at my mom's house. I had my drums set up, he was playing the guitar and said: 'Let's write a song' and I said: 'That'll be the day!' He said: 'That sounds like a good idea.' So, that's how it all started, and it took about thirty minutes or something like that to finish it.

When *That'll Be The Day* went to No. 1 in the States [September 1957] I think we'd already gone to New York. It was a thrill when it went to No. 1, but the *big* thrill was when it got in the charts and we got a call to work. A fellow named Irving Feld — I think he now owns the Ringling Brothers, Barnum & Bailey Circus — booked us for a seventeen-week tour when *That'll Be The Day* first started getting into the charts, and that was it. We thought: 'Well we're gonna play New York and all the big cities', and that's when we sorta felt like we'd made it. It was a great feeling.

The first tour, for Irving Feld, had LaVern Baker, Chuck Berry, Fats Domino and many others. Eddie Cochran was on it once in a while. He would come on a tour and then go out and do some other dates and then come back on the tour. Paul Anka was on it for most of the time, Buddy Knox, the Everly Brothers occasionally, and Jimmy Bowen. It was called *The Biggest Show Of Stars For '57*. Yeah, that was great fun. We all travelled on the bus together and I think Fats Domino had his car, so he and his band travelled in the car most of the time.

It was a three-month tour and we went to almost every state in the United States and part of Canada. A lot of places we played twice on the same tour: we'd be gone a month and then have to come back three weeks later. Usually we just played two shows, but at some of the venues in New York like the Paramount Theatre, there would be seven shows a day and all of them packed out. They would start about nine or ten in the morning, show a movie, then run the rock and roll show through, and keep on going till late at night.

The incident in my career that most elated me was the New York Paramount [Christmas 1957] *Holiday Show* in Times Square. We had four records in the charts and were a three-piece group. The bill was fantastic, including Jerry Lee Lewis, Fats Domino, Little Richard and the Everly Brothers, who are my favourites. Their record of *Cathy's Clown* is my all-time favourite.

There was no pressure in those days. We didn't have to do anything but play music and just drive around. They had a bus and they'd tell you when to get on it and we had no worries. I mean, we weren't getting *rich*, but we were making plenty of money to eat and pay for hotels, and it was just a good time. So, we didn't have much on our shoulders at that time. But I was very green as far as being out in the world was concerned. Joe B. and I were both seventeen and Buddy was nineteen when we went out on the road after the particular time that *That'll Be The Day* struck. Before that,

45

we had done some tours in Florida and I was probably sixteen then. We weren't *totally* green, but we sure looked up to the tall buildings when we got to New York.

Norman Petty was a good businessman and I didn't mind him having one contract for Buddy Holly and one for the Crickets. I thought it was fine, because we didn't know which records were coming out as 'The Crickets' and which were coming out as 'Buddy Holly'. We all just made the records and Norman Petty overdubbed the background vocals after we'd gone. Buddy and I produced *That'll Be The Day*: we set up what we wanted to do and who we wanted to sing, and arranged the studio, but after we got on the road we didn't have time to get all that together. We'd sort of go in and cut the vocal, and for the band on the actual Crickets records Norman Petty would hire somebody around Texas.

We hired some guys called the Picks for a while, and then some guys called the Roses. They'd overdub *[vocals]* on some of the tunes and that would be Cricket records, and that was the only distinction between the two — 'Buddy Holly' and 'The Crickets' — and that was a short period of time.

Buddy did one in New York, *Early In The Morning*; Joe B. and I weren't even there and they had a vocal group on that one. Being there didn't bother us; we were just making records and all the money was split the same whether it was Buddy Holly records or Crickets records. So, it was fun to have two records out at once in the charts instead of just one.

On our tour of the UK in 1958 we had a great time because we got to play longer than we'd been playing in the States. Over there, we usually did shows with twenty acts on and you would play three or four songs. When we came here we were told that we had to do thirty minutes. It was like a variety show here, which we enjoyed and it was just all new to us.

Vi Petty was with us on that tour; she is a great lady. She has re-done the studio in Clovis, New Mexico and always nags me about my smoking, but it hasn't stopped me. *[laughs]*

When the split with Buddy came, I just didn't want to move to New York. Buddy, Joe B. and I had all decided to leave Norman Petty and move to New York, but Norman talked Joe B. and I out of it. We weren't hard to talk out of it either, 'cause it's fun to be in New York but — I had just got married and my wife wasn't in the mood to move to New York particularly. It was an awfully big step to take and we were sort-of uncertain at the time about what exactly we did want to do. Buddy knew for sure that he wanted to move to New York and try it. Buddy, Joe B. and I talked about it and he said: 'I'm gonna move to New York, so I'll just work as Buddy Holly and you guys work down here as the Crickets, and if it works out then we're all happy; if not, we'll get back together.' So, we didn't really split as far as having a hassle or anything. But, of course, I always regret that we didn't go to New York now, 'cause things might have been different, you know, for Buddy. Hearing of Buddy's death was the lowest spot of my life.

I've still never thought how I felt about Bobby Vee taking Buddy's place on the *Winter Dance Party* tour after he died and then continuing to perform with us sometimes. As you know, we weren't on that tour and promoters are always involved with keeping the show going on. After Buddy was killed, I sure wasn't gonna concern myself whether that show went on or not. Bobby Vee and I have become great friends. We got to be friends in early 1960 when we were both recording at Liberty Records, and if that gave Bobby Vee a break then at least something good came out of the tragic events of the time.

THE CRICKETS

Song Hits, May 1958

After Buddy, the Crickets toured quite a bit in the States in the Midwest, but we never ever settled into a group. Somebody would come in, somebody would go out, and then people would go off and do different things. After thirty years, we are more settled into a group right now than we were all those different times. We toured with... oh, I won't even go through all the people. We had *Don't Ever Change* — Jerry Naylor and Glen Campbell were singing on it. But we never had a working group.

My lowest career points were Buddy moving to New York, and then later during 1964–65, due to the British Invasion, when there was nothing for

THE
SLEEPER HIT—
BREAKING WIDE
OPEN!

"REAL
WILD
CHILD"
by
IVAN

Vocal With Instrumental
Accompaniments
CORAL 9-62017

Billboard, August 1958

our music. Nothing! We loved the British music — it was great — and artists like Chad & Jeremy, the Beatles and Gerry & The Pacemakers. We worked, but not enough. It was all different.

I never resented not being a star act in my own right, but I did resent the business end of it. I feel fortunate that we had as much success as we had, and are still having now, that we get to go out and play to full houses and people enjoy it. The Beatles and people like that saying that we were an influence on them, that makes you feel satisfied. To be a 'star', as such, I got to pass on that anyway: there's too many people in your face all the time! *[laughs]* I've enjoyed about as much stardom as I need: I like to perform so that people enjoy it, but not the 'star' part.

I've had my taste of being out in front as a solo attraction too. Back in 1958, I cut a record called *Real Wild Child* under 'Ivan', which is my middle name. That got somewhere in the Top 100, although it didn't get Top Fifty, and I went and did a couple of shows as 'Ivan', but I always had more fun in a group.

In 1965, I cut *We Gotta Get Together* in Clovis under 'Jerry Allison & The Crickets'. I still enjoy being in a group and prefer to be one of the trio. I never did wanna go out and cut Jerry Allison records, even as a band. I mean, I like to have my old buddies on the road with me.

A lot of the records we did in the Sixties were made with some studio musicians and myself, and then once in a while a regular member of the group would play, and sometimes not. They were more 'produced' records — more so than a group actually going in and cutting a record like we are doing these days. I own the 'Crickets' name now. I just own it myself because Joe B. has been out of the business sometimes... well, you gonna talk to him anyway.

I have a farm outside of Nashville and I really enjoy just being on the farm and being laid-back, but we always enjoy coming to England probably as much as anywhere we've ever toured, and we've had fun every time we've ever been here. We got a call from a fellow, Jeffrey Kruger, to do last year's *Peterborough Country Music Festival*, which I thought was a key thing as we never thought of ourselves as country musicians even though we're of the country. But he called and we were sort-of not doing anything at the time. Niki Sullivan is an engineering representative and not interested, Carl Gordon plays ten days a year, and Sonny Curtis — who had a country career — had gone off to do his own thing and was playing a tour of England on his own, so I called Gordon Payne to see if he wanted to come over here. Anyway, when Gordon, Joe B. and I got together to work up some songs for the Peterborough thing — there was also a little tour connected to the *Peterborough Country Music Festival* — and we started practising and really had a good time. We'd all been friends for a long time anyway. So, we started having fun. Then a few more new jobs came in and we started learning more new songs. Then we started writing songs. That's how we accidentally came to get back on the road. We planned to work, at the most, two or three days a month and now we're working all the time and only *off* two or three days a month! This present tour is the result of Joe B., Gordon and I performing at Peterborough, and it's good to be back.

I met Gordon somewhere around 1972. John *[J.J.]* Cale was a good friend of mine from Tulsa, Oklahoma and Gordon is from Tulsa. And J.J. was at my house one time and said: 'Hey, there's this old buddy of mine from Tulsa. Gordon is, I guess, ten years younger than us, somewhere around that, maybe a little more, I don't like to think about it, he's so young. *[laughs]* But John Cale said that this friend of his, who was a good songwriter, was playing at a place down Long Beach in Los Angeles — where I lived at the time — and that he had some good songs. I had a publishing company at the time. In fact, I gave Eric Clapton a copy of *After Midnight*, but I guess I was never too much of a publisher.

John talked me into going down to Long Beach and it was Gordon Payne who was playing down there. I said: 'Well, come by the house sometime, I would like to hear your songs,' and he came by the next day. I published a couple of his songs and then he later cut them himself *[laughs]*, but that's how I met him. He started to work for Waylon Jennings shortly afterwards. Then, as it ended up, the Crickets started opening the show for Waylon, and Gordon used to come out and sit in with us all the time. It was about the time *More Than I Can Say* was a hit for Leo Sayer *[September 1980]*. Gordon tries to do the Buddy material as authentically as possible, and I think we have the best combination with Joe B., Gordon and me.

T-Shirt — our new single from our album of the same name — came from Paul McCartney's *Buddy Holly Week* songwriting contest, and in 1986 we visited him at his home studios and cut some records. Later, we sent him some tapes and he contributed his ideas for the album. It took us one and a half years to get the *T-Shirt* album together.

On nostalgia shows, I guess you play the sort of music that you like. We went through periods in the Sixties doing surfing music and other styles with synthesizers and this and that. Finally, we are back to playing three-piece music that we like to play, so I guess that keeps it fresh, and these days we do songs that we never even did with Buddy: Buddy, Joe B. and I never played *Not Fade Away* for instance, or *Rock Me My Baby*, on stage. Like I say, we didn't get to do that much time and these days we get to play an hour a lot of times, so we can play a lot of tunes including 'B' sides. But we have to get 'em out and learn 'em now because the only time we played 'em was on the records — songs like *Looking For Someone To Love* and *Rock Around With Ollie Vee*. So, that keeps it fun because you've got to think about it.

I think what gets *bad* about playing *Oh Boy*, *Peggy Sue* and *That'll Be The Day* is that you get to driftin' off, as you've played it so many times you don't have to think. It's fun to play the 'new' old tunes because you've gotta pay attention to where the breaks are and think about it. And we'll *always* play *Oh Boy*, *Rave On*, *Peggy Sue* and all those tunes because that's what people come to hear. But it's fun too, and what you're there for is to entertain people. If they want to hear *That'll Be The Day*, then it's fun to play. And we change it a lot, we get the audience to help us sing *That'll Be The Day*, and that's fun to hear them singing it back to you. I love the live audience reaction.

Talented Sonny Curtis balanced his career as a singer/guitarist in and out of the Crickets with an alternative existence as a highly successful songwriter responsible for such classics as *Rock Around With Ollie Vee*, *Walk Right Back*, *More Than I Can Say*, *I Fought The Law* and... the theme music for *The Mary Tyler-Moore Show*.

I was born on May 9, 1937 way out in the country in Meadow, Texas. It was real loose in those days and, at their discretion, my folks hadn't picked out a name for me when the doctor came out to deliver me. He told them to stop by the courthouse in the next couple of weeks and name me. They never did. When I was twenty years old in New York City, I was signing a contract for Southern Music and some reason or other their lawyers wanted to see my birth certificate. I sent down to Austin, Texas and when it came it had 'Unnamed Baby Curtis' on there, so I had to send two dollars down to Austin and name myself!

My father's name is Arthur and my mother — who is now deceased — was Violet. I've got three sisters: Ruby Mae, Aileen and Jean, and a brother, Pete. My other brother, Dean, is now deceased.

Bluegrass music was my earliest interest. How I got interested in music, as I remember, was when I was real, real small: a guy came over to our house one night and played the fiddle. He played *Listen To The Mocking Bird*, and I've been hooked ever since I think. When I was a child, I used to listen to the Sons Of The Pioneers, Eddy Arnold and Bill Monroe & The Bluegrass Boys. I learned the fiddle as a child, and my aunt taught me and my two brothers to play the guitar. She didn't know very much, but she was able to show me how to play *Little Brown Jug*, and when I learned it I couldn't reach all the way across the neck. I could only reach four strings, and there is a way to do it without reaching the bottom two. I went around all day long playing *Little Brown Jug* on the guitar. Apart from me and my two brothers no-one else in our immediate family was musically inclined.

Really, the guitar came first and then, as my brother Dean played the fiddle, I started hacking away at that as well. I don't play it anymore. Although I've studied the piano for arranging — as you need to know how to use it — I don't play and can't sit down and rip off *Poor People Of Paris* or anything like that. *[laughs]*

I sure can remember my first amateur performance — you wanna hear about it? *[laughter]* We had a grade school and a high school in Meadow, Texas, and it happened in the fourth grade. Every Friday morning, just before lunch, we had an assembly program at 11:30 with each class presenting something. Our class decided to do a radio program. Even though it didn't go out on the radio, we pretended that it did and this was for the whole school. The call letters for our radio station were 'Meadow, Texas FOUR'. I knew how to play *Good Ol' Mountain Dew* and *Give Me Five Minutes More* on the guitar and I was so little — gee, this sounds awful *[laughs]* — that they got a small chair for me to put my foot up, and I leaned the guitar down on my leg.

First, I played *Five Minutes More* and I was overwhelmed by the response. Man, I had lain in bed all night before *crying*, but I never did tell anybody that. I had already agreed to do it and I couldn't back out without being a twit. My mom sat right there in the front row and we had pre-arranged that I would look at her all the time while I was doing this, so that I wouldn't have to look at anybody else. It went down so well that I got to do an encore and I did the only other song that I knew which was *Good Ol' Mountain Dew* — and that went down even better, considering the lyrics are about getting drunk!

This success at school didn't lead to any other appearances — it meant I had to learn to play. After leaving school, I never did too much other than music. I was a bricklayer's helper one time for about fifteen minutes and then... oh, let me see... I got a job selling advertising for a local magazine. It was more like a programme that came out annually when there was a fatstock show or some kind of function like that, and I went all over the South Plains selling advertising for this programme on a commission deal. I'd go into these cotton and meal gin yards and approach the managers who were all old, tough, hard, tobacco-chewing Texans and I'd go up and say: 'I'm selling advertising for so-and-so-and-so-and-so' and these guys would look at me and say: 'Get outta here, man!' Oh, they were *rotten*! I sold a little bit, but said: 'Man, I'll *never* do this for a living.' We are talking about stuff where I wasn't going anywhere. I had no direction and was just bouncing around Lubbock like Buddy, Waylon Jennings, J.I., and Joe B. who was in a group called 'The Four Teens'.

I went professional when Buddy got his contract down in Nashville. Well, I guess 'professional' is when you get paid. If you are in the union you're 'professional', but I wasn't in the union and I was getting paid. We didn't have a musicians' union in Lubbock. I played with Tommy Hancock & The Roadside Playboys, but while I was in school I'd go around and do what I'm doing tonight: just play my guitar and sing. I'd play at the luncheons of civic organizations like the Lions and Rotary, sing a few songs and pick up ten bucks.

Ben Hall and I cut a record together one time, but it was just a demo. It was kind-of a religious song and he used to play it on his radio show — Ben was a local deejay on KDAV. He and I were good friends and still are. He lives in Nashville and I've been over to his house for Christmas parties and all that.

I first met Buddy Holly at his house. A friend of mine — Olan Finlay was his name — moved from Meadow to Lubbock, and he would come back down to Meadow at weekends and tell me about these two guys, Buddy Holly and Bob Montgomery, who were great pickers and they were bluegrass pickers. I had been on Bernie Howell's show on local television and Olan said that they had expressed an interest in meeting me and, of course, with similar interests in music, I wanted to meet them. Olan took me out to Bob Montgomery's house and we were there waiting for him when he got off the bus from school. We jumped into our car, his car, *somebody's* car and went straight over to Buddy's. Right after we met — and I mean within thirty seconds to one minute — we shook hands, got our guitars out and started playing music, which looking back seems rather strange.

There wasn't a real big personality clash between Buddy and myself. I guess maybe there were personality clashes between the two of us *somewhat*. It's hard to remember everything. You know, Buddy was real confident. I got a gig offered when Norman Petty called me to take the place of Jack Barnes who had left his trio. Buddy said: 'Man, don't go over there and play with Norman Petty, we're gonna make it big ourselves.'

And I said: 'About how long, man, is it gonna take?' and he said: 'About as long as it took Elvis.' And I stayed. I didn't go over and play with Norman, as I was having more fun playing rock and roll, and playing with Buddy and the guys of course.

Buddy could be a bit hard-headed and I was certainly hard-headed; I'm not saying it was all him. But, you know, when you're that age, man, you've got egos involved — and everybody's egos were a lot bigger then than they are these days! My ego, I have been able to kind-of shave it down quite a bit. *[laughs]* But I wouldn't say that there were real personality clashes to the point where we disliked each other.

At the time, I didn't really think too much about how far Buddy or any of us would go in career terms. With Buddy, I certainly must have felt that there was a potential, but I realized and recognized how hard it was to succeed. It's really strange, but you're the first person who has ever expressed the opinion — having seen him on stage — that he was, at the time, perhaps no different to any other pop act. I didn't rate him, I don't think, quite 'up there' with Presley or as good as the Everly Brothers. But I *did* think that he had an incredible feel for the music and an incredible voice for singing certain types of rock and roll, and I knew that he was extremely interested and dedicated. I'm probably the wrong person to ask for an assessment, probably a lot of people are. As the Bible says, you're

never a prophet in your own home town. I liked Elvis because I didn't know him. I knew Buddy real well, so maybe he was too familiar for me to assess.

You were asking me how I assessed him at the time and I think my answer is true, but, looking back on his talent and assessing it from where I stand now, I rate him much, much higher. He was only up there for about eighteen months and pumped an incredible amount of music into the system. Remember, when you really look at it for what it was and think about it, this was a simpler time for music — prior to the Beatles and when Buddy had never heard *What'd I Say?* by Ray Charles. His music had an *incredible* feel. I rate him real high, man. He made some things and he also broke some ground which nobody had ever done before — like adding strings to rock and roll.

Jerry Allison's contribution should also be remembered. 'J.I.', as I call him, is one of the most under-rated drummers in rock and roll as far as breaking new ground. I mean, drum shops all over the world should hang up a picture of Jerry because he sent rock and roll drummers all over the world into shops when he played that lick on the Everly Brothers' *('Til) I Kissed You.* The next week after he played that lick, Hal Blaine and great drummers like that had tom-toms tuned from here to yonder.

Not getting away on a tangent from your question here, but what is *appalling* to me is that they didn't invite Jerry and Joe B. to the Hall Of Fame when they inducted Buddy Holly. Man, what is the matter with these people? They invite all these flakes that had nothing to do with it. Did they never hear *Peggy Sue*? J.I. played an *incredible* drum thing on *Peggy Sue,* and played that incredible thing on *('Til) I Kissed You*, and it makes me mad that they didn't invite them. But, looking back on Buddy and his music and what he meant to rock and roll, and all the new ground he broke, and all the people that did copy him and were influenced by him, I certainly am happy to assess his talent a lot higher than I did at the time.

At the time, I probably did regret our split but I don't regret it now. I think it was the right decision and that I wouldn't be as good a talent as I am now if I had stuck around, and also I might have been on that plane with him. Whether I would have got much money out of staying, in view of Norman Petty's business acumen — well who knows the answer to that one? *[laughs]* Certainly, whatever I got would have been split right down the middle. I'm not talking about *his* part, I am talking about *my* part! *[laughs]* He'd have taken his part and then given me my part and split *that* down the middle, because that's what my contract with him said.

I did tour with Slim Whitman, and although I wasn't as flipped-out with his music as a lot of people were, he was a real good ole boy. I was more of a bluegrass fan — people like Sons Of The Pioneers, fiddle players, Chet Atkins and banjo pickers — but Slim Whitman had a real unique style and working with him on the road was like working with a star. He *was* a big star, and I was always happy to be associated with a big star back in those days. I will say that he was really a nice dude. Although I was just a flaky kid on my first time out on the road, he treated me with respect. I remember him grinning at me on stage and coming over when I was missing a chord or two saying: 'Now don't get nervous, everything's okay.' He treated me real nice, you know.

Touring in those days, there were certainly no problems with drugs. I remember guys used to come through town and drink a little bit — booze was always there but not drugs, not that I knew about. I was incredibly naïve.

No, I never played behind George Jones: that's another Sonny Curtis who runs a music store these days in Columbus, Ohio. I met him one time, it was really funny. This young lady came up to me one time with a guy when I was doing the show at the Grand Ole Opry House and Tammy Wynette was on it. He was playing steel guitar for Tammy and it was a case of: 'Sonny Curtis, this is Sonny Curtis.' But he was a nice dude, I liked him.

I agree that, after Buddy, the Crickets made good records like *When You Ask About Love*, *My Little Girl* and *Deborah*, and also that there was no great push or promotion. For one thing, we didn't really believe in it too much in those days, and I think we were wrong probably. But I remember J.I., Joe B. and I discussed it many, many times and were all agreed on it that the record — if it is any good — will sell itself, so what do you need promoters for? Well, you need promoters to get out there and *hype* everybody, because I think a lot of the time people have to be told that something is good before they like it. Earl Sinks was the chief vocalist at the time because I was viewed as too country to sing rock and roll. As a matter of fact I've had that problem all of my life: too country for rock, and too rock for country — big problem!

We didn't give Bobby Fuller *I Fought The Law*. It was recorded on our *[1959]* album, *In Style With The Crickets*. He found that album, liked it, and they really gave it pretty much the same treatment. They released it and it was a hit *[in 1962]*. I was living in L.A. and Bobby Fuller called me one day and invited me down to the studio where he was recording it. Fortunately, I was able to meet him that day, and that's the only time that I ever saw him. All I know about his death is that there is a big cloud hanging over it. They claim it's suicide, but he might have been mixed up with the wrong kind of people.

After Buddy died, J.I., Joe B. and I joined the Everly Brothers and played for them for about a year including a tour of England. I got drafted, and when I got out of the army joined back up with the Crickets and moved to L.A.. I did the *Bobby Vee Meets The Crickets* tour and also toured with the Crickets some, and at the same time toured with the Everly Brothers as their back-up guitarist. My favourite guitarist at that time was Chet Atkins. I was really influenced by Chet.

I love the Everly Brothers — they were great to work with. There was always a sort-of undercurrent in their relationship which I didn't understand, but they are brothers. They always seemed to get along when I was with them and, as I understand it, they are getting along well now.

All this I was doing together as well as writing songs and doing some projects of my own. I cut *Beatle Hits (Flamenco Guitar Style)* for Imperial and did a record for Liberty with Snuff Garrett producing it called *I Pledge My Love To You*. I was mixed up with Lou Adler, a big music business figure you've probably heard of. He produced a couple of records for me like *A Beatle I Wanna Be* and *This Is The Last Song I'm Ever Gonna Sing*.

Apart from my hit with Bobby Fuller's version of *I Fought The Law*, Andy Williams cut my song *A Fool Never Learns*. *Walk Right Back* was a big hit for me, as was *More Than I Can Say*. My songs were doing well enough that I wanted to get off the road and devote all my time to it. At the end of 1965, I quit the Everly Brothers and decided to stay in L.A..

Of my own compositions, if you press me, I would say that my favourite is *Walk Right Back*, but really it's hard to say what my favourite is, as I have three or four of them: songs like *It's Not Easy Being Fifteen* — which I wrote for my daughter, *I Like Your Music* and *Straight Life*. I still like it a lot and it's probably my most-recorded copyright. So, it's hard to say, you know. If I had the choice and could have written anything in the world that I wanted to write? Oh, I've thought about this a lot *[laughs]* — I may change my mind tomorrow, but I think right now I'm gonna pick *Hey Jude*; that's a terrific one. That or *Yesterday*. Gimme two: I'll take *Hey Jude* and *Yesterday*.

The lowest spot of my career was not during the English Invasion. That didn't really affect me, as I wasn't really anything other than a picker and a songwriter. To me, it just created store traffic and more good music. It was a great period and I loved it. I kept on writing my songs and picking my guitar, and it just seemed to increase my bit. I guess my lowest spot was when I got down to Nashville one time, when I was just starting out. I was working on the *Philip Morris Country Music Show* with Carl Smith and others, playing fiddle, and everybody in town wanted my job because I had the best job around. So Dale Potter, a great little fiddle player, got my job and they fired me. I elected to stay in Nashville and that was probably a mistake, because I learnt that I really *could* eat my straw hat! I got really broke in Nashville in 1957, and that was a pretty low spot because I was really having to watch my pennies. I mean, I got down to one meal a day for a quarter, and figuring out what I could get the most mileage out of to eat — like a bowl of chilli and a glass of milk for that twenty-five cents. That was a low time.

I enjoy touring now: it feels right. The door is open and people want me. The guitar I play now is a Martin acoustic model, and I like getting up and performing in front of an audience where you have eye-to-eye contact. There's a farm to pay for and I still have to work to make the payments. I'm content with live shows, my songwriting and TV advertising jingles, and I've always tried to grow. I'm content just gently canoeing along and don't quite have the desire to be a 'star'... but always remember the saying 'Better watch out for what you want in case you get it'!

Bassist Joe B. Mauldin joined the Crickets in March 1957, shortly after they had cut the seminal *That'll Be The Day*, and over the next eighteen months contributed to such Holly classics as *Maybe Baby*, *Words Of Love*, *Peggy Sue*, *Oh Boy!* and *Rave On*.

My name, like my father's, is Joseph Benson Mauldin and I was born on July 8, 1940 in Lubbock, Texas. Mother's dead and I have one sister, LaRue.

An early interest in music was forced on me at six years of age by my mother who made me take piano lessons. I didn't take it up, but I learned the mechanics and this and that. Later, I was a trumpet-player in the school band and then went on to the steel guitar. I was having fun but got nowhere. I think that I was a sophomore in the tenth grade at Thomas S. Lubbock School when I took up the bass: we had a group called 'The Four Teens'. I can't remember my first amateur performance but it must have been in the school band or the group.

As the Four Teens we used to play dances around the town, and I suppose this must have been my professional debut as we used to enter talent contests. I have no idea, and have never thought of what I would have done had I not been in this business. Buddy and J.I. asked me to join the Crickets. They both liked a group out at that time called the Spiders who had a hit with *Witchcraft*. Buddy and J.I. wanted a similar insect name for their group and came up with 'The Crickets' from a book.

My earliest influence has to be Elvis Presley, but I loved the early rockers — Little Richard, Fats Domino, Chuck Berry — and the rhythm & blues acts and artists like Clyde McPhatter. I got on well with Chuck Berry, who always had his own car to travel in when he was on the road touring. We became good friends and I used to have him stay with us when he was in Texas, but we haven't been in touch for years.

I can't remember where I was or what I was doing when *That'll Be The Day* went into the Top 100, but I was probably in Clovis, New Mexico mowing Norman Petty's lawn! *[laughs]* I take that back about his lawn, but we were down in Clovis. I never had a close friendship with Norman Petty, but he was okay on the mechanics of recording. There were no pressures when we got a No. 1, we just had a ball.

Even after Buddy Holly left, the Crickets were quite successful, but it wasn't really a group: they were never tight enough and always hard to get together. Someone was always away or something was happening.

The lowest spot in my

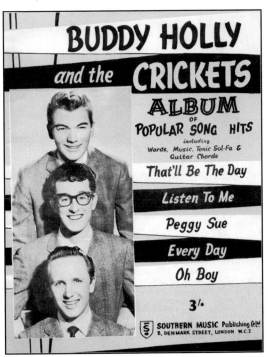

BUDDY HOLLY *and the* CRICKETS ALBUM OF POPULAR SONG HITS *including* Words, Music, Tonic Sol-Fa & Guitar Chords

That'll Be The Day

Listen To Me

Peggy Sue

Every Day

Oh Boy

3/-

SOUTHERN MUSIC Publishing Co Ltd
8, DENMARK STREET, LONDON W.C.2

life and career was in the early Sixties. I had been married only a few years —
married her in '58 — and was living in L.A., but things weren't going well for the
group and I was doing some work as a recording engineer. I couldn't get into
what they were all doing, and didn't want to get into the marijuana thing, so I
moved back to Texas.

My high spot has got to be our appearance for TV on the *Ed Sullivan Show*
and our 1957 New Year's Eve appearance on the New York Paramount show.

People ask why we are making a comeback, but we have always worked
on and off in the States. For myself, it's fantastic that we can come back over to
Britain after thirty years and play to packed houses for people who want to hear
us play our music. If the offer is right and the money is good, would you turn a
job down? Of course not, so it's the same with me. When the money offer is
right, I've always worked. Doing this tour gave my daughter the opportunity to
come to Britain for the first time and she arrives next week to join me.

The first time I played alongside Gordon Payne was at Peterborough
last year, but J.I. and Gordon have been together before that. We could play a
ninety-minute set, but I doubt if we could stretch beyond that period.

I have never minded the nostalgia and revival thing: I enjoy it and am
tickled to death. It makes people — including the young — ask for our old
records at the shops. I enjoy nostalgia — it's having fun and making money. The
more people want you, the more money you make and the more fun you have!

This Crickets threesome is the most enjoyable, and I have more fun on
stage than at any time. Our music is made up of fun tunes. We don't protest
about anything or have a message to give: we have fun playing our music and
the audience is having fun. We have no trouble keeping our material fresh. It's
easy for us to play, and we do it exactly to the original recordings — that's what
people come to hear.

Recalling the wonderful tour of Britain and the enthusiastic reception will always remain a great thrill. Words alone cannot be sufficient to thank you enough for your acceptance of my recordings.

My foremost hope is to be back with you real soon. Meanwhile —

Every Good Wish for a Merry Christmas and a Happy New Year

Buddy Holly

CORAL RECORDS

Business Representation :
GENERAL ARTISTS CORP.

Great Britain :
LEW & LESLIE GRADE LTD.

New Musical Express 1959 Annual

5

MAKE IT SAY SOMETHING!
Bo Diddley

Bo Diddley's vision of rock and roll was — and still is — quite unlike anyone else's. Heavily influenced by blues and doo-wop, he added African, Spanish and Caribbean elements to his music to create a truly unique sound. He was equally inventive as a guitarist, experimenting with sound effects like tremolo and reverb, and pioneering a hard-rocking style that has influenced successive generations of musicians.

My real name is Ellas McDaniel and I was born on December 30, 1928. You mention that you have also seen my name as 'Otha Bates'. I don't know where that 'Otha' came from, you need to forget about that. Forget that word, as it should never come up because I don't know where they got it from. My name is not 'Otha' and never has been. It is Ellas Bates McDaniel.

I started life as Ellas Bates, and was then adopted by my mother's first cousin. The woman that raised me — Momma Gussie McDaniel — is the same woman that raised *my* mother. I have never seen my father to know him. As many of us kids running around, we don't know who poppa is. We know who momma is, but poppa — maybe. *[laughter]* No discredit to the girls, although I am not saying they don't do weird things. Your momma is always there, but a lot of times you don't know which way daddy went. Sometimes a fellow can't hang: he can't cope with momma running her mouth and always chewing him out, so he takes a walk and you never see him no more.

I can't remember exactly when I moved to Chicago. I used to tell people that I was five, six or eight years old, but I think you could be right with five, as I started to play the violin at seven or eight. We moved because of the Depression in the Thirties. I can't say whether Chicago was a better place for blacks to work, as I was too young to know what the heck was going on. I didn't know anything about black and white, colour, or all the corruption crap that adults had going on. I think it was beautiful being a child not to be involved in that mess.

I don't know where my musical influences came from, I just know that I wanted to do *something*. I didn't know that I was going to end up as Bo Diddley. One day, I saw a man with a violin and wanted to play copy-cat. There were no influences at any time because I don't sound like anybody; everybody tries to sound like *me*. I listened to a lot of people, but I didn't pattern after them.

In Chicago, I went to school but I didn't do too well. As a kid I always thought that school was great, lovely, but I wasn't too educationally minded: I wasn't interested, you know. But I think that everybody should go and get that piece of paper. Knowing what I know today, I can truly say that — but school is not for everybody. It's all right for doctors and lawyers, but not everyone can be like that, and somebody has to be back here to do the dirty work. And I think that I was one who was cut out to do part of the dirty work, but on the other hand, somehow or other, I fooled people.

It doesn't *always* mean that because you don't go to school that you are illiterate, you know. I really believe today that if we eliminated some of the things going on in the classrooms, we wouldn't have so many bombs being built — but that would have to happen all over the world. In other words, *every* country would have to adopt the same idea. The more you teach people how to mix up this little grain of dirt and this little grain of sand, and put some horse manure on it, the bigger the bomb they will make. Colleges and places like that should be for science to find out how to get rid of all the diseases that plague us as human beings. They should be trying to stop the growth of whatever causes children to be born with handicaps and all this sort of stuff, and to try and weed out rapists and drug-users. This is what science should try to do instead of building bombs that are going to destroy us all at one little click.

I come from a very religious family of preachers, deacons and Sunday School teachers. They are all through my family, even now. I'm the outcast! *[laughter]* I'm not what they call a *devious* outcast, it's just that I'm one who doesn't go to church like I was brought up to do. I read my Gideon's Bible in my hotel room and I am a very religious person within myself. In other words: I try to help people.

I'm a rock and roller, and just like all the other rock and rollers that are going to perform on this show with me here tonight, we are all clean people. I can truthfully say that, because you will not come on this show — even if you sneak up and no-one knows you're coming — and find anyone with any dope or drugs. We don't fool with this mess: we *denounce* it. You understand me? We are from the old school. Guys might drink a little bit or something like that, but you won't find them falling all over the floor or in a state where they're having to be detained or locked up because they're drunk. We don't do this.

We are classified as very, very clean music. When everybody goes on stage, they are not doped out of their mind like a lot of today's musicians who have to get full of drugs before they can perform — we just don't do that. I think that drug-taking is ridiculous, and I think that the kids shouldn't be so rebellious towards their parents and adult friends who tell them to back off, because the grown-up stuff will keep.

No, I never played music with friends on Chicago street corners as some books have stated. My first performance was in Carnegie Hall, New York. *[laughter]* Oh, as an *amateur*... it was at the Lincoln Center in Chicago. There you go, it's been a long time. I played violin and won a scholarship and merit pins for my outstanding performance and stuff like that. At that time, I wasn't even thinking about the guitar and only turned to that instrument when I was thirteen or fourteen because Momma Gussie didn't dig.

As a teenager in high school, I formed my first group which was called 'The Langley Avenue Jive Cats' simply because I lived at 4746 Langley. My first appearance in front of a microphone was at the midnight club shows in Chicago — before that we didn't even know what a microphone was. Later on,

EVERYBODYS, "BEAU"

Rhythm & Blues, May 1955

BO DIDDLEY

we had another band with Frank Kirkland, Billy Boy Arnold, Jerome Green and Norma-Jean Wofford — 'the Duchess'. Norma-Jean is in Long Beach, Los Angeles, California now and Frank and Jerome are both dead. Clifton James was my original drummer and he did the *Bo Diddley* beat with me. You've probably seen him with Willie Dixon a lot — a little short dude.

Although sometimes people thought that Norma-Jean was my half-sister, we're actually no kin. We just used this 'she's my sister'. But in real spiritual life she *is* my sister. The Bible is right in that we are all brothers and sisters no matter which part of the planet we come from. People believe in God, whatever they call him in different religions. If they believe in the Book of

Genesis, then there were two people in the beginning and from those two people we got all different colours of people. The mixing-up of races on their own created other colours of people. So, if the Bible is right, we are all here through those first two people, that's all I can say. That's what we go by and that's what I was first taught when I stepped into church and learned how to read. So, when people don't believe that, and they tell me something else, I get a little bit weary, because then what *is* right?

From leaving high school until I auditioned and signed with Checker Records, I worked the Chicago nightclubs and had different day jobs. I used to be a foreman with a construction firm — what we, in the States, call a 'straw-balls'. That's a dude who's got substitute balls. I drove a truck, a big six-by-six stone truck, and I used to do road work like luting the pavements — which was levelling them before the roller went over them. I've done all types of jobs, so I know all about work and I know about *hard* work. I know about being hungry, and I've been there. I was an amateur boxer for a little while around Chicago. I didn't like it too well. *[laughs]* It was okay, but I like what I'm doing better.

I was also a policeman around 1972–74. I was a deputy sheriff in Los Lunas, New Mexico, Valencia County Sheriff's Department. We were nineteen miles out of Albuquerque and I knew Bob Foster, the World Light-Heavyweight Boxing Champion who was a deputy sheriff there, very well.

It was beautiful, man, you know, being an officer and the law enforcement. It gave me a chance to find out that policemen didn't have to be as naughty as some of them are. If they take into consideration that they were once teenagers, then they know that you only use force when you are forced to use force. Until that point is reached, you are supposed to be a lot, lot more intelligent than the dude you're about to arrest. You have a job to do and if you make this man create more problems — which can be done by harassing the person that you're arresting — then he will get angry. He may then say a lot of things, which might get him into *more* trouble, when *you* provoked him to do this because maybe he is not an adult.

I got the police job through being funny because I didn't think that they would hire a rock and roller as a cop, you know. *[laughs]* Three or four months after my application, I came home about three or four o'clock one day and my wife said: 'The police is looking for you!'

I said: 'Whaaat!'

Sure enough, when I went down there, I was the only black thing that was on the force.

I had never been in trouble with the police apart from getting locked up when I was eighteen years old, like many others. Any kid who gets past sixteen, seventeen, eighteen or nineteen without getting locked up is plain lucky 'cause he's bound to get hassled by 'the Man'. I got hassled *all* the time and reached the point where I almost hated a policeman because I didn't understand why they even existed. But when I got older, I started seeing that the role of the policeman was a wicked job. Somebody is always lurking in the dark trying to do you some harm, and the idiot that's trying to harm you doesn't know that you are out there trying to *protect* him! So, I joined the police department and I was glad to do it, man, and I'd do it again.

The kids in grammar school gave me the name 'Bo Diddley'. It's not jive talk or anything like that: I got the name not for being a bad boy, but because I used to punch out dudes that would jump little dudes at school. You know, little guys who couldn't defend themselves, and I'd take it up. I'd tell them: 'If you're gonna hit him, then you're gonna have to hit me too, baby!'

Then the big guy says: 'Well, I'll take both of you on,' and I say: 'No, no, no, only just one — me.'

Where the actual name came from, or what it meant, I don't know, but my mother said that, when she was a little girl in Mississippi, there was a man that used to sing and dance. He played guitar and harmonica and called himself 'Bo Diddley'.

The song *Bo Diddley* was written as a result of me and one of the guys in my band — Roosevelt Jackson — trying to write a song. The song was called *Uncle John* and I had to change and rewrite it. Yes *[laughs]*, the one with the rude words. They said: 'Why don't you use the name "Bo Diddley", man?'

It took me all night to figure out how to say: 'Bo Diddley bought his baby a diamond ring.' I just couldn't get it together. We stayed in the studio a long time with me trying to say in one breath: 'Bo Diddley bought his baby a diamond ring/ And if that diamond ring don't shine/ He's gonna take it to a private eye/ And if that private eye

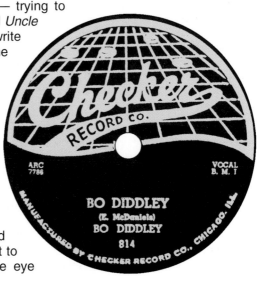

65

can't see/ You'd better not take my ring from me.' *[laughter]*

I have no idea why it took so long for me to get a recording chance — I never even thought about it.

My first meeting with Chuck Berry took place in the Chess studios. I ain't never had a feud with Berry — somebody lied. You see, a lot of times people try to make things up as they can't find nothing to put in their papers. They come up and do stuff that they think sounds like something that would have happened, and I don't like that. If you don't have the information, then you don't have a story — don't make up stuff!

I designed all those fancy-shaped and fabric-covered guitars like the 'Cadillac' just to be different. I've been much copied and people have traded on my sound, and that bothers me. Also the *Bo Diddley* album with my hits on that you just pulled up to show me is another example of a lot of mess that is going around which is very, very bad. It is very bad and ridiculous that this is happening to cats like myself. People are buying my records and they think that they are supporting Bo Diddley and they are not! They are unknowingly supporting thieves. I call them thieves because they have no intention of doing the right thing according to agreements. Whether the agreements were made twenty or thirty years ago, I am still here, I'm not dead, and if I die my kids are gonna be looking for the money, you understand what I mean? I got four children and seven grandkids. Nobody's gonna get away, so they may as well do the right thing because I'm coming! *[laughs]*

My favourite compositions out of my songs are *Bo Diddley*, *I'm A Man*, *Hey! Bo Diddley*, *Say Man*... oh there's a lot of them, man, a lot of them. I have an album out on New Rose Records in Paris called *Ain't It Good To Be Free*, and I just released another album on the Fan Club label of New Rose.

Yes, I did write *Love Is Strange*, which was a hit for Mickey & Sylvia and later on for the Everly Brothers. It wasn't my usual style, and when I first took it round people asked me if I was trying to turn into another Perry Como, so I put it under my wife's name.

You're right that the 1976 album, *The 20th Anniversary Of Rock'n'Roll* doesn't have much rock and roll on it. I don't like the album — period. I think it sucks. It's not me. A guy called Ron Terry came to me with the idea. Ron is a very nice person, but his idea of what Bo Diddley should have been was wrong. Nobody knows that better than me, because *I* am the person. I know what my public likes and what they expect from me because I am standing out there looking at them.

It's true that it's different everywhere you go, but that album was a very bad mistake because they put me into a situation where somebody says to me: 'What do you want to do? You just want to make money? Don't worry about it, just do it.' But it means *more* than just making money to me with my fans. It means being able to *play* this stuff for them. I can't play any of that stuff on that album. It's just not me and I hate it. I got two albums in my career that I literally *hate* because I had no say-so. *[Much laughter when it is suggested that I have brought them both to the interview deliberately.]* I had no say-so about a whole lotta things, but this was totally out of control.

You quote a very early review from 1957 of a Canadian performance that said I had a hypnotic act with a unique but limited sound, and mention that since then the 'limitation' comment has often been repeated. My reply to that is there are no limitations on my songs. I always have something to come out of the bag with. I'm fifty-six years old and I still write songs. I'm still thinking.

I'm in perfect health. I feel like the Rock of Gibraltar, and if you push me too far I'll shock you! *[laughter]* So, I tell other musicians — I tell cats — I say: 'Hey man, you know all this fancy playing and this fast finger-work and all that? To me, you're doing all this, and you ain't doing *nothin'*! Give me some soulful meaning, make your instrument *talk* to you. Make it say something to the audience, 'cause all this fancy fast stuff — deedle-deedle-deedle-deedle — it's *nothin'*. Make it *say* something! That is what I have developed: making it say something.

6

A WORD FROM THE WANDERER
Dion

Lead singer of Dion & The Belmonts, the most popular white doo-wop group of their time; million-selling solo artist with hits like *Runaround Sue* and *The Wanderer*; bluesman, folk-singer, gospel artist — Dion's amazing career history reflects the turmoil in his personal life as he struggled to find contentment as an artist and happiness as a human being.

I was born in New York on July 18, 1939. In those days, the Catholic Church insisted that you were named after a saint, so I was christened Francis Dion DiMucci. My father, Pat DiMucci, was a puppeteer in vaudeville and my mother, Frances, worked in a millinery shop making hats. My sister Joanie is a therapist today and married to a minister — she likes to work with teenagers. Donna, my other sister, is a beautician. I have no brothers.

I was educated at P.S. 45 until the sixth grade and I have just been inducted into the P.S. 45 Hall Of Fame with John Garfield and Carl Reiner. Then I went on to Roosevelt High School where I was a kind-of discontented teenager, restless and irritable. In total, I went to seven different high schools and was thrown out of a lot of them.

Musically, I was influenced as a real youngster by Hank Williams and later on by a lot of the black groups and singers who were coming out of the South like Fats Domino, Chuck Berry, the Dells and the Diablos, the Nutmegs and the Cadillacs. Basically, I liked rock and roll, a lot of country music, and blues. In the early Sixties, I got heavy into Robert Johnson.

No-one in my family played any musical instruments. I never sang in church choirs, but the churches used to hire me to do some dances. I used to sing at those Thanksgiving dances and other celebrations — for example when a monsignor became a bishop in the local Catholic church. The church was the hub of the neighbourhood, and they would ask me to sing with my group because I used to stir up things, to say the least.

I don't know about getting family encouragement for my musical talent: I was kind-of driven on my own because my family was very rigid emotionally: I mean they appeared warm on the outside but they were scared to death of feelings, and it was hard to express anything without anybody feeling threatened. So, music was a door for me, a way out to express myself without threatening anybody. It's always been one place I could go to be honest. I think I got encouragement, but mostly I was driven to music — it overtook me.

My first amateur performance was on the *Paul Whiteman Show* when I was thirteen. I sang two Hank Williams songs, *Jambalaya* and *Honky Tonk Blues*. This appearance didn't lead to anything much. By the time I was fourteen, I knew over one hundred Hank Williams songs. I got hung up on his music and just learned everything that I could get my hands on. It was a stepping-stone for me, a process of this learning and going on from there. I just used to digest Hank Williams, I used to inhale everything that he put out.

You ask me about religious influences. The Rev. Gary Davis, a priest in my neighbourhood, played blues. He played on the street corners of Harlem. I used to go up to his house, so I guess in a way he was a religious influence. He sang a lot of gospel music. There was another guy in my neighbourhood called Willie Johnson who used to sit on the stoops of the Bronx singing and playing his guitar — sang a lot of gospel songs, he influenced me. I had a mild Catholic upbringing, you know, with the big cathedrals and everything, but I never kind-of connected.

I was sent for music lessons, but I would take the money and spend it up in the pool-room and then I'd listen to Hank Williams songs and the groups on the jukebox, and I would teach myself new songs that I wanted to learn.

Moving towards music as a professional career, there was this guy in the neighbourhood who had a brother who was a songwriter who knew a friend who was opening up a record company. They knew that I played guitar, sang, and was causing quite a stir in the neighbourhood. People used to gather round me because I used to walk around the neighbourhood with my guitar. So they brought me down there, they liked me, and that was the beginning of a career for me. It wasn't like I knocked on any doors, it just happened.

If I hadn't gone into showbusiness, I would have needed an occupation where I could express myself by getting out and sharing myself with people — like painting or photography. It would have to be something in that vein because I like expression, self-expression, sharing my perspective, my thoughts and feelings.

The trigger to go solo from the Belmonts came after we did one album on which we put a record called *Where Or When*. This track was done for one of the company presidents of Laurie Records. I really liked this guy — he was like a father-figure to me — and, as *Where Or When* was his favourite song, we worked up an arrangement on it. It was way out of our back yard — it was something that didn't come natural to me — but we did it for him. The Belmonts liked that song and wanted to go further with it and kind-of wimp-out, so to speak, and do all of this neat harmony-pop singing. And that I didn't like. So, this caused a division, because I wanted to sing rock and roll and they wanted to sing standards. *Where Or When* therefore

became our swan-song.

Gene Schwarz *[founder of Laurie Records]* was what you would call a 'square'. In those days, we would produce our own records, arrange our own records, write our own songs — we just didn't get credit. But he had a knack, heard some things objectively and made an input — we got along. We disagreed on *some* things, but it wasn't a strained relationship. However, we were cautious. We were very suspicious of him because he wasn't one of us: he was a Jewish accountant with a whole different culture and approach. So, we looked on him as a square and certainly didn't just turn over everything to him, but he liked a lot of the stuff we came up with and had some good suggestions at times.

Ernie Maresca was a real character and gave us a lot of input in the early days with his writing. He was real help to us and, in a sense, very much a partner of mine. I used to bounce songs off him, and him off me.

As for having a say in production material, oh yeah, all of the time. Take a song like *A Teenager In Love* — it wasn't a song that came to me naturally, but I liked what the Belmonts did in the background. You know, they were doing this 'ooh-ooh-aah-ooh' which sounded kind-of nice and I wanted to put something on it. Even though it wasn't one of those songs that I could really get my teeth into, I knew that it was a hit, so we did it.

I had no regrets about leaving Laurie for Columbia, even though it wasn't a happy relationship. Columbia was a good company and it was a kind-of process for me. I was ready to stretch out and wanted to travel to Europe. With Columbia Records, I had a chance to go to England, France and Spain. They were a bigger machine who could get my music out to more people, so I made that move. Unfortunately, some division began there and it got into a time of disagreements which started to get sticky emotionally, so it was just time to leave.

At Columbia, *I* was the problem. I was changing rapidly. I had sung *Ruby Baby* and *Drip Drop*. John Hammond at Columbia — before he brought in Bob Dylan — he invited me into his office and said: 'I see you have a flair for the blues,' and started turning me onto a lot of records by Lightnin' Hopkins, Mississippi John Hurt and Robert Johnson. I got very hung up on these records and I started wood-shedding at my house and coming into Columbia with a lot of rural blues sounds. They didn't know what I was doing and it caused a lot of confusion because it wasn't pop-sounding to them. To this day, there is still a lot of unreleased blues stuff at Columbia that I was trying out with a lot of guys that I recorded with on *Runaround Sue*, like 'Sticks' Evans and Panama Francis who played drums, and all those good bass players. There was a lot of experimental material, and there is still a lot of good stuff at Columbia somewhere on the shelves.

My drug problem wasn't a factor at Columbia. I always had a drug problem, before I even started at Laurie Records. I started with drugs at the age of fourteen or fifteen. When I was at Laurie Records — at the time we had *Where Or When* out — I made a trip to a hospital in Hartford, Connecticut for a four-month stay, but I wasn't ready to deal with the root of the problem. My drug problem was progressive — neither moving to Columbia, nor a change in career had anything to do with it. It was perhaps the progression of the disease that started getting in the way of many things.

You mention comparisons between me and Bobby Darin, who was also an Italian American from the Bronx with similar roots. At that time, I wasn't really clear. Rock and roll was in its infancy, it was just starting. To begin with, I think that Bobby Darin was a club singer and he kind-of used rock and roll to get out to people, and he very naturally went into the clubs. For me, it was something different. A lot of these Italian guys like Bobby Rydell, Frankie

Avalon and others from the North who were in New York City at the time were doing the club thing. The record company was relentless for me to get into this because they thought that rock and roll was going to go away tomorrow. So, I tried my hand at it, but it was never me. It wasn't natural. Although I liked some of the arrangements and what I digested from listening to some of it, for the most part it simply wasn't natural. I didn't understand that I was a rock and roller at heart. I wasn't listening to that still small voice within me.

There were a lot of artists around me at the time who were making music that I really enjoyed listening to, and who influenced me. Roy Orbison — who I went to Australia with — he touched me deeply. Of course, I loved Fats Domino, who had this kind-of Cajun accent which he combined with a rolling blues 'happy' piano-playing style. Little Richard changed my life when I heard his records. The people that I was actually working with — like Gene Vincent, Eddie Cochran and Buddy Holly, who I was on tour with for two weeks before that fatal plane crash — were also very significant.

We affected our fellow artists. For example, these people had never heard of a Bronx-Italian rock and roll singer. You know, my music — which was black music filtered through an Italian neighbourhood — came out with an *attitude*. Ritchie Valens' music came from the body he was — Chicano — and played great rhythm guitar. Everybody just had a little different brand that they were bringing to the scene and we digested each other's influences.

Yes, I remember the whistle-stop touring package shows and what I got from them: I got a *headache*! Seriously though, there was a lot of music made on the buses and on those tours. I remember singing for hours with Sam Cooke and the Elegants, the different girl groups that we went on tour with, Little Willie John and Bobby 'Blue' Bland. God, those tours were just perking with creativity and you would soak it up like a sponge.

Of my own recordings, I have always loved *The Wanderer*. I like the drum riff and the sax sound on it. I like the song called *Lovers Who Wander* because I like the drums on that. *Runaround Sue* and *Abraham, Martin And John* are also favourites. Of other people's work, I would like to have recorded *Honky Tonk Women* by the Rolling Stones, and there is some good material on the Beatles' *Revolver* album.

I think God came into my life in 1968. It was then that I felt the connection with God — as I understand him — and started building a relationship in that area along spiritual lines. I am not religious, but I do feel like I have a relationship.

I don't like anybody preaching to me and I don't like preaching to anybody. I just share my experience, strength and hope with people, and if it can help somebody then that's fine. I've never been one to buttonhole anybody, put their back to the wall and, in a sense, say: 'Think like me, believe as me, do as me.' To me that's very arrogant.

From a personal point of view, without God I don't think that you could do anything. He is my substance. That's why I feel more powerful today than ever because that's where I get my health, my wisdom and creativity. It's all God-given. It doesn't come from drugs or even from me conjuring it up, it's a gift from God.

What made me come back and perform after many years of reportedly refusing to do so? Well, I had always performed, but I know what you mean. For years I hadn't sung my hit records as 'Exhibit A'. There was a lot I didn't

like about those type of shows and the things that I was offered. I didn't like the way that they presented that material, the context they put it in or how they formatted the music, so I stayed away from it. What changed? Well, they gave me the stage at Radio City Music Hall and said: 'Do a show for an hour and a half, and you can do whatever you want,' and I said: 'Thank you!'

You know, I like to take people on a trip, but not in the context of how they were then seeing and representing Fifties music. They had an idea of Fifties music like a Sha Na Na vibe, as if it was all very silly, stupid and ridiculous. This was kind-of insulting to my younger years, as I was serious when I did that stuff. Even though it is simple, I had feeling for it when I did it and it wasn't stupid, and we weren't silly — we were serious.

In a sense, writing my autobiography did help to unburden myself. In fact, since I have written it, I have changed because I saw patterns in it — behavioural patterns — that maybe I wanted to get rid of. I said: 'Gee, I don't need this,' and cut away a lot of excess baggage that I didn't need. Plus, I found out what was really important in my life, what really meant something to me: the people, the feelings, the music. I think that I got closer to myself by writing that book.

Looking back, I wouldn't change anything, because if I changed anything I may not be sitting here talking to you feeling as good as I feel about my music, about my life, about my children, about my wife. Just everything about my life brought me to this point. That is not to say that I am proud of *everything* I did, because I am not. There are sure things that I am *not* proud of, but I learnt from those things too.

The highest point of my career? There were a lot of major moments which stand out, like *The Wanderer* hitting the Top Five, and when I got a No. 1 record with *Runaround Sue*. I think even coming back to Radio City Music Hall and doing those few concerts was a high point. They were very, very touching and special kind of evenings for me which I'll never forget.

Being inducted into the Rock & Roll Hall Of Fame was unexplainable in a sense because it meant a lot — especially to somebody who has been making music as long as I have. It's hard for me to explain my feelings for all the artists who were there to thank me and who had voted for me. They were saying: 'Thank you for touching our lives and our spirits and sharing yourself with us. We thank you.' You felt like you had contributed something and had connected. Not that you are in it for approval all the time — not that I'm *not* [laughs] — but the idea of connecting just makes it all worth it.

For the highest point in my life, I gotta say that it's probably Susan and I having our children. Sharing these dreams of seeing things come true as your children mature and you let go of them, and liking what you see. They are very high points. And even to break through and work through all these little things in relationships with each other and come through the other end are very high points. That's what makes my relationship with my wife so special. We've walked through the valley together, and we been there with each other through the worst of times — not just the best. That's when you've got something — when somebody sticks with you through the bad times.

Certainly the lowest point of my life was when I hit a bottom with drugs in the mid-Sixties. It was like a living hell. I didn't like what was happening to me. You start blaming people for where you're at, you blame yourself, but you don't move anywhere. There are no solutions in your life and it's just like a bottomless pit. It's a bad feeling and it's a stuck feeling. That was the lowest point in my life and certainly my career, I think. But, you know, as they say 'the

darkest night is right before the dawn'. So that was another high, when God just reached down and said: 'It's your time!' and by His grace lifted me out of that pit.

Now that rock and roll has come into its own, they have these nostalgia shows, which I don't think are needed. For Paul McCartney to sing *Yesterday*, he doesn't have to put on a Nehru jacket or look like he did then. In fact, if he just sings the song as a song, it means more today listening to that than back then, because anything good is forever. So, I don't like the 'nostalgia' approach to things, although I understand how people relate to that sometimes.

I don't get frustrated at all when people want to hear my early work: I like performing it. In fact, when I come out with a band and do songs like *The Wanderer* and *Runaround Sue* and also Eighties material from a new album like *Yo Frankie*, anybody in the audience who'd never heard of the new stuff or the old wouldn't know which was which. Perhaps on record it sounds a lot different because of the technology, but not the way it is presented in my show today.

As for laying down a register of work on which to rest my career like Frank Sinatra, Johnny Mathis, Tony Bennett and others — gee, I think I have that. I have a foundation of songs that I can go out and build a whole career on, but I like the creative end of it and just like to keep creating. For me, I don't want to get into a rote, or the kind of bag where I just work over the old hit songs without doing anything new. So, I like new expression, but I also have no problem singing the old songs. In fact, they become more valuable to me as time goes on.

Looking ahead, I am now recording for Arista and we are going to be doing a tour in Europe. We are looking at a new album and I am excited about putting a lot of new songs together because we certainly became very visible with the album *Yo Frankie* here in the States and somewhat in Europe. That album was well received and I'm proud of it. I just hope to keep giving people some songs which really take them on a trip, make them feel and think, stir them, and persuade them perhaps. That's my job — it was always like that.

7

BIG BEAT FROM NEW ORLEANS
Fats Domino

One of the giants of the rock and roll era, Fats Domino at one time ranked third in global record sales after Elvis Presley and the Beatles. Born Antoine Domino in New Orleans on February 26, 1928, he was taught to play piano by Harrison Verrett, a musician who married his sister, and by his mid-teens was already performing in various clubs around the city. He was signed to Imperial Records in 1949, where he had a long and fruitful association with trumpeter/bandleader Dave Bartholemew that produced a string of million-sellers including *The Fat Man*, *Please Don't Leave Me*, *Ain't That A Shame*, *Blueberry Hill*, *Blue Monday* and *Walkin' To New Orleans*.

The interviewer's lot is not always a happy one. This one was carried out under extremely difficult conditions after Fats' show in a dressing room full of other interviewers and fans. Unlike the majority of interviews in this book which flowed easily into an edited conversational mould, this was very much a 'question-and-answer' session. Though he was affable, Fats didn't have lot to say for himself and appeared to find it difficult to understand some of our questions, which made for very slow progress. We also had the additional handicap of being put under a short time limit by his brother-in-law/manager, Reggie Hall, who left us in no doubt whatsoever that our presence was undesired. The first six questions were mine; the rest were asked by others who were present.

It's said that you are a millionaire. Why then, at 58 years of age, do you take to the road — which is a hard life — for tours, as opposed to playing selected dates like Richard Nader's rock and roll shows at Madison Square Garden, or venues in New Orleans or Las Vegas, etc?

Who says I am rich? People have been telling me that for years, but I know nothing about it. I am still playing piano on the road with a band, I have a few beers, and this is my way of enjoying life. One of my brothers-in-law died at the weekend. They buried him today, but I didn't want to cancel the shows and let the people down.

How much of an influence or help has your wife been?

A great help to me. We've been married thirty-seven years and she is the best wife in the world — and I'm not just saying that because I'm married to her. But she never comes on tour with me. Never has done.

Dave Bartholemew

Do you think that's why you've lasted thirty-seven years?

[Loud laughter from Fats]

Do you classify your music, and Dave Bartholomew's, as rock and roll?

It has been called all names: rock and roll, jazz, R&B, blues, blues with a beat. I was playing that kind of music when I started out in the 1940s. If you play it soft one way it's 'roll', and if you play it harsh it's 'rock', but I probably see it as blues music.

Songs like *Blue Monday* are my favourites, as they are about everyday life and happenings. It doesn't matter what name they want to give my music.

I want you to meet Dave Bartholemew, my partner who wrote all those records with me.

Dave, with Fats you created a very distinctive sound. No matter what Fats plays, as soon as the music starts, just like Chuck Berry's riffs, you know who it is. Did you and he create an 'individual' sound deliberately?

Yes, it was a matter of experience, and I knew how to write the songs and in what pattern.

Fats, did Alan Freed give you your big break as a black entertainer on his shows along with Chuck Berry, LaVern Baker and others?

Not really, I was already known before that time and cut my first record in 1949. I was recording before Chuck. He made his first record in when — 1955? I made my first in 1949, *The Fat Man*. I wanted to play it tonight, but I just couldn't get it going in my hands enough.

Billboard, July 1961

I had hit records before Alan Freed, but he played *everybody's* records — that's what I liked about him. He was the first to call it 'rock and roll', so he gave everybody a break by playing the records over in Cleveland before he got famous. He helped everybody's records and he paid for us to play. He got a name for rock and roll, but we played it for him.

Tell us about the Alan Freed shows.

I started with Alan Freed in the Fifties at the Brooklyn Paramount Theatre. The theatre people used to get to the theatre at nine o'clock in the morning. People had been there since five or six o'clock in the morning — queues eight, nine or ten blocks. LaVern Baker, Ruth Brown — they were on these shows.

We used to play his rock and roll shows, but he still called it 'rhythm & blues'; a real fast song he'd call 'rock and roll'. When you played slow, you'd be 'rolling' and when you played fast, you'd be 'rocking'.

Where did your influences lie?

I had a few, you might know. Have you heard of Amos Milburn? Mostly piano-players: Meade Lux Lewis, Pete Johnson, Albert Ammons... I heard their records, I picked up ideas from them. I was going to a private teacher but I had to get off that to do what I'm doing now.

The music from New Orleans in the Fifties was a 'friendly' kind of music. Was it a friendly city?

Oh, one of the best in the world! Everybody helped each other: bands just wanted to play. As a matter of fact, a lot of bands still do it — but not like we used to do it.

Does the new technology in music appeal to you at all?

Some people go to school for techniques, some people are born with it. All music is good, but there's a lot of electronics now. When I used to record when I made my first records, we only made one track. If anybody made one mistake on that track, we had to go all the way back. Now, if you make a mistake, if one horn makes it, you just go back two or three seconds and make a 'da-da-da-da', but in the Fifties the whole band used to go over and over it until they got it. Sometimes it would take eight hours to record one number! Now, you can record a session in no time.

Are you going to retire?

Retire? Are you *kidding*? No, I hope I'm playing music as long as I live because I *love* it! Music has been almost one hundred percent of my life. All my problems, any kinds of worries I have, I'm just about at the stage where they're ready to go away. I'm starting to do a lot of work again: I see I can't do without it. I never really stopped, I just didn't travel as much. I used to travel *so* much at first: I used to work 275 days a year.

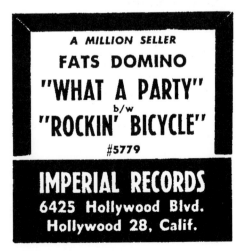

8

$1,000,000-WORTH OF TWANG
Duane Eddy

A gifted musician and great innovator whose creations raised him to the popularity of a vocalist, Duane Eddy enjoyed twenty-seven US hits between 1958 and 1964 — among them classics like *Ramrod*, *Cannonball*, *Forty Miles Of Bad Road*, *Because They're Young* and, of course, the ground-breaking *Rebel-Rouser*. The titles may have been somewhat contrived and the rebel yells a little over the top, but when more than lyrics were needed to express feelings, the twangy guitar spoke volumes for rebellion and teenage angst.

I was born Duane Eddy on April 26, 1938 in Corning, New York State. My father, Lloyd, did various jobs and the last thing he did was to manage a supermarket. Mother, Alberta, was a housewife. I have one brother and one sister — Glenn and Elaine. My first schooling was in Bath, then Penn Yan, New York. We moved to Tucson, Arizona when I was eleven, and four years later to Phoenix. I attended school in Tucson and graduated from Arizona Coolidge High when I was seventeen.

I received no formal musical education at all and am self-taught on the guitar. My parents always encouraged me and were both somewhat musical, but not to any exceptional degree. It was my dad's acoustic guitar that I first came upon when I was about five years old. He showed me a few chords and it became my hobby until I reached thirteen or fourteen, when I developed a serious interest.

As a kid, I found that I liked playing country & western songs and also played some steel guitar. My early musical influences, as I recall, were from the radio — artists like Merle Travis, Hank Williams, Barney Kessel, Les Paul, Joe Maphis, Mary Ford, Louis Armstrong, Ella Fitzgerald and later, of course, Elvis. It was just before the full rock and roll era, and country & western and big band music were popular.

Although I liked listening to jazz, it was never a real influence on me or my style. Ironically, the only lessons I ever had on a guitar were from a jazz guitarist, Jim Wybele. I only took two lessons, but didn't enjoy them — it wasn't my style — so I dropped them.

My interest in music never interfered with my school work. In many ways, the education I received in New York was superior to that in Arizona, so for the first few years much of it was just recapping for me.

By the time I was fifteen, I was buying — with my dad's help — a Les

Paul *Gold Top* guitar with a small amplifier. I started working in local Arizona bands, and spent most of my time perfecting my technique and learning from other artists.

I can't recall my first amateur performance, we just started anywhere we could — mainly with country groups in bars and clubs. Around 1954, I teamed up with a school friend of mine, Jimmy Delbridge. We used to do country songs together like the Louvin Brothers and the Wilburn Brothers and that type of thing. Jimmy and myself appeared on KCKY Radio in Coolidge and for a while we had a regular Saturday spot. This was our radio debut and we did things like country & western cover versions of hits.

Around 1955, I met Lee Hazlewood who was a deejay with KCKY. A friend took me up to meet him one night, and that is how our association started. Al Casey, the bandleader and guitarist also came into my life at this time, and I learnt a lot by sitting in with Al's band and by studying recording techniques from Lee, who was beginning to make demo records at Ramsey's Audio Recording Studios in Phoenix.

By 1956, Jimmy and myself were often featured on KTKV-TV's show called *The Country Hit Parade*. I suppose our local success created a demand for our first record and that is how we came to do *Soda Fountain Girl* with Lee Hazlewood's help. Lee composed that song and the flip side, *I Want Some Lovin' Baby*. These duets, as 'Jimmy & Duane', were recorded at Ramsey's studios in Phoenix and released on the Preston label. Some months later, Jimmy and I went our different ways and I did session work with Al Casey. I can't recall many of the sessions, but I worked on Sanford Clark's recordings and others.

In 1956, I was ready for a new guitar and traded in the Les Paul for a Gretsch *Chet Atkins 6120* and Bigsby tremelo which aided the 'twang'. I arrived at the twang sound by logic: I had been studying guitar sounds and styles for years and felt that a new sound could be created by building a sound using a bass lead. Nearly all of the hit records were played on the Gretsch with normal tuning.

Over the years, I have read that I used a guitar tuned one octave lower, but that wasn't true. However, around 1959, when I did *The Twang's The Thang* album, and in 1960 when I recorded *Because They're Young*, I used a Dan Electro guitar which *was* about a half-tone lower.

I played on the bass strings, because they are stronger and record stronger, and just constructed melodies as we realized that hot licks, riffs and jamming weren't going to make it or produce hit records.

Al and Lee co-wrote my material with me, and Lee and I had an arrangement to write most things together. One day, in 1957, Lee and I decided to do an instrumental and cut *Ramrod*, written by Al Casey. A few copies were pressed in an attempt to place it with a record company. It was

JAMIE
RECORDS
PHILADELPHIA, PA.

UNBREAKABLE
45 R.P.M.

RECORD NO.
1104
DE-3

GREGMARK (BMI)
Time: 2:04

Produced by
Sill & Hazlewood

REBEL—'ROUSER
(Duane Eddy-Lee Hazlewood)
From the Production Rebel-'Rouser
Starring John Buck
DUANE EDDY
AND HIS "TWANGY" GUITAR

released locally in Phoenix on Ford by 'Duane Eddy & The Rockabillies', but nothing happened, so we dropped the whole project. Al Casey had his solo *Caravan* on the flip-side.

Lee was always looking for new sounds and felt that Eddie Duchin's piano style imitated on guitar could with the right tune provide a big instrumental hit. Al couldn't come up with anything, but I played around with the Gretsch and the Bigsby, and that's how Al and I wrote *Moovin' n' Groovin'*.

Lee liked it, and he and his business partner, Lester Sill, got Jamie Records in Philadelphia interested. They put it out and it sold 100,000 or so.

We were in the studio the first time we heard *Moovin' n' Groovin'* played on *Bandstand*. On its first appearance in the charts, Lee called to tell me, but I can't recall what I was doing. It was very exciting. Jamie said to go back in and do some more, so we produced *Rebel-Rouser*.

The idea for *Rebel-Rouser* came at a session where Lee and I wrote it. Having worked one week on a rock and roll show in L.A. after recording *Moovin' n' Groovin'*, I came to the conclusion that I needed something to get me on the stage that would look good and sound good — an image if you like — so I pictured it and structured it. Thankfully, *Rebel-Rouser* was a worldwide hit.

We always went for dramatic titles that were cool and fitted the music: *Lonesome*, *Forty Miles Of Bad Road* needed those kind of titles: they were that type of song. *Forty Miles Of Bad Road* was named after our US driving expression: 'I've just done forty miles of bad road'.

To accommodate our recording, Floyd Ramsey located and bought a huge 500-gallon water tank to be used as an echo chamber. They set it up in his Audio Studio's back yard and attached a mike at one end and a speaker at the other. We were all amused to see someone chasing birds off the tank in the morning so that recording could start. If a police or fire siren sounded on the highway, it meant another take. We used a four-track Ampex deck and a new technique called 'stereo'.

In the first year at Audio, everything was cut using two or three of the available tracks and leaving one open. Lee Hazlewood would then have the tape overdubbed in L.A. with sax — usually by Gil Bernal or Plas Johnson — and rebel yells, mainly by the Sharps. When *Rebel-Rouser* was a hit in 1958, I hired my first sax player, Steve Douglas, and together with local recording musicians Al Casey, Buddy Wheeler and Bob Taylor, the Rebels were formed. I came up with their name from *Rebel-Rouser*.

One night, on *American Bandstand*, I was asked if I could close the show 'live'. I played *Ramrod*, and this created a demand for my 'new' single. Lee and I had intended *The Lonely One* as our follow-up but, in view of the reaction to *Ramrod*, Lee dusted off my 1957 version, dubbed sax and rebel yells in L.A., and had the 1958 version into the shops within a matter of days.

No conscious decision was taken to entertain — I just wanted to be a musician and there was never any alternative to that in my mind. It was Lee who thought that we should try an instrumental. Rock and roll was getting very big at the time, the scene was wide open and I just figured that I could do it.

My touring days were very enjoyable and I worked the best of them like the Irving Feld *Caravan Of Stars* . Irving Feld did all the best tours and I have some great memories. The first tour I did was with Chuck Berry and Buddy Holly. They usually had fifteen acts like Bill Haley, the Everly Brothers, Little Richard, Jerry Lee Lewis — in fact everybody but Elvis.

Many great friendships were formed in those days with artists like the Everly Brothers, and it was good to meet them again on the Dick Clark *American Bandstand 30th Anniversary Show*, with the likes of Chubby Checker, the Shirelles, Frankie Avalon, Fabian and Ricky Nelson.

There was never any rivalry or competition amongst the artists on these tours. People either liked your records or they didn't, and if they liked them, they went out and bought them. If you sold a million it was great, but there was no competition. The promoters got rich out of the tours. They paid us enough to pay our expenses, little more.

One of the best tours was my UK tour with Bobby Darin, Clyde McPhatter and Emile Ford, with Bob Miller & His Millermen to back Bobby and Clyde. My visits in 1970 and '71 to entertain US troops in Vietnam were also enjoyable for me.

My early publicity notes were not wholly accurate. Basically, I am quite a shy guy and have a deep love of the desert and its peace. I read all kinds of books, but never went shooting or fishing. I couldn't kill anything — and I haven't, except rattlesnakes — and fishing is so boring. I did genuinely like American history, and that is probably why the guy who wrote them thought I'd like hunting and fishing. I gather he found it all pretty funny.

I enjoyed my Hollywood days but, apart from being a non-actor, I was too shy. My film appearances in *A Thunder Of Drums* and *The Wild Westerners* were enjoyable too, and I formed a friendship with the actor Richard Boone. Also, as well as appearing on his *Bandstand* and *Saturday Night* shows, I did a movie with Dick Clark — *Because They're Young* — and had a big hit with the title track. Dick was in partnership with my manager and had a slice of Jamie Records, but got rid of it when Congress started the payola enquiries which ruined Alan Freed.

Although I had over twenty hit records, there was never any pressure on my part for follow-up records. I just didn't worry about it. We felt each record could be the last, but hoped that the next one would also make it. And when it did, it was great. I suppose that I was surprised in the beginning that

---

* Dick Clark took over with his tours in 1961.

something I had created — the twang — had caught on, but I liked the sound, and somewhere inside of me I figured that others would as well.

Towards the end of my main success, I got disgusted with things and wrote this song one day. It sounded like *Rebel-Rouser* sideways, so I thought that I would call it *Son Of Rebel Rouser* — my weird sense of humour and I am guilty. It was no-one else's decision but mine to issue *that* one!

Like children, I don't have favourites among my compositions. I liked them all, but if you push me hard I will probably express a preference for a non-hit I wrote called *Along Came Linda*. I was lucky I got the chance to records all of my favourite instrumentals on one album for RCA. I like today's technology in making records because, with the twist of a knob or a push of a button, you can do in a few seconds what it took us all day to do. That is wonderful, but I don't let the technology use me. I still remember the music. My own favourites are material by Les Paul and Chet Atkins. I like the multi-track and did it on *Lover* on my second album.

Producing for other artists like Phil Everly's *Star Spangled Banner* and Waylon Jennings has given me much satisfaction as a musician, as well as my spell as a producer at MCA with Jimmy Bowen and having my son, Christopher Duane Eddy, playing drums in my present band.

Looking back, like many others, there is much that I would have done differently. I still smoke cigarettes too much, but I never saw any point in giving yourself problems with alcohol and drugs.

I wasn't managed well, but don't want to elaborate on an aspect you could expand into a book. It was a hit-and-miss affair in those days when I started out. Basically, the businessmen we were involved with grabbed the money and ran. They figured that none of us would be around in six months time, let alone a year. We were living rock and roll, loving it, and believing in it. I get writer's royalties, and I get recording royalties from RCA but not Jamie.

I should have been more of a businessman myself instead of being nice to work with, co-operative and stupid. There should have been proper representation, but how do you know who to trust?

9

CRUISIN'
Frankie Ford

Frankie Ford shot to fame when his second release, *Sea Cruise*, made No. 14 in the US charts in early 1959. A New Orleans rock and roll classic, it paved the way for several smaller hits including *Alimony* and *You Talk Too Much* and a successful career as one of the most dynamic of all Crescent City entertainers.

My real name is Frank Guzzo and I was born in New Orleans, Louisiana on August 4, 1939. Some books have 1940 and 1941, but it's 1939. I am an only child. My father worked for a shipyard and mother was a homemaker — just a regular family.

In my family, I'm the only one that is musically inclined. From the time I was a child and we would go into a restaurant or something, I was always at the jukebox. It was the first place that I went to and I'd hold on, even in diapers, and dance. I've always loved music. My earliest recollection of music would be around the time that we lived in a little town called Patterson right outside of Morgan City. It could probably have been country music. They tell me that as a kid I used to sing *Pistol Packin' Mama*. I forget who did that originally, but it was a country record.

I remember driving into New Orleans with mother singing *Colinda* sometime in the early Forties. There were no major influences that I could put together from that time, only songs. Later on, there were influences from Tony Bennett, Frank Sinatra, Kay Starr and Hank Williams. When rock and roll came about, it was Fats Domino, Little Richard and that type of artist.

When I was playing in my high school band, the Syncopators, Clarence 'Frogman' Henry would help me with some things. He was working in a place called the Joy Lounge and I used to go to his house in the afternoons as he didn't live too far away. And, of course, when I started to work with Huey 'Piano' Smith, he taught me a lot. I studied classical voice extensively, but as for piano, I just took the basics up and then sort-of ran with it from there and learned the licks, phrasings and all that the New Orleans people use.

I don't know why I chose the piano. Even before then, when we lived in the country in Patterson, my mother and another lady had a card-party thing that they held every Tuesday afternoon in the lady's home. They played bridge and all of that. The lady had a piano and I used to pick out melodies on it. One of the lady's sisters taught piano and she said: 'While you're here every Tuesday, let me give him lessons,' and so I started that way. I can play any keyboard, but nothing else.

My family were always very supportive but never pushed me into it. Their attitude was: 'If you want to take it, then fine.' My father, when he bought a piano, said: 'You want this, you're gonna deal with it', but he never did force me. The lady who was teaching me told us that a piano was an investment as there was always someone who wanted one, but we always kept it.

I guess as early as I could talk and sing, I would do parties and family gatherings. When I was about six years old, my godfather — an attorney — did some work for his good friend Ted Fiorito, who was in Carmen Miranda's orchestra. While we were in Memphis, the orchestra was playing the Peabody Hotel and I sang *Pistol Packin' Mama* in the show. At six years of age that was quite a big deal and we have pictures of that. Of course, I didn't go on with Carmen, I went on with Ted Fiorito and the support show. Even as big as Carmen was, you still didn't follow children or dogs — it's the old vaudeville thing.

From there, I went on to taking lessons and working in vaudeville, charity and hospital shows and then into amateur contests. I won about thirteen straight and won the state championship. Then I was sent to New York to be on the *Ted Mack Original Amateur Hour* in 1952, and that's when you had to turn professional to be on television. So, on September 18 this year I will have been a professional for thirty-six years, and I've not done anything else. Always as a child I said that I wanted to be a singer, an actor, a dancer, so I don't know what else I would have done.

When I came out of school at the end of 1957, my manager, Joe Caronna, was also the manager of Record Sales — a record distributor — and I worked there and did everything possible just to be in the business. In addition, I was still working with the high school band three, four, five times a week. I was signed to Johnny Vincent's Ace Records at the end of 1957 or the beginning of 1958. There have been some bleak times like the 'British Invasion'— we've all had them — but I've never had any doubts about going into showbusiness.

My offer of a recording contract came up when I was working a club. A man came up and said the typical thing: 'I think you're very good, here's my card, give me a call,' and he took my number. He didn't call for the longest time, then he said: 'I'm going to come to a band rehearsal, I want to hear you a little better without the crowds and all that.' So, he came along and then told me that he wanted to use me, but not the band. They could be used as a back-up band, but he couldn't use them for recordings as they had all the professional musicians at the studio. So, having true honesty and all that, I said: 'Well, I don't want to leave my band.'

He said: 'Well, I'll let you know.'

One afternoon he called and said: 'Get down to the studio, the Man *[Johnny Vincent]* is here.'

When I got there, he said: 'Let us hear your original material,' so I played *Cheatin' Woman* and *The Last*

Billboard, April 1959

One To Cry.

'Okay,' he said, 'we're going to do a session!'

I said: 'When?' and he said: 'Now!'

So, I went home that night with a demo record.

It was actually at the first record session that my stage name came about, as they didn't know what to call me. My manager had a new Ford car and they said: 'What about Frankie Ford?' They liked the flow of it, and then my manager said: 'What about Frankie Lee Ford?' At that time Jerry Lee Lewis wasn't very big, but there was a Frankie Lee Sims. Anyway, I nixed the 'Lee'. I said: 'No, I don't like that at all. No, no, please not.' However, Frankie Ford I liked, and I still do.

Huey Smith wrote *Sea Cruise*, so I don't know how it came to be written, but Bobby Marchan was Huey's lead singer in the Clowns and he was ready to go out on his own. In 1959, Huey was riding high in the charts with *Don't You Just Know It* and I had my first record, *Cheatin' Woman*, out and was working in Philadelphia. I came back on the Sunday night, and I think on Monday night they called and said: 'Come into the studio, we want to put your voice on Huey's follow-up to *Don't You Just Know It*.'

So, I went in and Huey taught me *Sea Cruise*. He told me the words and I wrote them down. I still have the paper with all the mis-spelling and all my little notes about inflections and things like that. Then we laid down the tracks. We did *[the flip] Roberta* first, then we did *Sea Cruise*, and used the Clowns in the background for both recordings.

After the session was over, my manager said: 'Huey, you don't need a record now, but Frankie needs one. Let's put this one out on Frankie and the

next thing we'll put out as your follow-up.' So, I actually acquired it and I'm so thankful that I did get it! I thought that *Roberta* was the 'A' side originally, but Cosimo Matassa — who owned the studio and was the engineer — and I both thought 'No, no, no, it's the other side,' and we ended up right.

Sea Cruise took off in New Orleans and was very big. Then they did test markets on it. I was sleeping in the back seat of my manager's car and we were coming back to New Orleans from Jackson, Mississippi. He was listening to Hoss Allen out of Nashville, and suddenly he was yelling and screaming and woke me up. He said: 'Listen!' and I said: 'Well, yeah, good, they're playing the record.'

He said: 'No, that's *Hoss Allen* playing the record!' Then he said: 'Here it goes from here. That test market showed if it breaks out of Nashville and goes pop, it'll break nationally.' Then it moved to Bill Randle at WERE in Cleveland and Bob Green in Miami, and then Dick Clark picked up on it.

Even without *Sea Cruise*, one way or another I think I would have still been in this business. I would have had to look at different vehicles.

As for keeping *Sea Cruise* fresh after all these years... well, first of all I loved the song the first time I heard it. It comes at the end of the show and I do sing it with full meaning every time and try to do it as it was done then. I don't try to change anything about it.

You mention my reputation for being a dynamic entertainer and ask me about my restrained performance on Richard Nader's *Rock'n'Blues Reunion* tour *[1985]*. Well, I only had something like sixteen minutes, but I don't think that I was restrained. I did Little Richard, I did Fats Domino and I did Frankie Ford. Maybe some of the audience felt that it was a bit more formal than some of the rock and roll shows like the festivals at Weymouth and Eindhoven. It was just that the venues were a little bigger. Also I had a suit on that I wore on the Dick Clark show. I don't think that I was restrained, but I don't know whether it came off that way. It could be that as they seemed to be big venues some people might have been looking at it as if it was a television show, or something like that, with all those acts.

You have to give it to the promoter, the show was quite successful. He had one of each type on the show: you had a white rocker in me, a version of the Marvelettes, and Bobby Vee — the white young teen idol. Then you had Del Shannon who was the cross between country and rock, Bo Diddley explains himself and, of course, so does Rick Nelson. I thought it was a very good cross-section of American music, except for a black doo-wop group.

Regarding nostalgia: I have done conventions which have gone on for five days, and one of those days was the nostalgia show. I did one just a couple of months ago with Richard Nader in Chicago at the Park West. It had the Doves, Johnny Maestro & The Brooklyn Bridge, the Dixie Cups who did *Chapel Of Love*, and me. The people there just went wild, dancing and singing along. The producers told me that they had a disco night and a big band night, but that the biggest party and most fun was the nostalgia party. I think that everyone likes to look back, and nostalgia is always nice. If it was bad, you say: 'Well, it was bad but we had fun,' and if it was good you say how good it was. So, nostalgia is always here, and if the music is presented properly that is important.

Talking about my categorization as a rock and roll singer... in the Fifties, when rock and roll came about, it was 'rhythm & blues' — that's what we called the music. But when I started to work later on in 1959 and 1960 for Alan Freed, it was 'rock and roll'. At that time, if you were doing what you liked to do, and were successful about it, you really didn't care what they called it. I mean, it could have been called 'doo-wop', like the groups. I don't think that categorization is important, music is the catalyst for the whole thing,

From the time *Sea Cruise* hit the charts to the time that I went into the US Services in 1963, I was involved in the big package tours. These packages usually had at least five or six acts, and some of the big ones had something like twelve acts. You would go out and do your records, and we carried a big band. It was good training and hard work — just like I'd had before with the high school bands and the like. It makes a contrast with today when you're chauffeured around and pampered. I sometimes laugh at the things that are done for us now, but it certainly makes you feel that when you go out on stage you'd better do your job.

I have many memories from those touring days. In some of my shows I do songs by — as I say — my 'friends in heaven'. I was with Jackie Wilson on the night that he received his gold record for *Lonely Teardrops*, and was a friend of Ed Townsend and a lot of people. The *Rock'n'Blues Reunion* tour was really fine and so were the venues — particularly in the UK. Dave Nelson, Rick Nelson's brother, said in a program that he did about Rick that it was one of the finest tours he had done.

Any disputes between Rick Nelson and Richard Nader were kept off the stage. Rick went on and did Rick Nelson. No matter what you or anyone thinks of the promoter or the band, when you go out onto that stage you are professional and do what you're supposed to do and enjoy it — whether you do or not. That is what I do all of the time.

There are 40,000 funny stories from touring, but your book would be too long and I don't like to mention names. So many

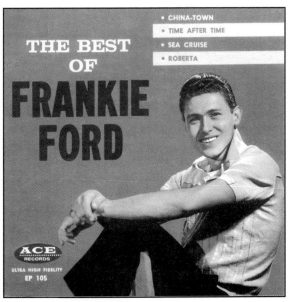

● CHINA-TOWN
● TIME AFTER TIME
● SEA CRUISE
● ROBERTA

THE BEST OF

FRANKIE FORD

ACE RECORDS

ULTRA HIGH FIDELITY
EP 105

funny things go on. I have one of the first Polaroid cameras and have photos of people losing their trousers, and getting pulled off the stage, and coming back in just their underwear, and people missing the tour coach. The coach left at 9 am prompt, and if you weren't on it, then you had to get to the next place on your own. You'll have to wait for *my* book — I'll have them all in there *with names*!

Jackie Wilson, Little Richard and Fats Domino are favourites of mine — so, so many that I worked with. It was quite a thrill for me to come up so fast that I found myself working with people that I'd idolized. Being on first name terms and spending evenings with them, that was special.

My relationship with Fats Domino is a good one. Although we did share the same label at one time *[Imperial]*, we never recorded together. I go to his home, and in fact he called me on my birthday last year to wish me happy birthday, and I call him on his. I have opened for him at a number of places in the States. We were at the Chicago Theatre the third week after it was reopened and then we were at the Fox Theatres in St. Louis and Atlanta. He is a beautiful, lovely, lovely man.

With the 'British Invasion', you certainly got us back for the Battle of New Orleans! I got out of the services at the beginning of 1965 and everything was closed in New Orleans. There are comments sometimes from the staunch rock and rollers that I sold out in the Sixties by going into cabaret. Well, if you hadn't sent us those packages that rock and rollers in the UK seem to detest today... Anyway, while that musical style was going on I went into cabaret, as I was trained for all kinds of music. I ended up owning four nightclubs at different times in New Orleans. Believe me, there was nobody working in New Orleans at that time, and that's when that great exodus went to Los Angeles.

You had the Beatles who started it, and then you had the Rolling Stones right behind them. Everyone in the world tried, then you had to get out and that was it. It was the biggest influence that Britain has ever had in music. Then you had to wait until the Seventies to get Dylan, Blood, Sweat & Tears and all of that in there. I was happy to see that era come about. But, back in 1965, there wasn't a single recording contract to be had in New Orleans. I think that the girls in the Dixie Cups were the only ones — that I know of — to beat the Beatles out. The Beatles had Nos. 2–10 in the charts and the Dixie Cups had *Chapel of Love* at No. 1. They were the only American act to beat them out, and it was a girl group.

There was an irony in the Beatles displacing the rock and rollers who had influenced them. When they were in New Orleans, they spoke about all the New Orleans flavour because one of their first influences was Little Richard. In fact, on the tapes found in Germany they did a song that I wrote called *Have You Got Troubles*. So, obviously I was in there somewhere, but that didn't help when I had finished my stint in the services and intended to go right back into what I'd been doing — because my career had been going well. Here, all of a sudden, there was nothing. Even in the Army Special Services I had my own show which toured all over the Orient to places like Guam, Thailand, Korea, Vietnam, Japan and the Philippines, entertaining the troops.

New Orleans has always had a happy atmosphere musically, and still has today. It's going through a little change now with going back to traditional Dixieland music. We are now in the middle of July and I have worked once in New Orleans this year, when I took part in the *Jazz & Heritage Festival*. In fact, last year I only worked New Orleans three times. I still live there, but I'm always out on the road.

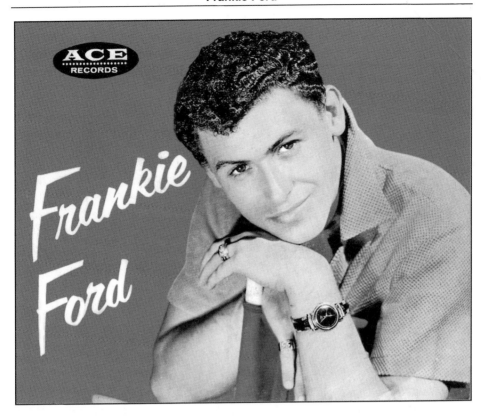

There have been a couple of high spots in my career. One of them was here in the UK, at the Royal Albert Hall, and the other was at the Hollywood Bowl. And of course, the Dick Clark shows like the *Saturday Night* show have always been special.

The lowest spot was when I got back to New Orleans from the service in 1965. I was so happy to get out — not that I'm unpatriotic or anything, but they certainly interrupted a good career. It might not have been so hard if I could have been taken down gently, but when I got back there was *nothing* and I had to go to clubs and look for a job. Of course, I managed. I always will and I always did because I had the drive and initiative. I went and found some place and said to the man: 'I'll build your business up if I can have a piece of it.' And so, literally, that's what I did. I took a little club which was very small and built it up so we didn't close until seven or eight o'clock in the morning. That was the quickest shock in my career — coming out of the service in 1965.

I have never hit rock bottom even then, because I've always had that drive. You don't wait around for something to happen, you go make it happen, and you approach it from any direction you can. Last year, I did over two hundred dates and I am going to do more this year, but you don't sit around waiting for them to come to you. You get out there with good management who will present the act, and you spend money to put back into your act. A lot of people just want to take out of the act. They don't want to put anything back into it or do any research or anything. I listen to my act and go as far as imitating my own records because, naturally, I'm not seventeen years old again — that doesn't happen. But no, no, no, there was never a time when I was down.

There are a lot of songs that I would have liked to record. Originally, I turned down *You Talk Too Much*[*] and had to acquire it later through the record companies to record it myself. Fats Domino turned it down and his brother-in-law, Reggie Hall, *wrote* it! There were others I would have liked to record, but that was the 'biggie'.

I was second in line for the song *Go Jimmy Go* that Jimmy Clanton did. It was written for Frankie Avalon first as *Go Frankie Go*, and then Jimmy was hee-hawing with it because he didn't know whether he wanted to record it. Then I figured: 'Well, maybe if he doesn't want it, then I don't want his hand-me-downs.' My manager said: 'If it's a hit song you'll take it because I know how you are.' As it happened, I didn't get the chance to turn it down as Jimmy did it.

I listened to an original tape of *For The Good Times* — the Kris Kristofferson song — and I said: 'I don't know. I don't like that too much.' It wasn't my particular style, but at the time I was doing cabaret stuff and it could have been very, very advantageous to my career. But I said: 'Well, no.' It wasn't presented properly — I have one of the original audition tapes that was sent to me and it was very bad — so that is something that I've missed.

Jimmy Clanton was a good performer, he was fine. He did Jimmy Clanton, middle-of-the-road rocker. He liked uptempo tunes, but all of his things on record seemed to come out slower. Oh yes, his hairstyle was distinctive: the bird's nest! Jimmy's now a born-again Christian and a preacher, and he's not performing at all other than Christian music. As I understand it — and this is hearsay — he won't even sign his old records or photographs. He says that he doesn't want to associate with that at all. I've seen him on television a couple of times. We toured together and everything, and we are still very good friends, but he is not performing at all.

Of my own recordings, one of my favourites is a pop thing that I did in 1960 called *Time After Time*. At that time, we saw the record business moving. It was getting back into big bands and things like that, and back into what you in

---

[*] The song was subsequently recorded by fellow New Orleans artist Joe Jones, who took it to No. 3 in the *Billboard* 'Hot 100' in November 1960.

the UK would call cabaret and we in the US call supper clubs and nightclubs. I wanted my career to go in that direction, to grow where you could do both, and in the States now I do both. So, *Time After Time* was one of my favourites. Of course, the all-time favourite is *Sea Cruise*, naturally, and I'm not just saying that because it was the biggest. I tease and kid about a lot of things, but I do say that I thank the Good Lord that the song came about.

I know that a lot of their hit records are not particularly liked by the artists who sang them. However, you have to remember that, at the time when you are seventeen and eighteen years old, record companies are selling millions of records over two or three months. They couldn't care less what you think, they just want you to sing it. I've had producers who gave me a lot of rubbish to sing and they weren't hits. Every now and then someone digs them out and I laugh at them, but there was nothing you could do. That was like having the boss say: 'You have to sing this and that's it!'

Looking back, we would always want to do things differently. Like I said, the songs that I turned down, I would have certainly taken today had I known. I still try as it goes along to do the best. No matter where it is, I walk out every night to do the best that I possibly can — whether it's in a little club of two hundred people or at a jazz festival with an audience of 65,000.

With over two hundred days a year on the road, my only hobby is trying to stay at home for a little while, because I haven't had a weekend off for eleven weeks and it'll be another twelve weekends before I do. Today is Saturday, and I'll get home on Tuesday morning and leave again on Thursday morning after being gone for two weeks. I have no wife or family, but my mother still lives just a short distance right around the corner from me and I have a big home life when I'm there.

I have gone into record production and we've done a number of things. I've produced a couple of albums on myself and a couple of records. My major end of it is performing — I like that better. My manager, Ken Keene, and I have also produced other artists. We've been together for twenty years and it just might be a working partnership. *[laughs]*

Billboard, January 1960

99

10

FABULOUS!
Charlie Gracie

Charlie Gracie's all too fleeting period of stardom in 1957–58 belied the considerable talent that lay behind it. A second-generation American of Sicilian ancestry, Charles Anthony Graci was born in Philadelphia on May 14, 1936, and not only looked the part but was also a dynamic and masterful guitarist capable of turning his hand to jump blues, swing, country boogie and rockabilly as well as the pop offerings through which he became famous.

It's twenty-nine years this year since I started out in this business. My father was a great influence on me: he was born in the Depression and would liked to have got into showbusiness but never had the chance. I am the eldest of three sons and he was delighted when I made it. Dad taught me the basics of playing guitar and singing before I went for professional lessons every day for six and a half years. Basically, I am a nightclub entertainer and cover the full field of music in my normal Stateside act. Being able to sing and play properly greatly enhanced my career.

I appeared on things like *Children's Amateur Hour* and won *Paul Whiteman's Talent Show* for a record five times. Someone heard me singing on radio and I was offered a recording contract in 1952. My father managed me in the early years, but for the past twenty-five years I have been with Barney Rothbart.

As I was born and raised in Philadelphia — fifty miles from the sea and ninety miles from New York in what they call the 'Eastern Corridor' — I can't claim Southern influences or the usual ones cited by US rock and roll singers. Joe Turner was my big influence, and some of the old-style big Eastern bands which were beginning to disappear off the scene. As rock and roll began to grow, other musical influences came in like black swing and country.

Looking back to those mid-Fifties years, we were all young and pioneers — even though we weren't aware of it at the time. I was one of the first with an electric guitar and, for all I can play most instruments, it is still my favourite. It's the same with rock and roll: my heart lies with it and it comes naturally. Apart from the music and pleasing an audience who bought our records and paid to see us, we weren't trying to drive a message at them. We espoused no causes or philosophy. We were not cult figures. As entertainers, we were seeking nothing: no messages, and no drugs or experiences. Drugs are the worst thing that happened to our country — they are an evil. Look at Presley: the poor man was smashed out of his skull as a result of drugs.

The records which gave me my big hits — like *Wandering Eyes,*

Greetings From
CHARLIE GRACIE

Butterfly, Ninety-Nine Ways and *Fabulous* — were really pop songs as opposed to rock and roll. In those days, our musical expression wasn't free as we were under contract and therefore had to do — and play — as we were told. But my stage performances were always my own. I played my hit records, but was able to play the music I loved which was rock and roll.

I derived a great deal of pleasure from both of my trips to the UK. My first visit was in 1957 for a few dates, and then I returned in 1958 for Lew and Leslie Grade to do a nationwide variety tour of the Moss Empire Theatre circuit. I loved it and the experience it gave me.

An amusing thing happened with regard to that British tour. It concerned one of your British lady artists, Dorothy Squires. I had never met her, nor even heard of her, but the press were running a big story on her objections to me getting No. 1 spot on the billing. We came over on the *Mauretania* and the story was received on ship. I played Southampton first with the Ted Heath Band before doing the London Hippodrome and then going onto the provincial dates. The press asked me what I felt about her objections. I told them: 'Gee, never! I don't mind what spot I do on the bill.' I had to be honest and admit that I had never heard of Miss Squires. Later on, we met and smoothed things out.

I didn't consciously go out to project an image by dressing in formal attire for my British theatre performances in the Fifties: I dressed in the same way that I would dress for an engagement in the States, where we always wore tight peg trousers and a long drape-style jacket. Later on, I discovered that my style of dress was similar to the fashion of the English teddy boys. For me this was a pure coincidence, although it greatly enhanced my standing with British teenagers!

Although I married young and brought my new bride to Britain in 1958, it didn't affect my career at all. I really don't think that the majority of fans were bothered whether you were married or not. I agree that in those days some managers and promoters went to great lengths to hide the fact that a male artist was married — just so the girl fans could believe that their idol was 'available'. However, I never accepted that line of thinking. Even a girl fan favourite like Pat Boone didn't lose out in popularity because he had a wife and children. By the way, I'm still married to the same lady.

Of my Fifties contemporaries, I was closest to Eddie Cochran who was a real fine boy and the nicest kid you'd ever want to meet. I miss him very much. He was at my home several times and we were good friends. I used to teach him licks on my guitar. The other guy that I worked with plenty was Bill Haley. He was from my area — Chester, Pennsylvania — and I was pretty upset when he died. Buddy Knox is a good buddy of mine, and Frankie Avalon grew up in my area and went to school with my wife.

You point out that I never seemed to get the publicity given to other artists. Well, I guess that I wasn't the type that attracted that sort of attention. Some of the guys that you mention, like Fabian and many others who were around then, have just disappeared. I am proud to say that I have only ever had one job, and that is the one I am still in today — showbusiness.

On the same plane, I only ever made one movie — *Jamboree* — in which I performed *Cool Baby*. I didn't have the tall dark handsome image of a film star, and equally I don't think it would have been my medium. While filming that movie, I met Jerry Lee Lewis and Fats Domino for the first time. Both were great guys — Fats more so. Despite what you read, all Yanks are *not* bigots, at least not in the North where I grew up and live. Besides, as a Christian, I love *all* God's people and can't speak for other men. I must say though that there are some people here that don't like anybody!

Record success or lack of it didn't make much difference, as I have always made a good living from my nightclub act and have never been out of work. Things went wrong with Cameo where I had a financial 'outing'. Plainly speaking, I considered that they didn't pay me properly for the number of records that I was selling for them. It ended up with me taking them to court and finally an out-of-court settlement being arrived at. They were powerful enemies from then on. Although I worked for many labels after that, they controlled most of the jocks and it was hard to get the right plays or exposure, so it was a tight squeeze for a while.

Today in the States, apart from my staple nightclub act — which as I have said incorporates rock and roll — we do a lot of variety and *Sounds Of The Fifties* nights where everyone dresses in period. I do a lot of these, and many college shows — which are on the same lines — for kids who weren't born when I was having my hit songs in 1957–58. We even have jitterbug competitions.

It's a great feeling to see original fans coming back to see me and bringing their children. This current tour of Europe and England is like a complete rebirth for me. We were in Belgium before arriving in England, and everywhere the reception and audiences have been marvellous. At one of the shows, a father came along with a really great-looking kid who was holding some of my original albums. After the show, I had some photos taken with him, so that I could take them home to show my own children. He reminded me of myself when I was that age. I think the kids now have had that music passed on to them, and they in turn find the same pleasure with our music that the previous generation found.

11

SEALED WITH A KISS
Brian Hyland

No-one is ever going to forget Brian Hyland's *Itsy Bitsy Teenie Weenie Yellow Polkadot Bikini* about the distinctive summer clothing of a two year old girl. More fittingly, he is also remembered for excellent recordings like *Ginny Come Lately*, *Warmed Over Kisses (Left Over Love)*, *Gypsy Woman* and the classic *Sealed With A Kiss*. An underrated talent whose live performances are still giving pleasure today.

My real name is Brian Hyland and I was born on November 1, 1943 in Jamaica, Queens — which is one of the five boroughs in New York City. My father's name is John Hyland and my mother's name is Gladys (*née* Kelly). Dad worked in the sales department of Peel's Beer in New York City. I was educated up to high school and went to the Franklin K. Lane High School in Brooklyn, New York, but have no idea what career I would have pursued outside of music.

Musically, my earliest recollection was of my brothers singing barbershop quartet songs and things like that around the house. That was real early, and then later on I was listening to Hank Williams. It was just kind-of odd in New York, and I don't really remember, but my mother told me later that in my pre-school years I used to sit and listen in the afternoons to country stations that we could get on the radio. But after that, I think that I became interested in the early rock and roll records by the groups in New York like the Five Satins, Frankie Lymon & The Teenagers, the Flamingos and the Platters. Then there was Fats Domino, plus the rockabilly stuff from Eddie Cochran, Buddy Holly, Bobby Darin, Elvis Presley of course, and the Everly Brothers.

I used to sing with my brother, Keith, so the Everly Brothers were real important to me, because I really learned how to sing harmony — and how to hear harmony — from listening to the harmony parts that the Everly Brothers did. Keith and I learned both parts, so that we could both do either part. At that time we both played guitars, and that is the only instrument that I play. My parents just let us get on with it, as at that time in our home it was just kind-of natural to sing as everyone was musically inclined. My brother played the trombone and he conducted the band at the church where we went.

My first public amateur performance is kind-of foggy, but one of the first would have to be a St. Patrick's Irish Night at our church when Keith and I sang a couple of Everly Brothers songs. From the first time that I started hearing those early records of the Everly Brothers, Elvis, and all those things, I thought that was kind-of a good thing to go after. In fact, I had a dream that I wanted to do that, and so I just kept after that dream and did it the only way that I knew how. In the interim I had a singing group — the Delphis — that I worked with. We did a lot of the doo-wop songs, practised all the time and played at some dances and things like that, so that was the next step.

We made a demo record at Christmastime one year and my friend, who was also in the group, and I would take the record along to record companies. We would cut classes in the afternoon and take the subway from Brooklyn over to Manhattan and hit all the record companies, or as many as we could. By looking on the directories in different buildings we'd see how many record companies we could go to. We would always get some encouragement from somebody who would tell us to come back next week and play it for Joe Blow or somebody else.

After we had been doing this for a while, we finally hit a lucky break with one of these people that we had played the record for, and it was in the bandleader Sammy Kaye's office. His arranger kind-of took an interest in me and told me to leave the group and just do a solo. This I did, and then signed a contract with their management company. They had a publishing company also, and I started making demos for them. One of those demos was a song called *Rosemary*, which they brought around to Kapp Records to sell the song. They liked the way that I sang it, so they signed me and they re-cut *Rosemary* — so that was my first record. It did nothing: zip!

Your question of how I came to record a novelty record like *Itsy Bitsy Teenie Weenie Yellow Polkadot Bikini* in 1960 is interesting, particularly as my first song, *Rosemary*, was a real pretty ballad. The *Bikini* songwriters, Paul Vance and Lee Pockriss, had been bringing that song around to a lot of people, and it just caught the fancy of the people up at Kapp who thought that it would be a good idea for me to cut it. I really didn't have much creative input at all being that I was only sixteen and didn't know much more than anybody else. They were looking for songs for me and had cut the 'B' side which was a kind-of novelty song in itself called *Don't Dilly Dally, Sally*. They had that ready to go, and it was initially going to be the 'A' side, but they weren't really happy for it to be an 'A' side. When *Bikini* came in, they thought that this may be a better choice — so that's the direction that they had in mind.

I don't really remember where I was or what I was doing when *Bikini* hit No. 1 in the States. A cousin of mine — Larry *[Fine]* of the Three Stooges — gave it a plug on their New York TV show. On the first or second day after it

---

* *Rosemary* and *Bikini* were both initially released on Kapp's subsidary label, Leader.

was released, I can recall driving around near Kennedy Airport in New York with my brother. We were getting a hamburger when we heard it coming from another car's radio. Drivers had the tops down on their convertibles and everybody in this car was singing along to it already. It was just like: 'Wow!' The record had only been out a day or so, and I couldn't believe it — it was so amazing.

No, I have never been embarrassed about that record, but for a long time I didn't do it on shows. It's a kind-of double-edged thing, because on shows if we don't do it then people come up afterwards and say: 'Why didn't you do it?' Then if you do it, people will say: 'How does it feel to do that song after so many hearings?' You can't win either way, so we just do it. I don't mind that people know the song, but may not know who sang it — it's just a memorable thing.

We had a string of something like three novelty records after *Bikini* including one about a donkey — *Lop-sided Overloaded (And It Wiggled When We Rode It)* — none of which were very successful apart from *Four Little Heels*. So, I was going down that road for a while and then I met up with two writers from New York, Gary Geld and Pete Udell, and at that point we started

doing their tunes. In 1961, we did an independent production of a song called *Let Me Belong To You*, which was taken to ABC Records. They signed me with that, and then the following year we recorded *Ginny Come Lately*, *Sealed With A Kiss* and *Warmed Over Kisses (Left Over Love)*. This was material that I was very happy with.

Unlike Frankie Avalon and others appearing in films at that time, it just never came up for me. In any event, I like being on the road and playing music more so than getting into that.

Not being easy to categorize wasn't done on purpose, but in a way I was influenced by things out there at the time. With Geld and Udell, after I was out on the road with

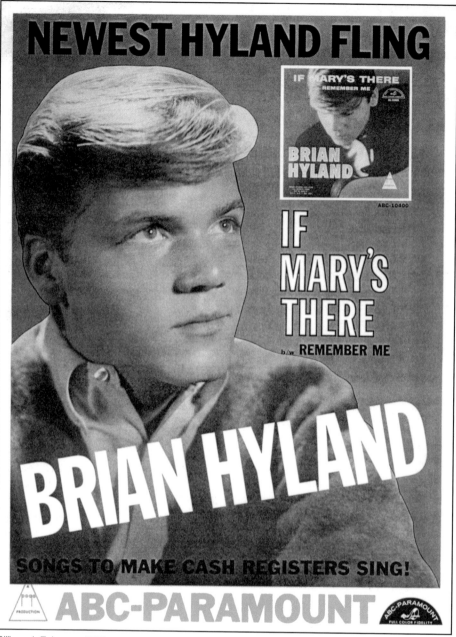

Billboard, February 1963

Sealed With A Kiss, I called them and said that currently there were a lot of really popular country records, and perhaps we should do something in that vein for the next record. I was hearing Faron Young and all these great records like *Hello Walls.* Anyway, having told them that, by the time I got back to New York they had written *Warmed Over Kisses.* We just went from single to single — we really didn't think that far ahead. It was what we wanted to do at the moment.

At that time, I was doing a lot of one-nighters on tours for Dick Clark's *Caravan Of Stars* and others with the likes of Bobby Vee, Gene Pitney, Jerry Lee Lewis and Joey Dee. You mention Gene Pitney sleeping on tour buses in the overhead racks — well I did that for one night. When I woke up, I was covered with sweat, so I didn't do that again.

I have memories of long trips with Bobby, Gene and all those other people. It's hard to remember specific stories or different incidents — there were so many — but I just remember having a real good time. Regarding Bobby Vee's story of me not taking the lens cap off my camera in Dallas, Texas at the time President Kennedy was shot — well I got *some* pictures on my camera, but only of the parade as there were too many people.

In 1964–65, I stopped having records that were successful in England and went with Philips Records. During 1966–67, I had hits in America while working with Snuff Garrett and Leon Russell — records like *3000 Miles*, *The Joker Went Wild*, *Run, Run, Look And See*, *Hung Up In Your Eyes*, *Holiday For Clowns* and *Get The Message*. We had a sort-of string there in the mid-Sixties with Snuffy. Working with another producer — in 1969 I think — I had a hit on Dot Records with *Tragedy*, which had been a hit for Thomas Wayne in 1959. Towards the end of 1970, I worked with Del Shannon and had a couple of hit records. Actually, one of those was the biggest-selling record I ever had, *Gypsy Woman*. It was a good song and a good record. So, I never really dropped out — I just kept rockin' along.

Of my own recordings, there are four that I like: *Sealed With A Kiss*, which has a special meaning to me, *Gypsy Woman*, *Ginny Come Lately* and *I'm Afraid To Go Home*. I guess those mean the most.

Looking at other people's records, off the top of my head I guess that there are a lot of things that the Everly Brothers have done that I would have liked to record. Songs like *Claudette*, *Sleepless Nights* — I love that song — and *Let It Be Me*.

Sealed With A Kiss has to be the highest spot in my career. We had a couple of records before that, and went to No. 1 with *Bikini*, but that was a novelty and came out of nowhere. When we came back with those other songs like *Sealed With A Kiss*, they were more meaningful.

There were, I guess, a lot of low spots like everyone has, but the 'English Invasion' wasn't really a factor because at that time we were working a lot. A lot of those tours with Gene and Bobby actually took place at that time: 1963–64. We were out on tour with the Yardbirds one time *[1966]*, when it was Jeff Beck, Jimmy Page, Keith Relf, Chris Dreja and Jim McCarty — so we worked right alongside all of those people.

I have never produced full-fledged, but with things I'm doing now I like to be involved with that part of it. Certain people's voices attract me. Right at this very moment one of my favourite artists is that dude James Ingram. There is also a guy here in England, Paul Carrack, who had a record out, *When You Walk In The Room*, a couple of months ago. I like the way Patty Smyth, who was with the group Scandal, sings. Also Dan Hartman and Simply Red's lead singer, Mick Hucknall.

Looking back at my career, I'm just thankful that I'm still working and playing shows. It's great. I don't think that I would do anything differently, even though it's been up and down and every other which way. That's just the way it has been and I can't change that.

12

GOT WHAT IT TAKES
Marv Johnson

Although chiefly remembered for his hits *You Got What It Takes* and *I'll Pick A Rose For My Rose*, Marv Johnson was justly proud of the fact that in 1959 his *Come To Me* was the first-ever Tamla release. Distributed nationally by United Artists, it was the first of nine consecutive hits produced for him by Tamla/Motown boss Berry Gordy Jr.

Marvin Earl Johnson is my real name, and I was born on October 15, 1938 in Detroit, Michigan. I have four children: three boys — including twins — and one girl. Both of my parents are deceased. Dad was an electrical lineman, fixing telephone poles in the storms and stuff, you know those guys.

My earliest musical influences were within the Gospel Church and the framework of the gospel. Then, there were certain early blues and jazz artists that I liked, people like Louis Jordan and others that people might not recall today: Clyde McPhatter, Sam Cooke and Jackie Wilson — those were my immediate influences. Clyde McPhatter had most of my immediate attention as a member of the Dominoes.

My education was high school in Detroit and just life. There were some things that I was interested in, like everybody else. Unfortunately, school deals with a lot of subjects that you may *not* be interested in, that you are going to get the basics for. I came through okay, but wasn't a particularly great student.

Being interested in music wasn't an immediate decision at any stage, it was a process of growing. My circumstances — paired with the fact that there was very little to do in those days other than the sports and music — led me to choose music. My mom and dad were not musically inclined at all and I had no formal musical education. I had a little piano knowledge — enough to know the chord structure and know how to explain myself to an orchestra that I might be working with.

I can still remember my first amateur performance: it was at the Warfield Theatre, Detroit, Michigan. It was an effort on my part to get in a talent show and to sing a song. I chose a song by the late Johnny Ace called *Cross My Heart*. I was placed among the winners and then hooked up with a group called the Serenaders. It was actually the *Junior* Serenaders, as the Serenaders were much older than we were. We toured with carnival shows all over, and from that I just developed a strong interest in continuing.

Turning professional just happened. Those are things that you can't really remember. If you're sincere in this business, you never know the moment that you turn professional because it deals with more than just getting a payment or salary. It means a full commitment to your art and doing the best you can at all times to please the fans. Had I not had any musical talent, then I was always interested in the military from the standpoint of aeronautics. As a matter of fact, the subject was my high school curriculum at the Cass Technical College in Detroit.

The biggest influence in my life was Dr. Martin Luther King, and that's the closest thing to anything in my experience that I may have learned about biblical behaviour. As I've already said, in music there isn't just one individual who can fill that spot.

My first record [on Detroit's Kudo label] was *Once Upon A Time*, and on the other side was a tune, *My Baby-O*, which was written by myself and a former member of the Midnighters, the late Sonny Woods. That recording, in 1958, was produced by Berry Gordy who came across me when I was working in the 3D Record Mart, Detroit.

My first hit was *Come To Me* on Berry Gordy's new Tamla label in 1959, and it was a national hit. As a youngster, you are always thrilled to know that you have accomplished something, and I felt *very well* about the fact that I was gonna be popular and had a hit record. Yes, it brought pressures, but there are always pressures on a young life. Being young, there's only a certain amount you know about life, and you're subject to a lot of pitfalls and things that you're going to encounter because you don't have the knowledge, or ability, to evade them. However, if you stick to your craft and you're sincere about what you are doing, you usually get around that, you know. Sincerity in what you're doing helps you get past a lot of things.

There *were* difficulties in belonging to a large stable like Tamla ran, as there were always some bits of political turmoil among the recording situation. You know: certain producers work with certain artists. You might find yourself waiting for an opportunity to do this or do that, or someone else getting a song that maybe you feel you should have gotten. Little stuff like that, but at Motown we managed to have those feelings and yet still get along quite well.

I was free to approach songwriters at Motown, but in a lot of instances they were busy because they were enjoying a string of hits on another particular artist and they wouldn't be as interested in you as they possibly could be. I guess, like everybody, there is a little greed involved too.

You had some choice of material, but it is best for an artist to follow the instruction of his producer, or the writers that are assigned to him, because your opinion isn't necessarily the best one for yourself when it comes to music.

TAMLA

1719 Gladstone St., Detroit 6, Mich.

UNBREAKABLE
45 R.P.M.

RECORD NO.
101
(G 1)

Jobete Music
(BMI) Time 2-15

Vocal Accompaniment
By The
RAYBER VOICES

COME TO ME
(Gordy-Johnson)
MARV JOHNSON

HERE'S THE BIG ONE

MARV JOHNSON

That's Where I Lost My Baby

AND

Let Yourself Go

UA 483
PRODUCED BY BARRY GORDY

Billboard, July 1962

Over a period of years, several producers and writers were assigned to me from within the Motown framework and from New York. They are too numerous to name, but I have worked with several people who are very talented and outstanding in music — Don Costa, Teddy Randazzo, Bert Berns, Bill Romero, Berry Gordy, Mickey Stevenson, Clarence Paul — quite a few of them.

Hits *do* matter, but if you stay in a profession, pleasing your audience and having a satisfactory feeling about your own efforts is more important than a few quid. In life, all our blood runs red, we have the same beating heart that may stop at any time, but it is important to get your values straight and to have some priorities other than a monetary one.

I am absolutely elated about nostalgia shows because I am a nostalgia artist. It's a good chance for me to reiterate what we attempted to do in the early years, and it's a pleasure doing it now having had the experience and knowing how to enjoy it.

I still enjoy the business, and keeping an act fresh every night is just nothing that you can explain to a person. When you are sincere about what you are doing and you're making an honest effort to please people who have paid their money to come and see you, then that's all it takes.

Audiences do differ throughout the world. In Europe, they are reasonable and intelligent without a doubt. We have some good audiences in the US, but some American audiences are more demanding and can be very hostile a lot of the time. If they come to see you on a show with other people, then they come to see one person. Instead of intelligently awaiting that person, they show everybody else how much they dislike them until their favourite turn comes on.

I haven't worked continuously, but quite a bit more than I did in the late Sixties and those years when

Billboard, January 1963

disco music was the main thing. When I wasn't performing, apart from a number of odd jobs in and out of the business, I worked in sales and promotion at Motown Records, so I've gotten some experience in the business other than that of a recording artist.

I've worked on productions of other artists like Sue Perrin and Hattie Littles. Off the top of my head, if I'd had the choice to record any song, there are a lot of Sam Cooke's things that I thought were very good. I could hear myself doing more of his songs than anyone else I've known. Also Clyde McPhatter's material. You mention Clyde touring the UK in 1960 with Bobby Darin and Duane Eddy without great recognition. Well, I didn't know that — it's really something. He was one of the greatest R&B artists who ever lived, you know. Of course, sometimes 'first' is also sometimes 'last'. 'First' has nothing to do with the generation passing, people forgetting and music changing. The record companies, management and people who are supposed to look after public relations for these people should let it be known, at least, that they have played these major parts in building the music and getting it to where it is. They shouldn't just leave a void as if everything was just there for the average guy who is born to just come along and take it. There have been a lot of dues paid for that stuff, you know, by guys like Clyde, Chuck Berry and Little Richard.

Yes, a lot of dues been paid.

I'm happy with my career. There's got to be something wrong with anyone that says they're not happy with the business like showbusiness — travelling around the world, staying in the best hotels, meeting people. They should really get out of it even if they cannot appreciate just those parts of it. Yes, it's hard work. Travelling is hard work, and it's no thrill once you do it continuously and relentlessly. You are presented with contracts to travel, travel, travel. They can be very unpleasant at times, but at the same time when you don't have a contract and obligations to some crowd, then you *really* have a problem. I imagine that I would have done things in my career differently, but to say what they are and where I would have them is just hypothetical for real.

The passing of my mom was the lowest spot in my life. In my career, the highest spot was probably the first realization that I was being recognized nationally by my peers and the public with a hit record — *Come To Me*. *You Got What It Takes* was a much bigger one and I was primed and ready to accept that fact more, but *Come To Me* was fresh, and it was the very first Motown record ever recorded — Tamla 101 — and it's *my* recording. I'm happy about it, and it's one thing I can relate to my children and grandchildren regardless of what anyone says.

Marv Johnson died on 16 May 1993 in Columbia, South Carolina.

13

STANDING BY
Ben E. King

Ben E. King's greatest performances were captured in the recording studios of Atlantic Records, initially as lead singer on the Drifters' classics *There Goes My Baby* and *Save The Last Dance For Me*, and subsequently as a solo performer. In 1987, a reissue of his biggest hit, *Stand By Me*, topped the UK charts thanks to its inclusion in a film of the same name and a Levis 501 jeans TV commercial.

For the record, my date of birth is September 28, 1938. I was born in Henderson, North Carolina, and my real name is Benjamin Earl Nelson. *Benjamin Earl Nelson* — now *that* would make my mother happy!

I started around 1956 and met Lover Patterson at that time. He was the manager of a group called the Five Crowns and I met him by accident when I was working in my father's restaurant at 119th Street and Eighth Avenue in Harlem, New York. Lover lived across the street and he came over one day looking for someone to fit into the Five Crowns, just to do harmony parts. He came over for a few days, and eventually I told him that I did a little singing and he said: 'Oh, great!' Lover then went back across to his apartment and brought the guys over to my father's store. There were no customers there, so we went right into the back of it and just rehearsed, and I harmonized with the group. Lover said: 'Great, you'll fit the group if you want to sing in it.' So, I joined the Five Crowns for a brief moment, and I guess that's basically how my career started in pop music.

I was with the Five Crowns up to the end of 1957. We were working at the Apollo Theatre as top of the bill, and at that time the group was still managed by Lover Patterson. On one bill at the Apollo, Ray Charles was the headline act and the Drifters were on the show as well. Somewhere around the middle of the week we were approached — through Lover Patterson — by George Treadwell, the manager of the Drifters. He asked whether we would like to become the new Drifters at the end of the week as his guys were breaking up. Apparently, he owned the group's name and could find guys any way he wanted and just call them 'Drifters'. Thinking that he was just joking, at the end of the week we went down to the office to talk about it all. We found out that the Drifters *had* broken up that week, so we started signing contracts and making arrangements to become the new Drifters.

In the black areas, the Drifters had been very successful up to that point. You have to allow for the fact that, back then there were very few black records being played on white radio stations which had the very strong play avenues that we needed to become exposed. As far as success was concerned, in those areas where their records were played they were very successful. They had *Steamboat*, *Lucille*, *Money Honey*, *Adorable* and all those things, so they had quite a lot of very successful records.

Why did they split up? Well, I imagine it's the same as it is today. After a while, I imagine you'd be feuding and fighting; the manager isn't doing his part; the agents aren't doing their part; the leader of the group is getting more money than everybody else. It goes into different avenues of why groups break up, but basically it's the same way that they are breaking up today. Being such a young fellow when I started, I never anticipated getting that much involved with the music business. My thought of the future was not geared to becoming a person in showbusiness, so I knew nothing of the politics involved in any of it.

I learned a lot from Leiber & Stoller, and they *were* an influence, basically because they were writing things that were different to what I'd ever heard before. The rhythm pattern, however, I *had* heard before because I'm from the South in America: Henderson in North Carolina. When I came to New York, the only music that I was able to listen to was gospel and regular R&B-type stuff. As I became familiar with the pattern that Leiber & Stoller were giving us to sing, it was more-or-less a Latin-type feeling that I had never really thought of getting involved with. *There Goes My Baby* — which I co-wrote — was supposed to be really a straight-off R&B thing. When I started writing it, I thought about a song that was written by Dee Clark or somebody called *Nobody But You.* That was the rhythm that I'd gone for in my head on *There Goes My Baby.* When I got to New York and we started showing the song to Jerry and Mike, they were saying: 'Oh, yeah, this is a great song!' Before I knew it, there were all these strings and kettledrums and everything else coming about, and a sound which I'd never heard before in my life. So, that's how it was born with all those different type instruments in it, but it was supposed to be just a straight R&B-type song.

One of the good things about being involved with companies, recordings, writers and producers during those times was their concern about what was going to happen with an artist, and this particular song was a hundred percent. They were there to actually concentrate on just you, just that material and to do the best they could for just you, just that material. It wasn't that they had you for an hour or two, and then had Aretha Franklin for the next two hours. They would spend all day, the next day, and on and on and on, really getting you geared to sing this particular song that they'd written or whatever. It was a tailor-made kind-of thing, and the pattern worked.

An artist's manager is outside that picture, because it's a world he isn't really familiar with. In most cases, it's bad news when managers get involved with what's right and what's wrong as far as music is concerned. They're not really that in tune to you as an artist; they're in tune to you as a person to sell. To put it another way, they have a tendency to overstep their boundaries, and they interfere to a degree where they can say either yes or no to a project that could make or break your career.

So, we were very lucky in that respect because, with George Treadwell, I've never seen him involved at any recording dates and I must take my hat off to him. He got the producers and the writers and that was it. He stayed in the managing areas, which was great, and I respect him for that. If I wasn't happy about anything recording-wise, I would complain and say: 'Hey, that's not

The Drifters' 1959 edition, with a youthful Ben Nelson leading the line.

happening.' A lot of artists were told what to say and what to do.

What made it much easier for artists such as myself, Solomon Burke, Joe Tex and Wilson Pickett — all of us from that world — was that the writers were brilliant enough not only to write very good stuff for us, but also they were even brilliant enough to arrange it for us and fix us up with a lead sheet in our key. So, whenever they would sing it to us, of course it was comfortable because they were familiar with the key that we would sing in. All it had to be at that point was good to sing lyrically. You can't lose with so much.

That standard of service isn't available today. Today's business is totally the opposite of what used to happen years ago — in *all* aspects. I don't think that they are giving the kids the best music *per se*. I think that, out of one hundred artists, there are about twenty that are doing very good work. Anything else is just *thrown* at you. I don't think that there is a great concern about lyrics or music in general. In today's music, there are very few people that are really using instruments. They are all just using a keyboard or a couple of keyboards. So, the only guys who are actually working today are the guitar-player and perhaps the bass-player. It's so mechanically done that it is frightening.

Lover Patterson

With some of today's music, they are packaging sex for youngsters. The love song today is a different love song. We didn't take you to bed; we made you hug and walk in the park. Today, they're taking you to bed. So, when you're eight or nine years old, you gotta think about going to bed: for what? You should be walking in the park holding hands. I know that it's a little bit cornball, but it's still good and that's still the way. You should try to hold that stage of innocence. It's a bit 'out there' now, and I think the artists realize it, but it has gone so far ahead and been so profitable that unfortunately everybody's heading in that direction. There are still the ones around like Lionel Richie and Kenny Rogers — a few, few of us that are determined to fight the odds and continue to write stuff that people still hum and sing as they walk around.

After taking on the Drifters' name, we came through some tough times. When we started out, we actually went on the road before we had our first record release. We got bottles and chairs thrown at us and booed off stage. Our station-wagon tyres were punched out and everything. That behaviour was based on the fact that we weren't actually the Drifters people wanted to see: they were Clyde McPhatter's guys. So, when the curtains opened, we got the full punch of it. After the first hit record, *There Goes My Baby*, things were much easier and the public accepted us. To make things even harder for us, we were all on salary, and the salary we were getting was a very, very small amount like $75 a week. I had just got married before I went on tour and found that I couldn't pay my hotel bills, feed myself and all those essential things, and send money home. When we got back off the road and back into New York, we were all complaining about the same thing. We had a very successful record and we were doing well with tours and records, but we had no money.

We went down to George Treadwell's office and had a meeting. I stood up, like a jerk *[laughs]*, and told him that we were very unhappy. He told me to cut the 'we' out of it, so I said: 'Okay, *I* am very unhappy, and for all that we are doing and all that's happening with us so far, we would like a raise.' George told us that no more money was available for us, and if I didn't want to stay that was it. So, I walked out then. That was in 1960. I was still living in Harlem, and when I got back there I told my wife, who understood because I had discussed it with her before going downtown. When I told my friends that I had just left the group, the reaction was: 'Are you *kiddin'*, man? You guys are the hottest guys in town!'

It was easier for me to quit, because I never thought of showbusiness as being anything but fun. When I first started with Lover Patterson coming over to ask me to join the Five Crowns, it was fun. When I was singing on the stoops in Harlem with different groups, it was all fun.

My reasons for leaving the Drifters then were purely financial ones: I just couldn't make ends meet. There were no other offers waiting in the wings. The only thing that saved me when I left the Drifters and walked out of the office that afternoon was Lover Patterson again. By the time I got to the elevator I was practically in tears. First of all, I couldn't believe that the rest of the guys wouldn't follow me, as we were all buddies. Secondly, I couldn't believe that I was actually fired for the sake of a few more dollars. Standing waiting for the elevator, I heard the door close behind me. I thought that it was my best friend in the group, Charlie Thomas. When I turned around to take a look, it was Lover Patterson who had become the Drifters' road manager. I said to him: 'Aw, man, what are you walking out for, where are you going?'

And he said: 'Well, I quit too.'

I said: 'No, are you kidding? You were making just as little as I was?' But at least he didn't have any responsibilities.

He said: 'No, don't worry, we're gonna make it.'

I said: 'No, I'm gonna go back to work.'

If there is any reason at all I'm able to sit here in this hotel room with you and talk about my career, it's because of him. He's the one that had all the confidence in me. I never had confidence in me or what I was doing as a lead singer. I never should have become a lead singer, anyhow. Everything was totally accidental as far as me becoming a lead singer was concerned.

The only way that I became a lead singer was after I had written the song *There Goes My Baby*. I was showing it to Charlie Thomas, who was doing all the lead singing when we became the Drifters. Because — for some strange reason — Charlie Thomas couldn't sing *There Goes My Baby*, I was showing it to him in the studio and kept rehearsing it with him. Jerry Wexler came across on the mike and said: 'Look, man, we haven't any more time to waste; *you* know the song, *you* sing it!' That's how I became a lead singer. I was just a baritone singer in the group, I wasn't really doing any lead at all. I didn't care about lead: I was having too much fun with the guys doing steps and ooing and ahing, so I never really focused on doing lead.

When Lover Patterson followed me out after we'd left the Drifters that day — because of his confidence in me — I was quite contented. First of all, because I'd done something I never thought that I'd do musically: I had recorded a record. That was enough for me, because in my neighbourhood I was a big thing. I'd had a very successful record, so everybody thought that I'd done enough then to have accomplished that. I never thought that I would achieve that in the first place.

So, with Lover's strength and determination, I continued. There were times when I was telling myself that I should go to work and he would say: 'No, don't go to work.' He would get me little jobs doing gigs here and there, and get me on at the Apollo Theatre with the Reuben Phillips band doing the records that I'd done with the guys before quitting the group.

My most memorable thing about Lover was the time I didn't have enough money to pay my rent and I went to him and said: 'This is it! I'm quitting. There's no way I can support a family like this.' He asked me what was wrong, and I told him that I couldn't pay the rent. He said: 'Okay', got out of bed — this was early in the morning about ten o'clock — gathered all his most valuable things together

BEN E.KING   ATCO Records

and went to a pawn shop. That convinced me. If he was *that* crazy, then I would go with it and we would see if we could make it work. From there, he introduced me to LaVern Baker, who took me on the road, allowed me to open up shows for her and showed me a lot about performing. Then, before I knew it, I started back writing again.

An agent I was with — Frank Sands — when I left the Drifters was responsible for 'Ben E. King'. They were trying to come up with a name. Years ago, there was a singer out called Earl Nelson, and I wanted to use the 'Nelson' part of my name, but they said not to use Nelson 'cause Earl Nelson is doing well, etc. They said: 'Call yourself Benny whatever', so I said: 'Okay.'

At the time, I had a favourite aunt who was dating a fellow by the name of James King and I thought: 'King' — that's great.' So I told them and they said: 'Great, we'll call you Benny King.' Then my agent, Frank Sands, said: 'We'll stick the 'E' in the middle, that' ll do it!' So, we put it together and that's how the name came about, and now I'm stuck with 'Ben E. King'.

Even after the split, Lover and I were still friendly with the rest of the guys from the Drifters. We all lived in the same neighbourhood and they used to call in. As a matter of fact, I wrote *Stand By Me* for the Drifters, and when they came by one day I told them: 'I got this song that you guys just gotta listen to!' I started singing it, and we started rehearsing it with them. I had a great bass part worked out that the bass singer was doing. They said: 'Oh, great, man, we'll go downtown so George can hear it!' So, we went to see him one day, stood up in front of him and did this song. However, we couldn't come to an accommodation, so I ended up recording it myself.

You ask me about the co-writer of *Stand By Me*, Elmo Glick. Well, I don't rightly know who he is, but I think he could be one of three people: Jerry Leiber, Mike Stoller or Ahmet Ertegun. I haven't figured it out yet. I almost did once. *[laughs]* But I honestly think that it is a pen-name for Jerry and Mike. They just *polished* my song. That was one of the things that happened in the business during those times: you found yourself with a writing partner that you never dreamed of. The publishers collect the royalties on the song; they send me my share and Mr. Glick his. *[laughs]*

It was an honour when Muhammad Ali — then Cassius Clay — recorded *Stand By Me*. I loved it. I saw him once, and he told me about it and we both had a big laugh. He said: 'Now I've accomplished both worlds. Not only am I the greatest in boxing, I'm the greatest in singing!'

I said: 'Are you *crazy*?' He did a pretty good job, I'll give him that. It wasn't all bad.

Why didn't I form a version of the Drifters like some of the others? I didn't feel the need to pick up the Drifters name and use it as an umbrella to protect myself when I was doing badly because I had a good start with my solo career — it was so strong. Also, Lover Patterson had such confidence in me at the beginning, that some of that reaped off and eventually I began to have confidence in myself. Up to 1965–66 I was doing great, considering that I was flip-flopping around in something that I didn't have a clue about. I had touched into a world that I knew absolutely, positively, nothing about — but loved it. Of course, I didn't like the politics, and still don't. I don't like the trickery, the slick agents and the slick companies. But music — yeah, I loved every note I could hit. I enjoyed it.

Today, I still don't listen to Ben E. King records. No, honestly I'm not joking. *[laughter]* I find it *hard* when they play the recorded tracks back and I have to listen. I am too self-critical, and that's the reason I don't listen to myself. I'm never satisfied as far as my performance goes. There have been very few records that I have been totally satisfied with once they were done. *Seven Letters* was a good one, and I like it very much; *On The Horizon* — I enjoyed doing that song; *I (Who Have Nothing)* was also enjoyable to do. There are a few that I can hear and I think: 'Oh, I did all right with that', but some — urrgh! I know the missed words, mispronunciations and everything, so I frown on those.

Whatever I did was natural and had feeling. Even today, I go with my feeling and try to avoid being so polished and overly correct about something. Like most groups, the Drifters' stage act is much too slick with little feeling. Very few groups today — if any — have that feeling, but the kids become in tune to that type of entertainment, and that's the bad thing. So, now for anyone to stand up there and sing with *total* feeling, the reaction is: 'What's he cryin' about?'

It's not the fault of the record-buyers, it's the way it's pushed at them; they haven't got a chance. They have to like something, so this is what they're giving them, unfortunately. There *are* some good acts out there, but in my opinion it's one out of ten.

Things haven't changed for black artists: it's just about the same, maybe even worse. Worse in the sense that there are other avenues to try to break through. People feel that,

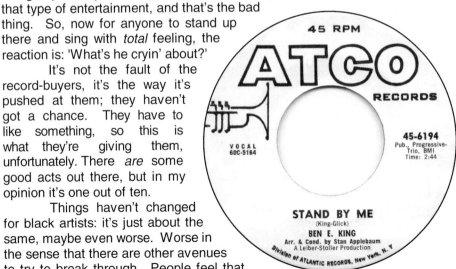

now, if you have a hit record, you can go and get a video and then go into motion pictures. So, there's still a fight to get a record; there's still a fight to, hopefully, get a decent video; and there's still a fight to get into motion pictures — if that's how far you wanna go — because they generally link like that.

I didn't do any motion pictures. I received a few offers, but have never been interested and wouldn't inflict this mug on anybody else in the world except on a one-to-one. That world to me is great; there is nothing wrong with it other than the fact that, unlike music, I don't think it has any feeling. It's okay in what it does, but it doesn't match the music world at all. My theory about acting is that anybody can act: if you can convince someone for the slightest second that you're telling them the truth when you're lying to them, then you're acting.

Acting to me is not a big feat. The challenge to me, is to sit down in this room and write a song, record the song, put that song out, and let it be a hit. Creation from start to finish. I am sure that the one who writes the scripts and stuff is the guy who gets the satisfaction. I know Paul Newman and others are great actors, but hey — like I say — if you can lie to someone and convince them that you're telling them the truth, you can act.

Getting back to black music: yeah, it is harder, and I don't think that there is any greater control, even allowing for the likes of Michael Jackson and Prince. In many ways, it gives people false hope and imaginations about what can happen — because they are *phenomenons*. They were well packaged and well planned. Years of planning went into both of those projects, they didn't happen yesterday. Those things were fixed to be the way they were. Now, if you get Warner Brothers Communications behind you with millions of dollars to promote me, if I've got an elephant on my back, then me and the elephant are going to do good. Know what I mean? But if you take a kid from the street, with his first project, and he's trying to bounce from a good record to a good video to the big screen, then I don't think it will happen.

It's easier for whites. I'll put it where it is — they are more marketable. You can find at least seven or eight top-name whites today that actually can't sing a note. I mean, let's be totally honest: they are terrible singers and terrible artists, but they are well promoted and the companies know that. I'm not knocking the companies — it's this business. They say: 'If we put a million dollars behind this guy here, we are guaranteed in a year's time to get back twenty times as much.'

Their argument is that the population of blacks that could buy videos and buy records don't really buy that much. They almost have to be *pushed* to buy because of factors like social status and unemployment. Also, blacks aren't so easily hyped. Just because there's a line going around the corner, they won't stand on it just to see what the hell people are going to see. They are not like that, basically because of economics again: they can't afford the money or the time. They have to screen out their spending really well before they buy something, even off a black.

A lot of black artists come in and try to be slick. I've seen them come and go with their slick videos and their slick songs. They don't make it. You have to convince blacks that you're *sincere*. Then they'll buy you and you'll last — but it's based on sincerity. The white market will accept whatever is going down — you just have to package it right and promote it. I can come through anywhere, man, and put a few hundred thousand dollars into something, properly promote it, and they'll buy it. I won't say that I'll sell out, but I will do all right.

Billboard, February 1963

Blacks in the music business have always been harder to sell. Yet, I have known the days at the Apollo Theatre where there were lines all around the corner for almost every act that came in there. As an act, you wouldn't come in there again unless you were sincere. If you weren't, then they'd boo you off the stage, and you would know right then and there that they were telling you: 'Hey, man, you're too cute and slick and we're not going for it.' So, I had my training, my learning, from the best grounds in the world and behind some of the best singers in the world, like Sam Cooke, Brook Benton and Lloyd Price. I've watched them, seen what made them work and what made people like them. There was no slickness, just a legitimate feeling coming from one person to another. So, that's all you really have to do: just be yourself. If they've accepted what you've offered them, give them that without being overly cute about it.

Today my audiences are predominantly white — even in the States — but I'll tell you what happens with that. It's because I have been fortunate enough, with the songs that I have been able to record, to capture black and white audiences, and it's always been like that. I remember my first time going down to South Carolina after I'd recorded *Spanish Harlem*: I went to the show and knocked on the front door of the gig which was at a private club. The guy opened it — he was white — looked at me and said: 'What do you want?'

I said: 'I'm Ben E. King.'

They never got a photo and didn't know that I was black. He brought me around the back, paid me off and put me back on the bus to New York! So that shows you that even way back then, in 1960, I had caught a white audience in South Carolina, but wasn't allowed to sing. At least I knew that I had an audience waiting in there! *[laughter]*

I've been fortunate — as have the Drifters, the Platters, the Coasters, Otis Redding, James Brown and lots of others — to have made a music that had no racial boundaries. So that's why, when I go to a show with the Drifters or myself and I look out, there is a strong following of whites. Another reason, too, is because blacks will follow you as long as they know you're around. If Ben E. hasn't got out any new records, then they don't know where Ben E. is at. However, whites will follow the name as long as the name is around.

Whites probably enjoy nostalgia more because they have a respect for what has happened. I laughed at the fact that, when Duke Ellington sadly passed away, there were queues of blacks all over the place — because I know that at every concert I had ever seen of Duke, there was a 99% white audience. I know that we are not a race to hold onto things. Most things are sold to us so fast and given to us like that, that we pick up each day little by little of what's going on today: whatever happened yesterday can really get lost, and we are that way about our music as well.

You also have to allow for the fact that we haven't got the avenues to keep us 'alive' as blacks. For example, you're constantly seeing what has happened to Jerry Lee Lewis and that Pat Boone is here. We haven't got those facilities to keep our public aware of where's Ben E. King; where's Chuck Jackson, etc. These guys are still alive, breathing and working: Solomon Burke, Wilson Pickett, Brook Benton — I could go on and on. We're still alive, but we are not news items and we haven't got anyone to tell our stories anyway. We have a black programme in the States called *Like It Is*, which is basically about political things, but once a month an old name may pop up.

A number of things went wrong with my career and, having been around the music business for a little bit of time, I have formed a few thoughts and opinions. Everybody is gonna have a slump time. They're gonna have that time when it's not gonna happen. I guess I got to mine around 1968. Other than the fact that the records weren't happening, I found that most of the writers who had been writing for us had gone to other projects and fallen in love with other singers. The company that I was with, Atlantic, were putting out other things on me, but it wasn't really happening. I went to another company called Maxwell Records and did a great project around 1970 with Bob Crewe *[the album 'Rough Edges']*, which I liked very much. Unfortunately, right after we finished the album, he filed bankruptcy for the company.

After that, I did a project with Bob Gallo and one or two other things — but nothing, of course, to match the impact of what I had enjoyed with Atlantic. However, I was still working and when the records weren't there it was probably the most valuable time of my career. All I had to survive with then was how good I was as a performer, as an artist to work onstage. I had to learn a lot and remember a lot of what I'd seen other pros do and put that into my world of entertainment. In my opinion, I developed into a fairly good entertainer based on not having the hits to lean on, which was great for me.

Regarding the 'English Invasion', I know that it played a part in cutting out a lot of American records. It's still happening today with the likes of Duran Duran, but during that time my style — if I had still been hot and recording successfully — would have stayed in there because what they were doing was more-or-less geared to where I was at anyway. Although the Beatles took over the charts at one point, artists like James Brown stayed in there.

The UK tours were all right financially, but at that time we thought that I should do some tours here as most of my records were being covered by other artists. I've worked with a lot of promoters over the years. Arthur Howes is probably my favourite, followed by Henry Sellers and Danny O'Donovan. I've been very lucky with agents here. I've never done a tour and not been paid, and I've never undertaken a tour where I've had to cancel and go home for any reason. In the States, I've been fairly lucky with agents because most of them are based in New York, which is my home base. Also, because they work with so many artists, bad news is gonna travel fast.

My favourite incident from touring days happened here in the UK on my first tour, which I did with Gerry & The Pacemakers and Jimmy Tarbuck, who was the MC. We were in the coach going to Scotland and I didn't know that they had arranged to play a joke on me where two guys get out of a van and stuff. Anyway, they pulled the coach over and I was told that it was an inspection and that we had to show our passports and legal papers before going into Scotland. I said: 'Oh, man, I didn't bring no passport. I haven't got any papers.'

They said: 'You didn't bring anything? Well, just get out of the bus anyway.'

We all had to stand against the bus. So here we are, and I'm standing against the bus with the band guys, Gerry & The Pacemakers and myself. All of a sudden, Jimmy Tarbuck comes up to me and says: 'Look, go around the back of the bus.'

I said: 'Why?'

He said: 'They're very hard here and they're checking all papers.'

So, I went to the back of the bus and stayed there for what seemed like hours. Needless to say they were all back in the bus looking down at me, rolling with laughter and killing themselves. All of a sudden one of them tapped on the window and said: 'Come on in!'

Later on, I did a show — *Live At Her Majesty's Theatre* — which Jimmy was hosting. When he saw me, he burst out laughing at the memory and the tears just rolled down his cheeks.

Regarding your question about why I came back into the Drifters, I'll tell you: I got a call from Faye Treadwell — who inherited the rights to the group when her husband, George, died — inviting me to join them. She told me that Johnny Moore, who is involved, needed someone to come and join him because one of the other members had left and we would make a great package. I said: 'Sure, no problem.'

For the past fourteen years I have been without a manager and having a lot of fun in the business doing anything that I wanted to do. I've always had a good rapport with the agents in the States that I've worked with, but the one that would cause me more problems than anyone would be the manager. So, really, not having a manager for such a long time has let me spread my wings and go anywhere I wanted. When I found out that I could come back with the guys, they made sure that it was financially suitable for me and that everything was right for us to team up.

As a matter of fact, when I got to sign the contracts to join the Drifters, Johnny Moore was out of the group. He had got angry with the management or agent situation and gone away with a group called Slightly Adrift. This left me holding the ball. I said: 'Hey, I didn't come back to take over!' I actually thought of being a part — not the centre — of the group. So, I was with Bill Fredericks, who is a very good singer and a person who had done a lot of good things in the UK, also Ray Lewis and Louis Price. Later on, Johnny Moore and the other guys decided they were going to come back and the agent we were with, who was Derek Block, got them back together and said: 'Now do you want to do it like you initially wanted?' I said: 'Great!' and came back to do it.

You ask me about adjusting from the style of my own performance to the slickness of the Drifters. Well, I tell you I've never had it slick in my solo performance. You know what, I make so many mistakes: I never sing a song the same way, I never know what I'm gonna do next. I'm fortunate to have someone around me at all times that's watching me and allows me the liberty of not just moving left and right and up and down — because they know that without this space we'd all go crazy. With the Drifters, yes, I am slick because they have slick beginnings and endings: da-da-da-daaa! Sometimes the guys do get cheesed off with the routines, but since I've been involved with the fellows here they've kind-of loosened their ties a little bit, and called me a bum. *[laughs]* But I say: 'Hey, man, don't take it so seriously, because we're supposed to be *enjoying* ourselves, you know.'Is it fulfilling? Oh yeah, sure, definitely; there is still a lot more feeling in me than just picking up a couple of dollars here and there.

We work much easier now. At the very beginning, I was making mistakes all over the place, but I've improved. On the early package shows, I agree that you didn't get much slickness. It was legit: whatever they felt, it just came out.

I will be honest with you and say that I don't know for how long I will go on with the Drifters. I still maintain my solo career in the States today, but not here just now in the UK because I'm working with the guys. Today my wife asks me: 'What's wrong with you, why are you drifting?'

This business is *hard*. It takes us away, and you have to be hard to survive. I think I'm half-nuts because being in this business makes you like that. I'm not a 'showbiz'-type person; I'm way out of the pattern of showbusiness people. I'm not into caviar and champagne: I got a bottle four weeks ago and it's still here with the cork in it. Now, the Meggazones for my throat on my table over

A SMASH!
BEN E. KING
"DON'T PLAY THAT SONG"
(YOU LIED)
ATCO 6222
ATCO RECORDS
1841 B'way New York City, N. Y.

BEN E. KING

SEVEN LETTERS

ATCO
6328

BEN E. KING
"THAT'S WHEN IT HURTS"
ATCO 6288

BEN E. KING
"TOO BAD"
ATCO 6231
ATCO RECORDS
New York 23
1841 B'way·

there — that box is *open*! Those are the things that I take seriously, but this business has ripped a lot of us apart — quite a lot. The only way I've survived is by always being very close to my family.

I'm married to my wife, Betty. My kids are Terris who is 27, Ben Junior is 25, and Angela is nearly 21. None of them are in the business, but one of my sons and I write together, and I think he is a very talented person. We've done a couple of projects so far, and two or three songs that will be going on albums. *[In 1980]* I did an album called *Street Tough*, and he did a lot of work on that with me. So, we stay busy, and because of him I am very in tune to today's music. The working relationship also allows me to remind him — if he wants to be involved in the business — how to get in it, and how to stay in it, and do good stuff. I think that he's a very good songwriter because he's not writing stuff that the kids are listening to. He's writing very good lyrics and there's a legit concern about really doing good stuff in the business.

I think that most songwriters and artists have only so much in them to come out. I've got about twenty-four scraps of paper lying around here. I find it very hard to write and probably have a thousand unfinished songs. Since I started this tour I've had at least two or three dozen. I just put down little bits and pieces and I haven't completed one yet.

It's hard for an artist who writes songs to have a favourite. It's like your children really. It would be different if I wasn't writing songs, then I would probably have a favourite, but because I write songs they are *all* my favourites. I don't hate any of the songs that I have recorded, basically because there are very few songs that I have recorded and not liked. Some of them I love a lot, but I must at least *like* them. There are a lot I would like to do that I know wouldn't go down well with an audience, and

that hurts most of all. I have never done *On The Horizon*. I love *On The Horizon*, but I know if I started to sing it they would say: 'What is he wasting his time for? We all know that song,' so I have never done it.

Looking back, I don't think that I would have done anything differently because I was totally ignorant from the very beginning. You can only change things if you know what you wanna change, but I got involved in the business and got a lot of success almost at the same time. To be totally honest, I wouldn't change a thing.

If my early career had continued at the same rate, I would probably have been in a velvet dinner jacket playing the big hotels in Las Vegas. I wouldn't have liked it, but I probably would have been there. Everybody seems to think that the top of the shelf is to work those big lounges in Vegas. I don't think that. I think that to work at a club like Castle's[*], where we are playing this week, to hear the audience singing along and screaming — hey, that's all right. That makes me feel good.

On the other hand, to know that someone is sitting out there because he wanted to take his wife out and she bought a new mink coat yesterday doesn't knock me out. They can afford a $50 dinner — so what? They don't come to see *me*: I just happen to be the guy appearing in the lounge tonight. I'm probably cutting my throat for Vegas, but that's okay, I'll make it without playing there anyway.

I call Las Vegas 'Plastic City' because nobody there really cares about you. It's all a hype game, a 'who-do-you-love' game. There are acts in Vegas who never had a record out. If they did, they would have one record out — because anybody could record it. But if the guy who owns the place likes you, you're in there. You mention your puzzlement as a youngster at the apparent US popularity of Julius LaRosa. Well, without taking anything from Wayne Newton, being the top money-maker in Las Vegas tells you exactly what the hell I am saying. Give me a break! Wayne Newton? I can find ninety-nine kids anywhere in the world that would outsing and outperform Wayne Newton any time of day. But the guys in Vegas say: 'Ah, I like him, I'll give him $20 million or whatever, let 'em roll!'

---

[*] Annfield Plain, County Durham.

I don't think that's for me. I still like to sing and enjoy what I'm doing. It's not just Presley who had a sad life, they *all* do. They won't admit it, but the ones that I've known — and I've known a lot of them — don't seem so happy. They're working those big rooms, man, they're packing them in and doing their number. They got the Rolls-Royce and they got the limo outside and they're high-rolling it. I knock myself out in that club every night, but I enjoy it, and when they come to see me they enjoy it. But when I come and see them in Vegas, I don't enjoy that. People there clap and say: 'Oh, it's very good,' but I say: 'Uh, man, something's missing here, man. The reality of what you're about and where you are, it's not blending properly.'

Unfortunately, I think that what has happened with me is what happens to most singers or artists that stay in the business much longer than the business anticipated: when you've been in it a long time, you're still fighting the odds because you still feel a part of it. So, you're kind-of pulling yourself up from where you were to now. There's a lot of friends that you've made along the way, as well as fans, that say: 'What are you going to do next?' And you look at them with a straight face and say: 'I don't know.' *[laughs]* But the challenge is wonderful, and to stay in the game today is very hard because everything is so 'rush-rush, push-push' and well packaged.

To break it down to where I would love it to be isn't hard to do. Don't get me wrong, it's still there. The hard part is to convince the backers to go with your idea and your feeling. It's like having a horse that you know has a good race left in him, and you just say: 'Hey, we'll mount him with the right jockey.' You don't put some fat guy on his back and think that he's gonna run well. Mount him with the right jockey and take a shot at it. It's a case of saying: 'Well, why not try to record an artist with whatever he feels that he is capable of doing, as opposed to all the other stuff that is turned out.' To me, one of the few artists who has proved that it can happen over and over again is Al Jarreau. He's a bit tricky with his things, but he still uses musicians. Another one who is making a fantastic comeback and doing great work is Bobby Womack, who is singing good R&B stuff again. There are still a few around, but very few. It's a thing they have got to come back to. They couldn't have done it throughout their careers as they wouldn't have survived — no way.

So, I have things in reserve. It's the same for all the guys in the Drifters. It gets hard, and you begin to question yourself about where you're going with this or that, what is happening in your life, and things of that nature. But it's easy, based on the fact that you still feel a part of the business. If you're still involved then you're a blessed person. There are a lot of guys who didn't make it for *one* year, and you're still standing out there. Yes, some artists will say that and not really feel it, but I'm sincere in my heart.

Life is much easier for me because I've done so many different things in so many different directions, and I've been similarly successful in all those things. It has been pleasurable, all has been good, and I've been blessed over and over again. When I worked with LaVern Baker, I was in awe of that. Not long ago, I did a thing with Average White Band, and recently I worked with Fatback Band and I've got a couple of songs on their new album. Each thing is a new burst of energy for me. It's: 'Wow, I'm doing something else!' It's a challenge. You feel: 'I'm still busy doing something. I'm still a part of something. I'm still here.'

14

LITTLE MISS DYNAMITE
Brenda Lee

Brenda Lee's powerful voice belied her small stature and tender years. Equally at home with driving rock and roll or soulful ballads, her versatility and sincerity shone through on hits like *Sweet Nothin's*, *I'm Sorry*, *I Want To Be Wanted*, *Break It To Me Gently* and *All Alone Am I*, gaining her a deserved reputation as the world's No. 1 female vocalist.

My date of birth is December 11, 1944 and I was born Brenda Mae Tarpley in Lithonia, near Atlanta, Georgia. My parents' names are Ruben and Grayce, and dad was a carpenter. I have a brother, Randall, and two sisters, Linda and Robyn. No, I wasn't a cousin of Elvis Presley and never did hear that piece of publicity *[laughs]*, although we did have our photograph taken together.

I went to schools in Georgia, Ohio and Missouri and to high schools in Tennessee and California: we lived in Augusta, Greensboro, Elberton, Atlanta, Lithonia and Conyers. I left Lithonia, I believe, in 1954.

While growing up, there were really no musical influences for me by way of the radio: we didn't have one, so I didn't get to listen. My mother used to sing me Hank Williams songs, and my influences in music were through the church. No-one in the family had any musical talent. I was about three years old when I started to sing and never have learned to read music. I *wish*, but I have never done it. My earliest recollection of performing was doing a little local television show, on WAGA out of Atlanta, called *John Farmer & The Ranch Boys*.

My father died when I was seven and my mother was certainly supportive, so I would say yes, there was encouragement. I helped support my family after dad's death, and later on when I started to do well, I did support them. I don't remember feeling any pressure on me — I don't think you do when you're a child, especially when you're doing something that you like.

The schools in our area always had a competition, and when I was about five years old I performed for my sister's school, singing *Take Me Out To The Ball Game*. There was a trophy and I won. Her school got the trophy and I got a box of candy, but I wanted the *trophy*!

After that, I was in the *Starmakers Revue* — a kind-of talent show — and then the TV *Ranch* show. When I moved to Georgia, I was on a local radio show there with a deejay called Peanuts Faircloth, who did a weekly show out of a record shop every weekend, and I used to do a TV show in Augusta — I think it was called *Orange Blossom Special*. My first paid performance was a little bit before the 1955 show in Swainsboro, Georgia, when I was paid $35.

133

No-one managed me as a child and I didn't have a manager until I was about ten years old, then Dub Allbritten — who also managed Red Foley — managed me until his death seventeen years later. Management-wise, I was always treated fairly — I was one of the lucky ones! I had good management, good people around me, and I came out of it very well when I wasn't a minor anymore.

In 1956, I was in Augusta, Georgia working when Red Foley came to town. Peanuts Faircloth took me over to the auditorium and asked Red — who at that time had a network television show on ABC out of Springfield, Missouri — if he would let me sing a song on the show. He was kind enough to do that and I appeared on his show, the *Ozark Jubilee*, and became a regular.

My name was changed from Tarpley to 'Lee' when I was doing the *Ozark Jubilee* television show in Augusta. The little stage manager — Sammy was his name — just thought that 'Lee' would be better than 'Tarpley' on a marquee. It was shorter and easier for people to remember.

A New York columnist, Jack O'Brien, saw me on that show and wrote up a very good review. As a result of his review, I went on to do the *Perry Como Show*, the *Steve Allen Show*, the *Ed Sullivan Show*, sign my contract with Decca Records and move to Nashville, Tennessee in 1956 to start recording.

At Decca, Owen Bradley and myself were in charge of my material. We did some other songs at the first Decca session, but *Jambalaya* was the first record issued and *Bigelow 6-200* was the flip-side. *One Step At A Time*, I believe, followed *Jambalaya*. *Let's Jump The Broomstick* was just a song that had been submitted to us that I liked. It wasn't a big record in the States, but it was a big record for me in England *[1961]*. *Sweet Nothin's* was written by a great writer and friend of mine, Ronnie Self, who I had met in Springfield, Missouri.

Ronnie Self wasn't contracted by Decca to write for me. He just happened to give me a lot of his songs, but other people — including himself — recorded his work. His main association is with me, but he was a good singer on his own and had some rockabilly records which are kind-of cult favourites now with people back in that era. He was a great writer.

At that time, I was still going to school and worrying about cheer-leading, being with my friends and all that kind of stuff. Being so young, singing was almost a secondary thing to me in those years. Although I loved singing, I didn't want to get my hopes up too much and get disappointed again, as we had several records out before *Sweet Nothin's* that really hadn't done anything.

So, I was very excited when *Sweet Nothin's* charted in both the US and UK in 1960. It laid around for about six months after it was released and didn't do anything. We thought that we had another flop on our hands. We were really frustrated and disappointed, and then it started happening in Cincinnati, Ohio. It started being played and all of a sudden it was a No. 4 record in the US. I can't pinpoint where I was when it charted, but I was probably on a promotion tour trying to get it going. We worked very hard on that record.

No, there was never any temptation to leave school early. I loved school and, as a matter of fact, wish that I could have gone on to college. I loved being there and being with the other kids. I think it kept me more normal and more stable than if I had quit and had a private teacher on the road — I didn't like that.

Had I stayed in school, I would have done something in the medical field. Yes, it's been a fair swap: I hope that maybe I've brought some kind of enjoyment to people's lives through what I do. I know that they've brought a lot to mine by letting me do what I do. So, I hope that I have touched some people's lives. Possibly I could have done more as a doctor, I don't know. If I hadn't been a singer — which is my first love — that's what I would have done.

As I've been doing what I wanted to do, and having a wonderful time doing it, I've never felt that I have missed out on very much in other areas of life. I know people may find that strange — singing from the age of six, etc — but I don't look at it that way.

I only did one package tour in the US — an edition of *The Biggest Show Of Stars For 1960* — and it was good. I enjoyed it, and I'm glad I got to experience it as we worked with a lot of people on the tour and it was fun. Back in those days, I didn't know what I made from a tour — that was handled by somebody else — but I got a lot of nice relationships and made a lot of friends: people like Duane Eddy, Fabian, Jimmy Clanton, Bill Black and Chubby Checker. Bill Black is dead now and I don't think that Jimmy Clanton performs very much.

One of the funniest things that happened was when Dub Allbritten took me — at age fourteen — to play the Paris Olympia in 1959. They had never even seen a picture of me before, so they had no idea what I looked like. I was booked solely on the strength of my voice. They kept asking for a publicity picture, so we sent a photo of me taken when I was

twelve years old but they kept writing back asking us to send a more recent picture and we didn't understand what they meant. Dub finally figured out that they thought I was much older, so he actually planted the story that I was a thirty-two year old midget and it got us a *lot* of publicity! *[laughs]* The crowds were real big, so it worked well. It was funny. My lack of height has never bothered me except you get frustrated when you go to buy clothes and a lot of the times can't get things that fit.

After rock and roll and upbeat numbers, yes I did move on to big powerful ballads with strings, but I don't know whether we were looking for a particular style or anything. We were just doing the best songs that we could find. Some of them happened to be the big ballads and we just did them accordingly, and I became known for those things.

There was never really any rivalry between Connie Francis and myself: Connie and I were different and we weren't doing the same things. We became friends right after we met, which would be when she had her first hit at age eighteen, and we have remained friends until this day. I had my first hit when I was thirteen, so I guess she's five or six years older than me.

Actually, we have never toured together. We talked about it, but it has never come about and I would like to tour with her now. She is still singing and packing houses, although she doesn't work a lot by choice as she has a nervous disorder.

It was very exciting to be the No. 1 female vocalist around the world. My twenty-million dollar record deal with Decca in 1963 was unheard of at the time. I was very honoured because it was a feat that not many people have achieved or will achieve. It's very hard to be a hit in foreign countries. You have to go over, romance that audience and continue to go, and a lot of American acts just won't do that.

I have two daughters, Julie and Jolie, who were born in 1964 and 1969. Had I thought about my marriage to Charles Shacklett, in 1963, from a career point of view, I may not have done it. He was who I wanted to marry and that's what I wanted to do. Fortunately, it didn't have any affect on my career at all. I think that is because I wasn't a sex symbol like Annette, Fabian, Elvis, Ricky Nelson or any of those people, and I wasn't a threat to female fans. I had a lot of female fans, and I think that they were my friends and that they were happy for me.

In the 1970s and 1980s a lot of people thought that I had gone into semi-retirement, but I didn't. In the early part of the Seventies, I was having No. 1 records and hit records. Then, in 1976, I decided to stop recording for about three years because I felt that what was happening to music wasn't where I wanted to be or what I wanted to do. So, I stopped recording, but I didn't stop working. I was still appearing, doing TV and all kinds of stuff.

In 1979, I came back with a record called *Tell Me What It's Like*, and I was nominated for a Grammy in 1980. The same year, I made a film — *Smokey And The Bandit II* — with Burt Reynolds. Ever since then, I've been recording and have had Top Ten records in the country field instead of the pop field. Country & western isn't my first love — I love *all* music.

I stayed with Decca[*] until 1986. It was a wonderful relationship and we parted ways amicably. I have nothing but good to say about the company: they treated me very well and I was happy to be with them.

I can't say that I enjoy getting on a bus, or getting into a car, or getting on a plane to travel hours and hours and hours to get somewhere. That gets tiring, but after I get there I love the performing. I love the stage-work and I love to sing, but I think as you get older some of the stuff that gets you to what you love gets a little bit tiring on you.

I don't get tired of singing my hits: I have a lot of reverence for them. Fortunately, with the help of Owen Bradley, we chose good songs that have lasted and stood the test of time, so I don't get tired of singing them. The songs stay fresh to me because they are well written. If you have been fortunate enough to have hits that people remember, I think you owe it to them to do those hits. But I don't think that there is anything wrong with doing new music. I put new music in my show any chance I get and it doesn't have to be *my* music, it can be somebody else's music I'm doing. It just depends on whether I like the song and I can sing it — that's what I do. When people come to see you, I think they want to hear the old things and expect to hear them, but I don't think that they close their minds to you doing anything else... only if you do the *old* ones first! *[laughter]* Yes, that's right!

Of my own songs, I can honestly say I've liked everything that I've ever recorded, but I guess *I'm Sorry* is one of my very favourites. *Johnny One Time* I loved, also *Rockin' Around The Christmas Tree*, *Coming On Strong*, *All Alone Am I*, *Break It To Me Gently*, *I Wonder*, *Fool No. 1*, *As Usual*... the list goes on. Every time you hear a great song which becomes a standard you think: 'Gosh, I wish I could have recorded that', but that's not to be.

[*] Decca became 'MCA' in 1972.

I don't know whether I've had the highest spot yet. I have had an awful lot of nice things happen to me — from performing for heads of state to playing for fans on the back of a truck in Alabama. It's all been special to me. I've won every major award that you can win throughout the world, and I've sold over 125,000,000 records. With help from a lot of people I've done some wonderful things. This tour is a highlight because I haven't been over here in a long time. So, I don't think that the highlights quit, or you can just choose one and say that was the best thing.

The lowest spot in my career was *not* when I went to Elektra in 1973, as I didn't actually join them, although people thought that I did. When I was off of Decca, I really was not 'off' Decca as I had a twenty-year recording deal with them, I was just not recording. In the interim, a friend of mine, Terry Woodford, called me from Muscle Shoals and said: 'Why don't you come down and let's just experiment, do ten or twelve sides and see if we can come up with anything?' The people from Elektra then called me and wanted me to sign with them! All of a sudden, it got out that I was recording for Elektra — which I never did and never was.

I've had such few low spots, but I guess the lowest was when I stopped recording for those two years or so — I missed it an awful lot. I missed not being in the studio and I missed not being able to be creative in the studio, but I'm not hard to live with at all and wasn't over that period. Those were my frustrations and I didn't put them off onto other people. It was a down time for me, but it was my own choice to do that as I thought it was the best thing to do, and it turned out that it was.

I like the old way of making records better. I like all the musicians there. I don't like overdubbing; I like to do my part there with the musicians. I don't like coming back in and singing to a tape. Progress is wonderful, I guess, and we all have to do it, but sometimes I think that you can get too technical and too good, and take all the guts and the feeling out of things.

With my career, I don't know what I could have done differently, actually. For many, many years I breathed, ate and slept it — I guess that's what you have to do during the early years. Personally, I would have made more relationships. I would have made more time for people, especially people that I grew up with and went to school with. That's not to say I'm still not close

Billboard Music On Campus, March 1965

with them — I am — but I missed a lot of things. I would have made more time for my brother and sisters. When we are sitting around telling stories, nine times out of ten I'm not included in them because I wasn't there; I was on the road working. So that hurts sometimes, you know. I missed seeing them grow up; they missed seeing me grow up. I wish my dad could have been alive to see some of the things that I've done. Other than those few things, I wouldn't change a thing.

15

EVERYBODY'S DOING A BRAND NEW DANCE
Little Eva

Young and talented singer Eva Boyd was in the right place at the right time when working as a babysitter for husband-and-wife songwriters Gerry Goffin and Carole King. Her spirited demo of a new tune called *The Loco-Motion* caught the ear of label boss Don Kirshner and the rest is now pop history. Forty years on, Little Eva's big hit remains one of the most popular dance records of all time.

I was born Eva Narcissus Boyd on June 29, 1943, in Belhaven, North Carolina. My parents were David and Laura Boyd. Dad did many things — a Jack of all trades. He worked on the railroads laying down train tracks; at the sawmill where they cut the lumber for furniture; in cotton fields — anything to make a living. The original family was thirteen, and there are eleven of us — seven sisters and four brothers — still alive.

I went to Belhaven's Elementary and High Schools and my first musical influences were the school glee club, and relatives that sang and played piano and organ. A first cousin was very influential in training me: she conducted the school glee club and all that. My family is musically inclined. Mom sang, my dad didn't. *[laughs]* I was involved with everything I could sing in at school and church, and any kind of musical programs that they had in our neighbourhood. My first amateur performance was a talent contest at Belhaven Elementary School and I won it. Certainly, there was family encouragement and they are very proud of me.

I always sang and wanted to be a singer. I always admired Mahalia Jackson the gospel singer, LaVern Baker, Ella Fitzgerald and Pearl Bailey. When I do things other than rock and roll songs, a lot of people say I remind them of Pearl Bailey, especially my sense of humour. That isn't coming to the fore right now as I'm kind-of tired.

My first visit to Brooklyn, New York, was in 1961. Then, after I got out of school, I went back there to stay with my brother Jimmy and his wife Shirley. It was through my sister-in-law, Shirley, that I met the Cookies — Earl-Jean McCree, Dorothy Jones and Margaret Ross — who were working as background singers for artists like Neil Sedaka, Mel Tormé and Tony Orlando, who worked with the songwriters Carole King and Gerry Goffin. Shirley told her best friend, Earl-Jean, that she knew somebody that could sing. They

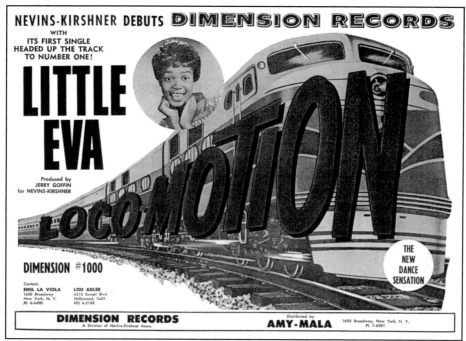

Billboard, July 1962

auditioned me, thought it would work and introduced me to Carole King. I auditioned as a background singer for Carole and Gerry, and they took me on. I was a singer on Tony Orlando' s records.

When I went to audition to sing back-up with the Cookies, Carole asked me if I wanted a job babysitting her daughter, Louise. I took the job and lived in with them. We got along fine. When I did *The Loco-Motion*, I was still living with them. They paid me $35 a week. Back then that was a lot of money for a sixteen year old girl — a *lot* of money. But actually, I made a lot of money doing back-ups. I could make up to $300 for a single side, and $1,500 for a session — which is one side of an album — so just think about the whole album! Mmmm, good money.

Goffin & King wrote *The Loco-Motion* for Dee Dee Sharp and I did the demo record. I didn't see anything in that demo for me; it was done for her. I did a lot of demos for female singers, and that's how they came to take it into the producer, Don Kirshner, so that he could listen to it for Dee Dee Sharp. Although I didn't know it at the time, he immediately thought that it would be a hit with me. He said that it had 'hit' written all over it.

Not long after that, they called me and told me to listen to the radio. Having no idea what they were talking about, I turned the radio on and all of a sudden I heard the intro to *The Loco-Motion*, but I thought they'd recorded Dee Dee Sharp. Then I heard my own voice! Needless to say, I was shocked. I was thunderstruck, and all I could say was: 'Wow! Wow! Oh, that's me, that's me on the radio. That's me!' I was so amazed and so happy. They didn't tell me they were going to release it with my vocal, they didn't tell me at all. It was the first record release on Don Kirshner's new Dimension Records label. So, it was just great.

We never discussed it, but I guess the other girls in the Cookies backing group were happy for me. I had joined the Cookies, and now at Dimension they were my backing group, but by that time they were also recording and later had hits with *Chains* and *Don't Say Nothin' Bad About My Baby.*

We made up *The Loco-Motion* dance when they made the song, because they wrote a portion of it at home. I put my little bit in about what I thought it should be like, but basically Gerry was the one who came up with the notion for the dance before the record came out. Actually, I envisaged the dance when the record came out with me singing it, so some of the lyrics were interpreted from what I would do to it. I made up my dance — you just do what the record says — and, of course, I elaborate on that when I do it on stage.

Nobody told me how to sing on that demo record or to style it for Dee Dee Sharp. I just did it the way they wrote it, and when I went into the studio I just sang it the way Carole sung it, except it was my version. It was just a demo record.

I can't remember where I was either when *The Loco-Motion* charted or when it got to No. 1. I just know that it was great. It was wonderful, not only to get to record, but to have a No. 1... you just can't describe it; it was amazing. Even today it still does the same thing for me thinking about it. I hear it on the radio now and I still go: 'Wow! That's me. That's me singing.'

Had I not got into showbusiness at that point, I guess I would have just continued to sing back-up. I wanted to be in the music and I didn't care how. From that time on, I was managed by Don Kirshner.

No, I didn't get everything that I was entitled to. You know the story. No? Oh, you didn't read that part, huh? Well, it has been written many times.

My family lived in North Carolina and they signed power of attorney over to my manager. I got $50 a week and expenses and that was it. When I toured the UK with Brian Hyland in 1963, I would be receiving $50 a week plus expenses with the rest going to my management.

I *knew* about it, but I was young. I wasn't the only one. We weren't into the business part of it, none of us were. Basically, we all did as we were told and took what they gave us, which was a weekly salary. I don't know how much anybody else got, but that's what I got. I don't dwell on it.

But there's a good side: I now get my royalties, but I didn't start

THE **loco**-MOTION

Words and Music by GERRY GOFFIN and CAROLE KING

Recorded by LITTLE EVA

on DIMENSION Records

ALDON MUSIC INC. • NEVINS-KIRSHNER ASSOCIATES, INC.

06009

60¢

to get them until 1992. Actually I started getting them through the manager I have now, Gary Cape. He called Rhino — who own the publishing — told them where I was at, and that's how I started getting my royalties.

As a result of having a hit record I did some tours, television, and theatre appearances at places like the Brooklyn Fox Theatre. The other guys and girls looked out for me because I was really young — people like the Shirelles, Ben E. King, Sam Cooke, Chuck Jackson, the Drifters, and everybody who had been out there a long time. They looked out for us young people.

The publicity people made up a story about my name, but it wasn't true. I was always known as 'Little Eva' at home. My daddy's sister was called Eva, so they called her Big Eva and me Little Eva.

There was no pressure on me for a follow-up record to *The Loco-Motion*. I didn't worry about things. We were young and didn't get tied up in things like: 'Oh, man, I hope I have another hit record' and all that, you know. Actually if you *have* a hit record, you tend to take it for granted. You don't think about the next record — we didn't. I imagine they do that now. We were just in love with what we were doing, and I don't think any of us cared what was going to happen next.

The follow-up was *Keep Your Hands Off My Baby*, which reached No. 12 in the States, followed by *Let's Turkey Trot* which made No. 20. Then there was *Swingin' On A Star*, a duet with Big Dee Irwin, which charted. My final chart hit was *Old Smokey Locomotion*, in the middle of 1963. That one was Gerry Goffin's idea. Even though he and Carole wrote together, Gerry was the main one for the lyrics and Carole for the music. My last single on Dimension Records was *Wake Up John*.

Incidentally, after I left the Goffin and King household, two of my sisters — Idalia and Mamie — went to work for Gerry and Carole. Mamie didn't work out, but Idalia got to release a record on Dimension called *Hula Hoopin'*, but it wasn't successful. Idalia and I can sound very much alike, and people thought that *Hula Hoopin'* was me under another name. It wasn't for her anyway — she wasn't the type — so Idalia went home and got married. *[laughs]*

Carole King and Gerry Goffin weren't on the management side of the business, but I do believe that much more could have been done for me and much better. You take it for granted that they are gonna look after you. You don't think about it until all of a sudden — bam! Then they tell you: 'Well this is going on, and you're not going to be on Dimension any more, you're gonna be on this label.' That's actually what happened to me. I had no say about it; I didn't know that it was going on. When it happened, I wasn't even at home. I was on the road somewhere and came back. They had a *right* to do it because they owned the label and they owned me.

I wasn't able to earn the good money I had been getting as a backing singer when I was on the road touring and doing concerts in my own right. I lived well, had a nice apartment, clothes and food — they took care of all that — but as far as money in my hand was concerned, all I got was the $50 pocket money that I mentioned earlier. I thought that, as I was so young and getting so little, they had money in a trust fund for me. Don't ask who told me, as I don't remember all that. In 1964, I found out that there wasn't anything — not for me anyway. So, I didn't have any funds at all.

I was still with Nevins–Kirshner when I found out that I had been moved to Amy Records. Because they still owned me, I thought that my bank account had to be somewhere. I called Nevins–Kirshner and was told: 'Bank account? You don't have a bank account.' They said that the money went on producing records, buying clothes and all that. In effect, Nevins–Kirshner stopped managing me when they got rid of Dimension. Business is business — I realize that — and some people have just got business minds. They are movers and shakers; they make money and that's it.

Al Nevins, the other half of Nevins–Kirshner, was a wonderful person, but he died only months into my career. He told me that I didn't belong in the business, and that I was going to get hurt. I believe that if he had lived, things would have been different with my career because he seemed to care a lot more for me. Anyway, that's the way I took it from the conversations that we had.

I left the business in 1971 but still did odd gigs until 1972, when I quit completely. Although not singing professionally for the next twenty years, I was still singing in church, schools, and at bar mitzvahs and weddings. During this time I got married and had a family. For work, I just did anything that I could. Before I came back in 1992, I was managing a restaurant and doing most of the cooking. I'm a *great* cook! Oh, yeah, I can cook.

When Grand Funk had a No. 1 in the States with *The Loco-Motion* in 1974, I didn't really know anything about it until I started coming back myself. In those years, I just left the business alone and didn't keep up with what was going on. I knew that they had a record out because people told me, but I just wasn't into it at all. I didn't listen to rock and roll, or have anything to do with it.

People magazine did an article on me in 1987, and it started the whole thing up again, but I didn't do anything about it. I made an album out in Malibu in 1989 called *Back On Track Again.* The guy that I recorded for didn't do anything with it for years, but I know it's now out on CD as several people have brought them for me to sign. I haven't seen a copy of it in a store, but I have a CD out there somewhere.

In the same year, Gary Cape — who is now my manager — called me and asked me to make a comeback, and over the next few years he persisted. My comeback in 1992 was the result of Gary Cape convincing me over a period of eight months. I don't know quite how he did it, but he took a survey of public opinion about me. He sent out these flyers and got this great mail about me and where I was, etc.

What finally triggered me to do it was the fact that he said that I should do it for *myself.* I started thinking about that. I mean, here I am cooking, and partly on welfare, with food stamps and stuff like that. I practically got off welfare 'cause I was working, but I could live better still by getting back into showbusiness. But that wasn't the deciding part. The deciding part was that I needed to do it for *me.* So, I took a look at what I was doing and how miserable I was. You gotta *love* what you're doing! I like cooking, but I don't like it all *that* much. One day I said: 'Man, this doesn't make any sense, I don't gotta do this.' So, hey, I called him and said: 'All right!' I signed the contract and sent it back to him.

Actually, when I came back in 1992 after twenty years, I wasn't sure that I could do it. The first performance was at the Nassau Coliseum in Long Island, New York. I went on and did this doo-wop concert for the promoter, Richard Nader. He asked for me and I went. That night, when I came out onto the stage it was like 22-25,000 people out there and they all stood up. And they just yelled and they screamed and they yelled and they screamed. This went on for six or seven minutes. Richard Nader was out there trying to introduce me and these people were going crazy. The whole place just stood up. I hadn't sang a drop: I hadn't sung *nothin'*! When they had quietened down, he came back out onto the stage and told me to go ahead and sing. After all, he couldn't say anything. The band started up and I did my two songs: *Keep Your Hands Off My Baby* and *The Loco-Motion*. By the time I got to the end of *The Loco-Motion*, they were at it again: the 'trains' were all over the place. It was so pretty. Richard Nader came out and said: 'You know, I knew she could sing because I was told she could sing, but when she opened up her mouth I knew that she still had it. Then I lost control of my own show!' The people just wouldn't let him open his mouth.

Up until that show, I was still sceptical, wary, and scared. I was thinking: 'I'm older, I don't know if I can do this.' But when I went out there and those people stood up, it just overwhelmed me and gave me confidence and courage. I sang my heart out that night! I did it for myself as well as the people. After that, I felt like: 'Yeah, I can do this.'

It has taken me some time to get to where I am now, to get back into the swing of things. It wasn't so much the singing; it was the entertainment part, because you have to have confidence and stage presence. It took me some time to get back into that.

Actually, I was in the church and I had lost all of that. I am still careful about what I do: I'm particular about how I move. I don't want to be vulgar, even though I dance and all that kind of stuff, because I'm in the church. Although I am not religion-crazy, there are standards that you have to keep. I like having fun — I have fun when I'm out there onstage — but there's certain places I don't go. As I say, I'm not 'way out there', but I've found out that I can do what I do and *still* be a church member. I love what I do and it's a talent. Our talents are supposed to be used and that's what I do: I sing. And if I *don't* sing, then what am I gonna do, cook chicken again? I don't really wanna do that.

I have no trouble keeping my hits fresh, and I am now rehearsing some new stuff other than rock. I sing a little jazz, a little blues, a little soul, but I can't sing new material on a package show like this one. We sing the 'oldies but goodies' on these tours, and if you go to do a show somewhere else other than a package tour, then you can sing your own material.

Of my own material, my favourite song to sing is *Keep Your Hands Off My Baby*, but my favourite fun song is *The Loco-Motion*. I don't have a favourite artist, and can't really think of someone else's material that I would have liked to record. Outside of performing, I like to sing — naturally — and listen to music of all kinds, not just rock and roll. I love gospel, jazz, classical, pop, longhair stuff — I just love music.

I like nostalgia shows, not only because they give me a second career, but because of people's reaction all over the world since that show at Nassau Coliseum. And I've travelled all over the world again: this is my second childhood and, yes, now I'm getting properly paid in my opinion. *[laughs]*

I saw Don Kirshner not that long ago. Richard Nader's wife died — and his son almost — from smoke inhalation when they had a fire. We did this big doo-wop benefit for him and his children. By then, I was on top of the world again and the past didn't bother me. I used to harbour bitterness, but after I got into church I learned that wasn't good, and you gotta forgive and move on. That's one reason why I didn't want to do that kind of singing again. When I saw him, I didn't have any animosity towards him at all.

Friendships in the business? Yes, I'm friends with everybody and there are strong friendships on this tour with Bobby Vee, Chris Montez, Johnny Preston and Brian Hyland. I have toured three times with Bobby, Chris and Brian, and twice with Johnny.

Looking back, would I do anything differently? I really don't know how to answer that. If I had the knowledge that I have now, it *would* be different. But even today young people don't have that knowledge unless they've got someone doing it for them. You just don't have the business acumen to know the ins and outs of the financial parts.

I think my lowest point was when I wasn't doing this. My mom died too, and that's another reason why I quit. And, of course, finding out that I didn't have any money saved for me.

My high spots are the whole thing: I have never got over it. It's amazing to me that I had a hit record — such a phenomenal hit record — and that it's *still* a hit record, 'cause it is. I'm making a living off this legend: the song is a *classic*. It's been No. 1 two times — only one of five songs — and who else can say that? There aren't too many of us, you know. It's beyond explaining, 'cause it just doesn't happen to everybody but it happened to me. So, I am just appreciating it.

16

LET'S DANCE
Chris Montez

Pop culture owes a debt to Chris Montez, who not only contributed the all-time classic *Let's Dance*, but also provided the inspiration for the famous collarless jackets adopted by the Beatles. Later on, a collaboration with trumpeter/bandleader Herb Alpert in the mid-Sixties resulted in a succession of hits in a laidback Latin style typified by the breathy *The More I See You*.

My real name is Ezequiel Christopher Montanez, and I was born in Los Angeles, California. My mother and father were called Zoraida and Isaac, and I had four brothers — Isaac, Gilbert, Fernando and Adolfo — and four sisters — Suzie, Sally, Connie and Helen. My nickname was 'Zeke'.

Listening to the radio, my earliest musical influences were Johnnie Ray, the Everly Brothers, Ricky Nelson and Bill Haley & His Comets.

My brothers all played guitar, so I got my playing ability on the guitar by singing Mexican ballads with them. My first amateur performance took place in a little dance hall in Hawthorne, Los Angeles with my brother Fernando. We did this acoustical, and sang some of the songs that I had written. Unfortunately, he froze up on me in the middle of a song when he was supposed to do his solo. He was supposed to play lead guitar, but he disappeared on me; his knee got the trembles and he couldn't stand still, so he just bounced off. After that, I continued to perform at different dance halls and parties and formed a little group. Basically, then I sang nothing but rock and roll songs in the Ritchie Valens style.

I got my general education as far as music is concerned after this period. My mother was very proud of me and my brothers and sisters still are. If I hadn't gone into showbusiness I have no idea what I would have done, but I would probably have become an artist, as I did a lot of artwork back then.

Our groups went through different names, but at one time a little trio we put together was called 'The Rhythm Dukes', and then we had 'The Invincibles'.

Recognition came after I made a demonstration record. Some publishers heard it and said that they would like to record some music with me. That's when it all began.

The song that they finally liked was one I had written called *All You Had To Do Was Tell Me*. They helped me to finish the lyrics and the record was a very good-sized hit in America, but especially in Los Angeles. This was my first record release and I think it came out early in 1962. They also asked me my full name and when I told them, they said that they would give it some thought. Later on they said: 'How about Chris Montez?' When I told my mom what they wanted to name me, she said that it sounded nice, but it was quite a change and took me some time to get used to it.

Let's Dance was written for me by Jim Lee, who was my producer at the time. We collaborated on my music and it worked. The song wasn't really tailor-made to my existing style. Although I was singing some of the uptempo Ritchie Valens numbers at the time, *Let's Dance* was different. But it has become a classic pop record, and its success .

I can't remember where I was or what I was doing when *Let's Dance* charted, but it was climbing every week. I thought: 'Wow, it's going to get up there, it's going to make the Top Five, you know; it's going to get *higher*! It was exciting, and I was thrilled because it was like something that you'd more-or-less planned all of your life. Like when you say: 'I want to do that, I want to do something like that one of these days' — and all of a sudden you've done it!

All of a sudden, you're an overnight success and have a chart record which gives you a lot of recognition and presents a lot of opportunities. No movie offers were ever received, but people are telling you that you've got to do TV here and go there, that they're setting up this tour and that tour. As a young man, I was excited by all this activity and pressure, although at the time I didn't realize that it would be such hard work. On some of the package tours, like Dick Clark's and the Sam Cooke tour, we would be doing three and four shows a day in the theatres we played.

Looking back at my early touring days with the package shows, I have some great memories, but no particular ones. I haven't any recollections of learning as an artist, but I did learn that there had to be a better way than running around like a rag doll. I think that it is important for any individual who becomes successful to be aware of what is going on in his life — contractually and direction-wise — and to watch out for himself.

I remember touring the UK with Tommy Roe and the Beatles in the spring of 1963. What did I think of the Beatles? I thought that they were *lousy*! *[laughs]* No, seriously, all of a sudden there was something new going on because I found that people were wearing black and trying to imitate them. Well, I tell you, I had a jacket with me on that tour and it had no collar on it. I don't know why, but when I used to wear it — and I wore it a few times onstage — everyone wanted to buy it from me. It was strange. When we finished the tour the Beatles said: 'I hope that you don't mind Chris, but we're having our new suits designed like that round-collared jacket you brought with you.'

I've met a lot of people in my career, but have never had long-lasting friendships. I toured with Smokey Robinson and we became good friends, and also with Sam Cooke and Jerry Butler. During tours with black artists like the Sam Cooke Show — which in addition to Sam included the Drifters and Smokey Robinson — I was asked to get out of the tour bus in Southern parts and order food for them, as it was easier that way. That was the first time I saw segregated rest-rooms and, being a Mexican, I never knew which one to go into as there weren't any 'in between' rest-rooms.

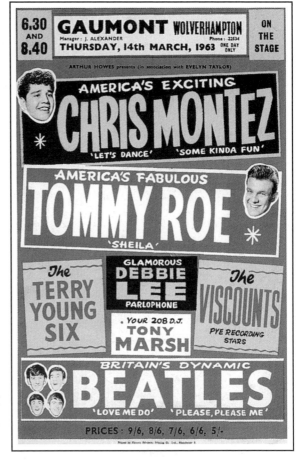

For me, there were no idols or pecking order in the business of appearing on shows. Once I had seen other artists do their songs at rehearsal, I knew what they did and that was that. I just did my job and off I'd go.

I never had a problem with alcohol or anything like that in coping with the pressures of showbusiness — I still don't. I figure that what is the point of trying to be successful and working hard in your life only to destroy yourself? Anyway, I believe in the Lord, and He's the one who takes care of me and keeps me in balance.

I was lucky to have written *Some Kinda Fun* as a follow up to *Let's Dance*. It kept me going pretty well, and I had a roll going. For the time, I thought that I was managed well — other than the shortcomings that I had with my contract, and being short-changed on my royalties by the record company and the manager, Jim Lee. The record company's name was Monogram, but it was distributed by Era.

In the early Sixties I would be earning $300–$500 a week, sometimes as much as $1,500–$2,000 — it all depended. There would be times when you would have to pay your own hotel bill out of that.

All of a sudden, after *Let's Dance* and *Some Kinda Fun*, I was stuck in the middle of this tragedy of royalty statements and my manager, Jim Lee, had taken most of the money that he wasn't supposed to take. In order for me to break the contract and leave him, I had to give up everything and not sue him — otherwise I would've been unable to get out and be contractually stuck for another five years. I just felt so let down because of the hard work that I had contributed towards my career, but I said: 'Oh, I can do it again. I'll just get out and go back to school,' and that's what happened.

We've got another
one of those wonderful-type hits
that <u>everybody</u> can play
and <u>everybody</u> will buy!

CALL ME
CHRIS MONTEZ

A&M 780

656-5330

Billboard, December 1965

I now had time to finish high school and go to college at the Sunland Conservatory of Music, California, where I got my certificate in classical musical composition. My instructor there was Harold V. Johnson, who helped me a lot and was a big influence on my composition. At Sunland, my studies included piano and guitar as well as the writing of fugues and études, etc. After that, I studied jazz improvisation and composition at Dick Groves' School of Jazz in L.A. That influenced my style for both the composition of standards and jazz standards.

It was during this period at college, around 1965–66, that I met Herb

Alpert for the first time. He offered me a contract, but I said: 'No, I've had this bitterness, and I don't want to do the contractual bit as I'm going to end up losing again.' However, it worked out well, and I had hits with *Call Me*, *The More I See You* and others on A&M, which was Herb Alpert's and Jerry Moss's record label.

In the late Sixties, I did four albums with them and we had a lot of hits in the States. I did tours in the UK and Europe, then came home and studied for a while — I just wanted to. After that, I left A&M and went to CBS International, which was their company for Europe. I wrote a few songs and we made Top Five with the first release *Aye No Digas (Oh Don't Tell Me)*. We started selling a different blend of music all over.

Over the years, I have toured throughout the world. Recently, I have been touring Germany, Austria, France and Spain and have just returned from Japan. Australia is the only place in the world that I haven't visited, and that is what they are planning on after this current UK tour. When I am not working, my hobbies are running, and I used to do a lot of boxing.

My favourite record of all time is Johnny Ace singing *Pledging My Love* — a most beautiful song. He and that recording were a great inspiration for me. One of my favourite lady vocalists today is Whitney Houston.

Of my own records I don't have any favourites; *Let's Dance* is just a song. But, the highest point in my life has to be making the charts with *Let's Dance* and receiving a gold record for world sales and a silver record for sales in Europe.

Looking back at my career, I regard it as a long experience. With hindsight, I would have done things differently — a little better. I would have protected myself more by getting better representation and being aware of what was going on.

Today, I am doing a lot of songwriting now and I'm in the middle of producing something for myself, but I *do* miss the simple ways of recording. Today, you can lay down more tracks on a record, but my approach is this: 'So we have more tracks, but do we have to take more time?' Because, if the basic *feel* isn't there then what is the use of doing it?

17

THE VOICE OF THE DRIFTERS
Johnny Moore

Pop music history will remember the Drifters for their supreme on-stage professionalism and a succession of charismatic lead singers including Clyde McPhatter, Ben E. King, Rudy Lewis and... Johnny Moore, the voice behind hits like *Adorable*, *Under The Boardwalk*, *Saturday Night At The Movies* and *At The Club*. Often overshadowed by the solo success of his peers, Moore was the cornerstone of the group for several decades, singing lead on no fewer than fifty-one of their single sides and can justifiably lay claim to the title 'The Voice of the Drifters'.

I was born on December 14, 1934 in Selma, Alabama. I have a wife and three kids with me and two grown daughters. Mom and dad are both dead. My father was a barber and mother worked in a hospital as a receptionist. I have a sister in Cleveland, Ohio. Educationally, I graduated from high school.

My earliest music influences would be in the early Fifties: groups like the Dominoes and the Orioles; singers like Roy Brown, Ella Fitzgerald and Nat 'King' Cole; and also the big bands of Count Basie, Louis Jordan and Duke Ellington. There were no musical influences in the home, I just happened to take it up and sing around the neighbourhood in people's homes. We had a group called 'The South's Youngest Gospel Singers' and played churches occasionally.

My first professional performance was at a place called Gleason's in Cleveland, Ohio with a group called the Hornets. There were five of us in the group and we made $7 apiece that night and thought it was all the money in the world! I joined the Hornets when a guy named James Long, who was one of the lead singers in the group, was looking for a tenor who could sing falsetto. As I had a knack for doing that falsetto bit at the time, he asked me to join the group and I did; it worked out just fine. That would be when I was at high school in the ninth grade.

After I started with the Hornets, it was easy to consider going professional. I wasn't obsessed, but I liked it very much and more-or-less geared my life towards a career in showbusiness. My parents didn't try to hold me back or push me, they just let me do what I wanted to do for myself — the decision was all mine. Had I not gone into showbusiness, I wanted to be a fireman or a long-distance lorry driver. Thank God, I've never had to take either of them up.

My first spell as a Drifter started in November 1954 — when I was recruited from the Hornets — and lasted until June 1955 when I left. I then returned to the group in August '55 and made my first Drifters record, which was a number called *Adorable*, in September '55. Bill Pinkney, one of the Drifters,

Johnny [back row, third from left] with the Drifters, 1955.

auditioned me with the rest of the guys in the group. Bill asked me if I knew any of the Drifters' material, which I did. I went down to see them, sang a couple of their songs and next day — Thanksgiving Day 1954 — I was a Drifter! The day after that, I was on my way from Cleveland, Ohio to Atlanta, Georgia.

My range was basically about the same as Clyde McPhatter's and that of David Baughn, who had succeeded Clyde as lead singer and from whom I took over, but the styling was different. No-one controlled how I sang, I just did it myself. The only 'control' came from the record company, Atlantic Records, as they picked the songs along with us — but that was it; we did what we wanted to do.

Adorable was the first hit, followed by *Ruby Baby*. We were touring when the first record charted. As a matter of fact we were going through Tennessee, as we headed towards Indianapolis or some place like that, when we heard this radio station broadcast from Nashville. This station, WLAC, which played all the black music at the time, had a power of 50,000 watts that more-or-less went all over America — north, south, east and west. They were playing our record, *Adorable*, and I said: 'That's us, that's me!' We just sat quietly in the car, driving along, listening to our new hit — the first one I did — and it was *fantastic!*

In 1957, I left the group again when I was drafted into the US Army. I was stationed in Germany for eighteen months. I did a few things in the Officers' and NCOs' clubs, but you couldn't continue your career in the services. They were in control there and you had to do military things. *[laughs]*

On discharge in 1959, I went solo for about five years on Sue Records with Juggy Murray as President. I recorded a few things with him, but unfortunately for me I didn't get a hit, so a successful solo career never happened, not at all. I was never as fortunate as Ben E. King or Clyde McPhatter in that respect.

Sooner or later, he met Ike and Tina Turner, and his attention turned to them as they were more-or-less — and I say this tongue in cheek — the 'black act without a white sound' for white audiences. He told me: 'You sound too pretty: you don't sound black enough.'

So, he switched to Ike and Tina Turner, and I found myself back in the Drifters again in 1963 when I left Juggy. His assessment didn't bother me. I thought that it was an underhanded compliment really. My first hit back with the Drifters was *Under The Boardwalk*, so I guess that I do sound 'white'. That record is No. 13 in the all-time Top 100 records, so I didn't do too bad, did I? *[laughter]*

I've thought a lot about putting out a solo album, subject to agreement with Faye Treadwell. I'd love to do it, but I've never been approached. It's a matter of backing, opportunity and seeing whether or not it would be worth my while really. Let's face it, this is a business, and I'm not in it for the cheering and the pats on the back: I'm in it for the gilt. If it ever comes about, I'd go and see Faye and tell her that I wanted to try that venture outside of my work with the Drifters, and see what happens.

If I had the chance to record any song, it would have to be *On Broadway*. I know that it was a Drifters record, but Rudy Lewis sang lead on it and it's my favourite record.

The first record would normally be a hot spot of a career, but the highest spot for me was when we appeared in New York's Madison Square Garden about 1973. We got a standing ovation from 23,000 people and the hairs on my arms stood up — I haven't got them on my head so they couldn't stand up there! *[laughter]* That was a highlight.

My lowest spot was in 1981 when Faye and I — for whatever reason — had a falling-out and I left the Drifters... *again.* I put together something called Johnny Moore & Slightly Adrift and it didn't happen. I guess it was destined not to happen. That was a *downer* and I don't want to talk about it.

If I could change anything, I don't think that I would have left the group in 1981. I would have stayed with

THE DRIFTERS

Under the Boardwalk

ATLANTIC

2237

it and battled through whatever crises Faye and I had to stay with the group. Sometimes you listen to the wrong people and you start being swayed by another person's opinion. It may not be your opinion at all, but if you listen long enough sometimes they can sway you into going their way. I think if I had to do it all over again, I would hold her down and make her talk to me so that we could squash out our differences and stay together. Had we done that, we probably wouldn't have all these other guys using the Drifters' name and all that kind-of stuff. I would like to have stayed with her and kept it like it is now, a happy family.

Today, there are probably between six and ten other Drifter groups running around the world. That's quite a bother for us, as it cuts our market down. I think that Mrs. Treadwell is now going to make an assault on them, telling them that they are plagiarising her Drifters' name and have no right to do so, etc. She is going to deal with them and stop it. It insults us, and it insults the people who love the Drifters and their music when they go to see these phoney groups who are singing our music and pretending to be us. The group's name has been with the Treadwell family for over thirty-five years now. Faye Treadwell is a battler, and since her husband died she's brought the group from the lowest to the highest, believe me.

I think that Faye Treadwell considers me her leader of the group if only for longevity — thirty-four years *[laughs]* — and a few records I made for her! Yes, I got my Christmas bonus last week and I'm wearing it *[shows off jewellery]* — look. So you see, it works out fine when you get along with somebody doesn't it? *Build* the bridges, and don't burn them behind you!

Faye will pick the show that she wants done on a tour. She picks the songs, and obviously she will designate who is gonna sing them. Then she'll come along and look and see if it's coming on how she wants it. If it's not how she wants it, she'll raise hell. Yes, she's in control of what we do and what we sing. Matter of fact, she's in *total* control because, as President of the Drifters, that's her job. Of course, we talk it over and try to co-operate with her. Usually we agree with her, but life's too short for silly arguments, so we try to give her whatever show she wants. Faye, in consultation with myself, hires and fires when necessary. That's why I'm back here now with her. No names, but I didn't want to share the stage with a certain guy, so he left and I'm back.

On tour, I've shared a stage with Jackie Wilson, Brook Benton, Sam Cooke, Little Richard, Bo Diddley, Chuck Berry, Jerry Lee Lewis, Paul Anka, Bill Haley, the Everly Brothers and Buddy Holly — it was fantastic! Right now, my favourite artists are Stevie Wonder, Barbra Streisand and Aretha Franklin.

The first time we came to the UK was in 1965. We did a London Palladium show for Lady Hoare and her cerebral palsy charity. We

The Drifters

SATURDAY NIGHT

AT THE MOVIES

Atlantic

2660

were guest artists appearing with acts like Des O'Connor — it was great.

In the late Sixties, we were still working and touring, and there were various breakaway Drifter groups formed by Bill Pinkney, Rick Sheppard and Charlie Thomas, but Faye Treadwell — who took over in 1967 when her husband, George, died — kept her group intact. I stayed with Faye Treadwell because as far as I was concerned the Treadwells owned the Drifters, 'cause when I first started back in the 1950s they had the group. In order for me to be a Drifter, I felt that I had to be in the group controlled by the Treadwells.

No, I have never tried to buy the group name, but I don't think that it would be for sale anyway.

We work some three hundred nights a year. How do I keep the same act fresh? I keep it fresh because I *enjoy* it. People always ask me that question, and I find myself answering it differently all the time. My pat answer is that our songs are 'situation' songs. However, the reason we are so successful, is that almost anybody can come along to the show and think that they could sing those songs. Our songs are so simple that everyone can sing right along to them, and the audience helps us to do our show. I'm looking at the happy faces, old and young — I mean *old* and *young* — and it keeps me going. I never get tired of it because I get the energy from the people themselves. When I perform on the stage for them, their faces say to me: 'Oh, we're really enjoying this tonight! Come on guys, let's go Drifters!' That gives me my 'oomph', you know.

Yes, there were a lot of special needs people in last night's audience. They could be me or you. I play towards them, giving them an extra little caring, but I keep it even and never overdo it or go over the top as they would sense that and be offended.

You ask me about the slickness of the act and what discipline we employ to keep it tight. To answer that I have to go back a few years to when the group consisted of Joe Blunt, Clyde Brown, Billy Lewis and myself. We had this sort-of 'discipline' that you call it for the slickness — not being over-slick, but being cohesive. However, today we don't have that real slick Drifter look. Now why that is could be down to individuals. I'm not putting anybody down here or calling anyone names, but we are lacking this 'cohesive' thing that we always used to have, and that people were more-or-less familiar with seeing us do. We don't have that now, but we're going to get it back because I'm going to *insist* that it comes back. I *insist* that we look professional on stage. So, tell people to bear with us a little while. We're gonna rehearse, rehearse, rehearse and get it right.

No, it never bothers me being anchored to a group like the Drifters — are you *kidding* me?

18

PURE GENE-IUS
Gene Pitney

Singer, multi-instrumentalist, composer, arranger, producer — talented Gene Pitney had all the prerequisites to make it big in the music industry. And make it big he did, averaging over three hits a year in the USA between 1961 and 1966 with a host of dramatic ballads like *Only Love Can Break A Heart*, *I'm Gonna Be Strong* and *Twenty-Four Hours From Tulsa* that were to become his trademark. Firmly established as an international star by the mid-Sixties, he continued to enjoy chart success well into the next decade.

Gene Francis Alan Pitney is my real name. I was born on February 17, 1941 in Hartford, Connecticut and grew up in Rockville, which is in the same state.

In those days, towns were different to what they are today. Everyone in Connecticut had a front porch and people used to sit outside their homes. It's a shame, but that's gone now. As a kid, I always sang and used to buy those books containing the lyrics of all the top songs. In the afternoon or early evening, I used to sit out on the front porch and sing — with this real high pure tenor voice that I had — not realizing that people in the street were listening to me. I just loved music and used to sing the songs that I knew from listening to the radio. People only recently told me that they used to sit out in the evening just to hear me sing. However, I had no interest in singing in front of people — as a matter of fact, I was terrified.

The first time that I ever had a 'do' would be one St. Patrick's Day when I was seven or eight years old and in the third or fourth grade. I attended a parochial school with nuns — who broke many rulers over my head — and this school was right across the road from the public school. Anyway, I remember that the school nurse came and took me over to the public school. Unknown to me, they had assembled all the classes into the auditorium and I had to sing *Tola Tolara Tolar*. I had never ever stood in front of an audience singing before. My heart was pounding. God, I was a wreck! So little was coming out, I didn't know whether they could hear me. I wasn't worried about *singing*, I was worried about getting out of there!

I always had a natural interest — I always loved music. In school, I sang in choirs. I sang in church. Playing instruments came much later: I was driving a car, having just got my driving licence — so I had to be sixteen or seventeen — and was going ice-skating in the adjacent town of Manchester, some fifteen miles away from where I lived in Rockville. As much as I loved music, I never ever had any intention of playing any kind of instrument and didn't even know what I was capable of doing. I was skating for a while, when it started to snow very heavily. I had a 1935 Ford Coupe with a rumble seat which cost me $40 when I first bought it, but by this time I had a '48 Mercury engine in it. It was candy-apple red, had white-walls on it and an awning on top. However, I didn't have any snow tyres on it, so I thought I had better get out of there and go home.

I was driving down a little back way to go back to Rockville — this place is still there today — when I stopped at a place called DeBaldo's Music Shop and signed up for guitar lessons, and I don't know why! I was just ice-skating — I never intended to — I saw the neon sign, and I drove in and I stopped. That really was the start of everything. Had I not done that, I don't think that anything would have ever happened musically at all.

My family loved to hear me sing. My mother especially was very, very proud of the voice that I had. They used to drag me up in front of relatives and everything — which is the worst thing that you can do because you can really end up going the other way. It's like being told that you're going to do something; if you're bull-headed enough then you're definitely *not* going to do it.

Once I did start with the guitar and everything, my mother encouraged that. I found out after a few lessons that I was natural to playing any instrument, because I took what I learned on the guitar and transposed it onto the piano. We had an old piano-player — the mechanical type that you pump — with a roll of music. It had this beautiful sound to it like the old pianos had, it was called a 'tack': when you pushed a certain lever on it, these little pieces of metal came up behind the things that thumped the strings and made a great sound like a rinky-dink piano. That was really the thing that I wrote on most of the time — I *loved* that sound.

From there — to make a long story short — I could play guitar and learned to play, like, four chords in three or four keys. At that time, the Top Twenty was *all* three or four chords — no more — so you could play everything that was going on. You thought you were brilliant after about five lessons!

The next natural step was to start a band, which I did in Rockville High School. It was a very small school, so I had the only other guitar player, the only piano player, the only drummer and the only saxophone player. We were called — embarrassingly — Gene Pitney & The Genials. We just did it for the hell of it. There was no intention of ever doing anything or having any success, especially a career.

I was the only one who had a car and, in order for five of us to fit into that car, we had to work out one afternoon, logistically, how you would fit in a set of drums, the amplifiers, the equipment and five people — three in the front and two in the rumble seat. It would only fit one way: if you put one thing in wrong, then it was all over. *[laughs]* It was really fun.

At that time, record hops were the big thing where kids would go. The big local disc jockey would go to a big hall or local ballroom, and the kids used to come by the thousand. We used to play at these things and just loved it. If we made $10 a night we were lucky, but we just didn't care.

I graduated from high school in 1959, so I was in it from 1954 to 1955, and at that time most people were listening to, like, the Presley influence — but I wasn't. That really wasn't my cup of tea. I was really into the black groups, who I thought were coming out of a combination of country & western and rhythm & blues. I remember driving back to that same town I mentioned before, Manchester. I used to go to this little cafe — a diner it was — 'cause theirs was the only jukebox that had a record called *Gee,* by the Crows. I've always said that I thought this recording was the first rock and roll record. Funnily enough, I was in Australia on a tour a couple of years ago and mentioned this in a conversation. A guy who was there, who knew all the things from the Fifties and Sixties said that it *was* the first rock and roll record! I almost fell over, because I'd always thought of it as that.

It was a *dreadful* record: you listen to it today and you have to laugh. It was all off-key, and all they did was a 'gee-doo-dee-doo' introduction and then the vocal came in, but it had whatever it is that rock and roll has. It wasn't the fact that it was good or bad, or had a good or bad lyric. It was just that 'rock' feel that was so infectious, it was to go out and become the biggest thing in the world.

Artists like Kay Starr were important. I used to play her songs like *Wheel Of Fortune* all the time. I can't say who else, and I can't say who influenced me as, growing up younger than that, I used to sing all the time, so anybody could be in that category of influence. I used to sing the songs of everyone that I could think of: Gene Autry songs, Hoagy Carmichael's *Old Buttermilk Sky* — things as far back as that when I was only a kid of six or seven years old. Whether they were influences or not, really I don't know.

The things that really sparked me, that I used to turn the radio dials to hear, were the Penguins, the Robins and the Angels. Also, right along at the same time, Ben E. King and his group, the Drifters, when they came out with some of the early stuff. I used to love to hear them. Clyde McPhatter was a favourite, as I have the same twist in the high-pitched voice that he had. I used to love what he could do with a lyric like *Seven Days* and things like that. It's a pity that he died very early.

When I had that band of mine, we were invited by a friend who managed a theatre to a record hop in Branford, Connecticut, on the coast. It was there that the proverbial fat man with a cigar came up to me and said: 'Do you wanna make a record?' And he's the guy that took me to New York for the first time. Now, I'm a green kid from Rockville, Connecticut and that was like a major trip, so I was just like a nervous wreck when I went in there. But once I got started working around the different offices and everything, bumping into different people and meeting people who were just involved in the business — not so much even the acts — I loved it. I loved the excitement of it and the possibilities of being successful.

I think that right from that point on — and at that point I was out of high school and going to the University of Connecticut's Electronic School — it made life very difficult, because the whole thing at that period of time was: 'You gotta get a college education!' I think that things have changed quite a bit today, because a whole load of people who went and got a college education *still* didn't have a job.

It concerned my parents. My dad was English and Irish, and my mother was Polish and French. Her mother — my grandmother — was from the old country, from Poland, and they *worked!* I mean, the work ethic was *ridiculous.* In her eighties, my grandmother was still working out in the tobacco fields! My mother's brothers — three of them had college educations and two of them were doctors, and the other was a very successful businessman. The only one that wasn't educated — and brighter than all of them — was my mother, because the girl was always the one who was last.

NOW MOVING UP FAST ON ALL TRADE CHARTS!

GENE PITNEY · I WANNA LOVE MY LIFE AWAY

MU 1002   PRODUCED BY AARON SCHROEDER

A NATURAL INSTRUMENTAL FOR OPERATORS

CHUCKLES FINNEGAN · FUNNY BONE

MU 1004

MUSICOR
R E C O R D S

DISTRIBUTED BY UNITED ARTISTS RECORDS · 729 SEVENTH AVE. · NEW YORK 19, N.Y.

Billboard, February 1961

They understood the opportunities that were in the States, so naturally my mother wanted me to go on to have an education. It was a *terrible* fight, and I even had some of the businessmen in the town take me to one side when I was standing there with my guitar. I had excellent marks at school and everything, so as far as they were concerned I was mad to ever pursue anything in a crazy world like rock and roll as opposed to getting a degree in something. While I was going to theory classes in electronics, my mind was still writing songs. At that point I knew that I was going to either self-destruct in both of them, or I should take a semester or two off and go and try the music business. If nothing happened, I could always come into school again. I've never looked back.

At the time the fat man took me into New York, duets were very, very popular, so what he did was he tied me up with a girl. He knew her manager in New Haven, Connecticut — the lower part of the state — where he came from. They put us together, thinking that it would be more possible for us to be successful as a duet than it would for a single at that time. We were called 'Jamie & Jane' and the first record was *Snuggle-Up Baby.* Jane's real name was Ginny Arnell. We had two records on Decca, but nothing happened. They weren't *bad* records; they were all right, but no success. Decca were very bad at promotion at the time as well. I could also see that I really wasn't cut out for that type of thing with a duet, and I wanted to go out on my own.

So, we went banging on doors again, and I ended up on a very small label called Blaze Records. The guy who ran it was really a unique individual, a very bizarre type of guy. His name was Herb Abrahamson. Herb was one of the original creators of Atlantic–Atco–Jubilee records, but due to a marital situation within the group he kind-of got bounced and the other ones ran the company.

As a result, he started up these new independent and small labels, and we had a record come out that — even listening to it today once in a while — was very, very good. It's called *Cradle Of My Arms [Blaze 351].* The only problem with it was — and I didn't understand 'cause I didn't know enough about the business and how it worked — it was released right in the middle of what was called a payola scandal. Anything that came out new, and especially by a new artist, at that period of time was just death. Nobody would play the record because they were all afraid that they were being scrutinized by the government. Nobody would even let you into the studio. I went out on my first promotional tour, the first time I'd ever been out of my home state except for New York, and when I came back... talk about being *depressed!* I thought it was a personal thing, like there was something wrong with *me.*

Around this time, when I cut *Cradle Of My Arms,* they got very creative and wanted to call me 'Billy Bryan'. They didn't want 'Gene Pitney', and at this point I'd had no success so I couldn't argue with anybody. It was after that they scared me to death, because they actually wanted to call me 'Homer Muzzy'! I suppose it was original thinking, like an Engelbert Humperdinck-type thing: make it weird enough and it'll catch someone's ear or eye. It scared me to where I said: 'That's it! If I'm going to have any success and continue on in this business, it's going to be with my *own* name!'

My break, when it came in 1961, was kind-of like a 'lateral' type of success. I knocked on the doors and, because of the high pitched nasal sound that I have — which *is* kind-of odd — a lot of people were interested. They said: 'Yes, it is unique and it's different, but mmm... not sure.'

So what happened was, a publisher, Aaron Schroeder, heard not so much the vocalist in the beginning, but a songwriter. I started writing for him as a staff songwriter and I did a demonstration record for him in the studio of one of the things I had written called *(I Wanna) Love My Life Away.* Well, he heard the demo that we made, and I have to admit that he was very objective about it,

Billboard, June 1962

because he listened to it and said: 'You know, that could be a hit just like it is.' He said it just like that.

The label, Musicor, was formed as an independent with United Artists and they released the record. It took a *long* time — it wasn't one of those overnight success things. I went and did promotions at every record hop and on every television show all over the country. It was a very catchy record and had a good hook to it — when it comes to the chorus part — but it wasn't a big record by any means. I think it made the Top Twenty, something like that. But it created the *sound*, and I had done so much promotion with it that it introduced the face and who I was.

That was the start of going on. I always say that the first record is hard, but it's not as hard as the third record. The second record you can always get away with because you can get it played based on the strength of the first one being successful. However, if the second one isn't successful in sales after everyone has played it, then the third one is *really* the difficult one. If you can get away with the third one, then you can have a string of them.

We worked *so hard* on one side of the second record. Again, being naïve as to how the whole business worked, if I'd known what was going to happen, or what does happen in this respect, we wouldn't have spent all the time on it. We worked on the side *Take Me Tonight*, which was Tchaikovsky's *Pathétique* melody. It was a beautiful song and it was a beautiful recording, but the other side was a demo that we put on which we hadn't worked on because we just wanted a 'B' side. Unfortunately the demo 'B' side sounded more like *(I Wanna) Love My Life Away*. As a result, disc jockeys automatically went with the 'B' side, and not the side that we wanted for the 'A' side.

Louisiana Mama was the name of the 'B' side. It was good, kind-of like a steal from a Chuck Berry-type of a rhythm where you almost write the rhythm right into the lyric. And to this day I keep getting huge cheques for that song — as a writer — from Japan. Somebody in Japan made a big, big, big hit out of that. Every four or five years or so, somebody puts it out on a LP or a single and makes a big smash out of it again, and the cheques start coming in again.

Of my hits, I was a 'B' side liker. *[laughs]* Whenever they had two songs to put out, they always asked me which one I liked and then went with the other one. For instance, with *The Man Who Shot Liberty Valance*, which was probably, worldwide, one of the biggest records I ever had, I loved the other side which was the Leiber & Stoller song, *Take It Like A Man*. This was not just a great song lyrically and melodically, but the string-work and everything on the arrangement just sent chills up my back when I was doing it in the studio. Things you'll never have heard of before like *Teardrop By Teardrop* and *A House Without Windows* — these were basically LP songs, but to me some of them were better songs than the songs that were hits.

Twenty-Four Hours From Tulsa was a terrific song and it had all the ingredients. Burt *[Bacharach]* likes to write, like, a narrative-type song with a story to it. *Tulsa* fitted exactly with the way I like to twist with phrasing and everything.

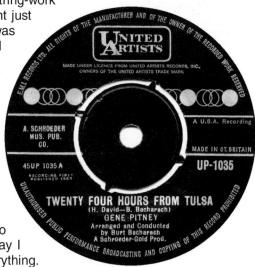

Billboard, July 1963

It was the first big record that I had outside of the States and it was the one that really opened the door. I'd had some success before, but that really was the biggest one.

Every country has a different song which is your identification/ association song to them — it's strange. We did Canada a couple of years ago and I found that *Only Love Can Break A Heart* was the monster song for that market. In England it's *Tulsa* and *I'm Gonna Be Strong*, but *Tulsa* is the one that the majority of people associate with me. If they hear *I'm Gonna Be Strong*, they'll know who it is and they'll applaud the song, but if you just say *Tulsa*, they say 'Gene Pitney!' Go to Australia and it's *The Man Who Shot Liberty Valance*. In Italy, it's a song called *Nessuno Mi Puo' Guidicare* as a result of me coming second in their *San Remo Song Contest* in 1966. Everywhere you go, it's a different one.

I love it when other people record my hits, but it's even better when they record songs that I have *written*. I never felt annoyed that my creations were given different treatments, as clearly they were versatile enough to be handled like that. I love to hear somebody take a song that you wrote and think of in one way, and change it totally by doing it in a different direction with a whole different interpretation. I think that's terrific, and I get the biggest kick out of that. Fortunately, the songs that I felt were the best songs have been done and been successful, even though they might have had different twists.

Never in a million years would I have thought of Rick Nelson doing *Hello Mary Lou*, although I don't know who it was written for. On the other hand, with *He's A Rebel*, I actually remember sitting in the car listening to *Uptown* by the Crystals. It was the first song to which Spector added cellos, violas and kind-of 'R&B strings'. It totally flipped me out, and I remember where I was, sitting in the car and everything when I first heard it. I said to myself: 'I'm gonna write their next hit!' — not ever thinking that it was even possible. I couldn't believe it when that happened and he actually used *He's A Rebel* to launch his record company.

Phil Spector didn't really produce my recording of *Every Breath I Take* in 1961: he was one of a million people who were all shouting at me. If a bomb had dropped on the Bell Sound Studios in New York that night, the whole music business would have changed. It was a session with Bacharach & David, Mann & Weill, Leiber & Stoller, Phil Spector, Schroeder & Gold, and Alan Lover. They were all in the booth at the same time because each one of them had a song that was represented on the session.

It wasn't that working with Spector didn't appeal, but Phil was such an odd guy that you never knew what was going to happen next. I don't know whether I could work that way. I mean, he'd be there, and then he'd be gone. His brilliance was one of those things that was a very thin line. He was one of those people who would walk into the publisher's office and have them play songs for him. When they'd played about four bars of anything, he'd say: 'No, no, no, no.' Like any businessman, the publisher would play the third-string stuff for him, trying to move that first. Then, if he turned all that down, the second string. And then, finally, if they had to, they would come up with the best. I watched him and the minute *He's A Rebel* was played for him — we knew it was a hit ourselves — he just grabbed it and ran saying: 'That's the one I'm looking for! Thank you, goodbye.'

As far as working with him, I don't know what would have happened. I agree with you that the high-pitched sound of mine would have been able to counter all the bassy sound of that 'wall'. I *did* like working with the guy, and he was brilliant at what he was doing. It's hard to say whether we would have been successful together or not, but it has never bothered me. I have had enough success for one man.

He's A Rebel has to be the most successful of my songs. If you can get into the Top Ten in the three trade magazines — which at that time were *Record World, Billboard* and *Cash Box* — you get an award from BMI if you're a BMI writer, which I was. I went to the BMI dinner to get this award and I remember Don Kirshner, who ran Screen Gems/Columbia and had under his umbrella the likes of Mann & Weill and Goffin & King. He came over to me from his table and said: 'My company has won five awards tonight, but the greatest and the most futuristic-thinking song of the whole batch was yours, and I would trade all five of them for that one.' I thought that was one helluva compliment.

To be honest with you, I can't really tell you the titles of the songs that I thought were the most creative because in the beginning, when I started

writing, I used to write kind-of like what the Beatles got away with after they were first successful. When they started changing directions, started changing chord structures, and changing tempo in mid-song — I did that in the beginning, not knowing that you were not supposed to. I didn't realize that I was writing in an era that was very Presley-dominated, and very three- or four-chord dominated. So, with the stuff I wrote in the beginning, I always got the same answer — that it was very interesting and it was very unique. However, what they were trying to tell me was: 'Who is going to record it?'

I didn't know that there were rules that you had to play by as far as fitting into the charts at that time. So that stuff — which I have no recollection of now — was probably the most creative I ever did. I don't even know what happened to them. I've got boxes and boxes of stuff. My mother passed away in 1982 and, although I didn't realize it, God, she had a room with everything in it from my paycheck when I worked in the theatre as an usher, to the first speeding ticket that I ever got. Everything you could think of that a mother could collect, she had it all. So, somewhere in the middle of it all may be those songs.

No, I never had the chance to go into films. I had so much trouble just trying to keep up with what I was doing. Also, I'm very strong-minded and don't know whether I could get along with them. Maybe if I'd had someone who was really good in the management area to thin out some of those things and delegate this and that, it would have left me time to be able to concentrate on something else. Then I probably would have attempted it, but I just didn't have the time.

I did oodles of tours for Dick Clark. Alan Freed wasn't really into the package shows part of the business — Dick Clark had most of those — but I did the Brooklyn Fox Theatre for him. I think the show lasted a week, and I don't think that I could have taken any more. You used to roll out of bed at nine o'clock to do the morning show, then you would do an afternoon show, and then two night shows. God, it was something! It was probably the hardest week I've ever put in in my life. You were forever either on stage or waiting to go on stage. There were so many acts on there that if you did two songs you were lucky. Everybody in the world was on. I think on the one I did, Little Stevie Wonder was closing it with the very first No. 1 that he had, *Fingertips (Part 2)*.

Dick did things that Alan would never have thought of doing. Alan was taking money for playing records, but there was no law against it at that time. Dick is a very, very brilliant man and what he did was to go into all the associated businesses with the power that he wielded from the TV show and everything. He went into part-ownership of a pressing plant; he owned publishing companies; he owned everything where he could benefit. In other words, if an act came along and they said: 'Look, we wanna put this performer on your show,' Dick would say: 'Well, it would really be nice if Ajax Publishing owned half of that song.'

That was his way. It wasn't money in your hand, it was owning part of the act. And, as he said in the Congressional Inquiry that they had, it may have been — as far as they were concerned — *ethically* wrong, but there was nothing *legally* wrong with it. It was then that they passed the law that made it wrong. I've since talked to him about it and he said: 'My God, if I'd ever been allowed to stay in some of those companies I had...' They have gone onto become multi-multi-million dollar operations. He had to divest himself of them, otherwise the legitimacy of him doing the show and being, like, the daddy of rock and roll would have been out of the window.

Dick was king of the one-nighter things. One of the ones I did for him was seventy-two days long. There were sixty-eight playing days with four days off, and we used to stay in a hotel every third day. This meant that you would travel all day long, you would get to where you were going, do a show at night, get back on the bus, drive all night long and then probably a good part of the next day again before you checked into a hotel. Then you'd stay over that night, and then the next night start all over again with the same thing. We did one show a night, and two — including a matinee — at weekends. If they could have put two shows on every night they would have done so, but there wasn't the time as the travelling distances were so vast. When I got over here in the UK and started touring, I heard people moaning about doing a two hour trip. I had to laugh, because we were doing 800–1000 miles a night without even thinking about it!

The camaraderie on the road was terrific: it was one of the big things. It's so different now that it's hard to even explain it to anybody. When Dick stopped doing the tours, or when I stopped doing the tours for Dick, I started putting shows out myself and I became the producer. I might have had sixty-something people on two buses. If you were out with a load of people for thirty or forty days, living with them twenty-four hours a day, eating, sleeping and travelling, then you really got to know them and made a lot of friends. Eventually, as the costs for everything got higher and the acts demanded more money, it became impossible to have that many successful people together at one time: you would have had to charge $50 a ticket for someone to come through the door. So, the amount of people on one show got less and less, and then when this word 'superstar' came along — it really got ridiculous.

At the outset, you would usually have a support act and then the main act. They had support acts for a long time, and they were subsidized by the record companies. Support acts were getting exposure before the main attraction, but when the record companies started to have trouble about four or five years ago, they chopped their budget and stopped subsidizing new acts. Today, it's usually down to one act. At home, they make announcements for so-and-so, which tells people that it's an eight o'clock show and that the artist will be on stage from eight o'clock. They found this necessary as some people would go to the theatre, but they wouldn't go inside to watch the support acts. So, the whole reason for having a support act on there — to get noticed by the people — was getting defeated anyway. Now the act just goes on, does it, and walks off.

The time that you had to take care of yourself properly on the package tours was limited. You had to really love what you were doing and be in really good shape to do it. Dick Clark has written in one of his books about what I did, because to me ingenuity was the name of the game at that time. You really had to think of ways to make it easier for yourself, and I found out that I could fit into the bus luggage rack. I went and bought one of those air-mattresses that you blow up for the beach and put it on top where the luggage would go. I was skinny enough not only to fit in there, but I could roll over — which is the key to the whole thing otherwise you'd never sleep. The cord that comes along to keep the luggage in helped me from falling out, and by the time we got to where we were going I'd had a great night's sleep.

I had very little trouble in getting paid by promoters as I was with the William Morris Agency. They were big enough to get a big part of the money up front, and they were also big enough that if some promoter didn't pay you, then they weren't going to get any more acts.

You mention artists like Chuck Berry not getting paid in the early days. Probably Chuck had to work for a lot of people that were independent dealers. I don't know anything about his management or what it was like in the beginning, but I'm sure that for a lot of acts — especially the black acts — at that time it was very difficult, as they had people looking after them who were almost as naïve as they were. So, they would get sent out with a promise of being paid, go do their show and ask for payment, and the guy was gone — vanished. I was fortunate enough to have good people around me from the start, so I didn't have much of that to contend with.

In the early Sixties, the going weekly rate for pop acts on package tours would range from $2,500 for the majority of them to $7,000 for a top guy. I don't think that many would make a $1,000 a day. Taking inflation and everything else into account, the buying power of those amounts of money was considerable. The thing that no-one takes into account is that it was only seventy-five cents to get through the door to see a show as opposed to a $10 or $12 ticket today.

When I produced shows, I instituted a policy for acts which made me not very popular with management and agencies. I saw how so many acts were getting ripped off. We were paying an agency or manager — let's just take a figure like $5,000 a week — and in conversation I'd realize that the act was only getting something like $1,500 and being told that amount was their fee. The other $3,500 was being spirited away. So, I made it a point in the contract that the artist had to be paid. The cheque had to be handed from my representatives or myself directly to the artist.

There wasn't a lot of big egos or arguments over the billing order on those big tours. People were just happy to be out there working, being able to travel, and everything else. There may have been a lot of naïveté about what they were doing, but it was the beauty of that period of time — especially of the Sixties. I was at school in the Fifties, so I don't know much about that time. I just went and watched some shows.

Even if getting ripped-off was a part of it, there was still something beautiful about the whole thing. That's a funny thing to say: you didn't get paid, but it was still great. I go and I see a lot of that — people who I worked with, who are now completely out of the business, and maybe had one hit.

In the States, about a year ago, I was playing Detroit, I think, or maybe Minneapolis. Anyway, a couple of the guys came out who'd had a couple of song hits *à la* Beach Boys stuff — about the cars, the beach and everything. They came to the hotel and I was talking to them. Now, they were guys who were kind-of roly-poly, had lost their hair, and were in different jobs and everything. But one of them said: 'Boy, I'd give my life to go back out there and do that again!' There was just something about it. They'd had the most wonderful times of their lives. They had scrapbooks — and, I mean, it was only a short time that they'd had. If they were out there for a year, it was a lot of time. So, there was *something* about it that I find distinctly missing today.

I formed many friendships and relationships. I did a lot of tours with Len Barry — who came from a Philadelphia group, the Dovells, before he split off; Bobby Goldsboro was a close friend; Johnny Tillotson and Dobie Gray. There were very few that I didn't get along with.

Yes, there were many amusing incidents, and just as you asked the question two came to mind — except they were amusing after the fact. We were somewhere in the lower part of the Midwest — I don't know exactly where it was — it was right in the corner of a state, but I can't recall the cities. But anyway, I had a stomach or bladder infection, thought that I was going to *die*, and ended up going to a hospital. When I arrived there, I was wearing a very lightweight poplin suit and the sweat was coming right through it — that's how bad a shape I was in. There were a lot of people in the waiting-room and I could tell that I was going to pass out, or something was going to happen, so I went over to the nurse and said: 'Look, you can either take me now or you can pick me up and carry me later.'

She looked at me and said: 'Yeah, I guess you're right. What is your name?'

I said: 'Gene Pitney', and she — honest to God — gave me papers to sign, and asked me to sign them for her daughters or whoever. I couldn't believe it!

Anyway, they took me right in, and the first thing they did was a urine analysis. It was full of blood and the doctor told me to go straight to the emergency room. He didn't call an ambulance or anything. I don't know why, but I hadn't taken my tour manager or anything; it was just me.

I went outside onto the sidewalk and was holding onto a parking meter when a guy came out and asked: 'Was that you just up in the doctor's office?'

I said: 'Yeah.'

He said: 'Where are you going to?' and I told him that I was going to the emergency room at the hospital.

He said: 'Well, you're never gonna make it. Get in the car and I'll take you.'

I thought: 'What a good Samaritan!'

The radio station that was advertising my concert that night had a hot-line and if you phoned in with some kind of news they gave you $25. What I *didn't* know was that, after this guy dropped me off, he called the station to tell them that he had just taken me to the emergency room — and I lost half my audience that night!

The antibiotics they can give you are amazing. Within an hour of taking one in tablet form, I felt so good that I got the doctors to sign me as fit to do my performance on condition that I signed back in again after the show. Anyway, that went off, the show went off, and I was better, but the tour had travelled on without me. So, I had to fly from wherever we were and meet them in Detroit.

We were going over the Canada border in Detroit to do a show in Windsor, Ontario. There were beds on these buses and, although I was still under the weather and not feeling that swift, I said: 'Look, it's none of my business, you do what you want other than on that stage, but I know that there are some of you people that are smoking those 'expensive cigarettes'. For my benefit, seeing that I am the owner of this tour and the guy responsible for everything, if you have anything with you that you can get caught with, or anything, please leave it behind as we go through customs into Canada.'

So everyone said: 'Don't worry, Gene, everything is all right, we'll take care of it.'

I went and lay down on the bottom bunk and we went through into Windsor, did the show, turned around, and came back out again to where we were staying in Detroit. I figured that it was my responsibility — again — to get up and thank them, even though nothing happened.

I said: 'Look, I know that nothing happened, but I want to thank you all for whatever you did to take care so that there were no problems going in and out of Canada.'

One of the guys came up and said: 'Gene, we want to show you something', and he lifted up the mattress of the bed that I was sleeping on, and there was more pot and God knows what else, and they'd put it all underneath *my* mattress! It was done as a joke, and there were a lot of really, really funny things that happened and a lot of strange things.

There was one tour where the last date was in Wheeling, West Virginia, and we had to fly there from Newark Airport in New Jersey in an old DC3 two-engined plane. We got up into the air and I was in the last seat on the right-hand side. I happened to be looking out of the window and they had very, very small flaps on the wings. Something came out from one of the flaps — just a very short distance — and this liquid went all over my window. I thought 'Ah!' and sure enough, to make a long story short, it turned out to be the hydraulic system. This thing had lost its flaps and lost its brakes, so what they had to do was by-pass Wheeling and go to Pittsburgh which had a jet runway and a longer one. It also had this big giant link chain across the end of the runway which they can lock up and it catches the nose wheel.

So, they had to come out and make an announcement and it was, like, a training stewardess they had on the plane. She was as white as a sheet, and a lot of people on board had never flown before. They could tell something was wrong because the tour manager came out of the cockpit with this stewardess, and it was like one of those 'let's sing a song' situations. You could tell from their faces that they were terrified. Anyway, she had to explain that they had lost the hydraulic system, and that means that you can't float in: you've got to aim at the runway. I had a bottle of Scotch in my attaché case, so I was all right. I noticed the intercom system and, as the microphone was back near me in the galley, I went and got on the mike. I said to them all that I hoped they had enough sides cut in the can for a memorial LP. There are still hand-prints on that plane where they were hanging onto the sides of their seats! They landed and everything turned out well, but the terrifying thing was that we had to get off that one and back onto exactly the same type of aircraft and fly back to do the show at Wheeling. Luckily, it was the last show of the whole tour. It was really funny if you looked at it that way, and because I'd flown enough it didn't bother me that much.

Billboard, October 1961

I've had a lot of high spots in my career, but I think that the first one — and most terrifying for someone who was still pretty green, but also from a little tiny town — was doing the *Academy Awards Show*, because I was the first rock or pop act ever to do it.

There haven't been many low spots, but at one point I did bow out when I thought that my popularity — like a lot of single acts — was about to lose favour with the public. I now have three sons, but in the early Seventies I had two boys around two and three years old. I'd been travelling up to that point where I really needed forty-eight hours in a day. I was trying to keep up with not just the American market, but everywhere we'd gone to seemed to turn out successful, like the foreign language markets and the country & western market. It meant that so much was demanded from you, because for each one of those you had to have songs that were relevant to the area that you were functioning in.

So far as doing tours and then coming back and trying to satisfy all these different things, the pressure that was on me was just incredible. I looked at it one day and the thing that opened my eyes was when the Internal Revenue people were trying to figure out where to tax me as far as what state I lived in. You have to be somewhere for six months of the year to be considered domiciled, and for years I wasn't anywhere for six months. I just thought: 'That's it! I'm going to break this off and not be what I call an 'absentee daddy'. I'm gonna spend some time and grow up with my kids.' I see too much of that, where the guy works all during the week, comes home, plays golf on Saturday, does whatever on Sunday, and then wonders what happened when the kids are up and they're gone.

This would be around 1971. I remember coming home and doing a local television show in Hartford, Connecticut, and I sang two songs — *Early In The Morning* was one of them. While I was on the show — which was like a local Dick Clark-type show — I was talking to the host, Brad Davis. I said to him that this would probably be the last time that you're gonna be hearing from me for quite a while. I remember my mother-in-law telling me that she had tears in her eyes when I said that. I told him that I was going to try and keep it down to, like, six months working out of the year, and spend the rest of the time doing what I wanted with my kids. So really, I think that I picked a choice time to back off from pursuing my career.

I don't think that there is anything like performing live and realizing that you did something with an audience and that you left them with something. I mean, last night was a standing ovation and just a crackle in the air that you could feel. I just feel that there is nothing like that. Probably if I wasn't capable of doing that kind of show, it would be a different situation, but I think that I'm a much better performer now than I ever was in the Sixties when I had all the hits. There is a lot of internship that many acts don't have a chance to do today.

Even when I was doing all those one-nighter tours that I've mentioned, the shame of them was that they were not readying anybody for a career. All they were doing was saying: 'Here is the guy, here's the meat that sang the song that was a hit!' And you'd get up and do two or three songs that were hit records and be gone. I mean you didn't learn how to ply your craft. You only really learn your lessons and how to ply your craft when you get in front of a concert audience and try to hold them for say an hour and a half, or maybe more so a cabaret audience.

That's one thing, looking back, that I would have changed. I would have spent much less time doing those tours. To me, they were an absolute waste of time and a waste of creativity. I would much rather have spent the time being locked away doing some writing, doing anything creative, because they were totally worthless. All they created was some money. That doesn't take away from the travel and memories I talked about earlier, but if I had to take one or the other, then I think they were a waste.

Regarding nostalgia shows and getting stale performing the same songs, I have probably a very strange concept. I don't like the nostalgia aspects at all, and as a matter of fact have stayed away *totally* from any nostalgia shows. They've haunted me to do these Madison Square Garden things. The reason is that all they are doing is putting you on display as being the guy who sang the songs from a period of time, and they consider you as a Fifties or a Sixties act. They're putting the meat up there again in front of the people saying: 'Here's the guy who had the hits.'

On the other hand, if you allow me to go in front of an audience and I say: 'Okay, it's my show and I've gotta do the full program myself', then I don't mind putting those songs in the show at all. I worked very hard to make them hits and, having spent so much time looking for good songs, they've stood up to the test of time. If I'd had garbage songs then it would really hurt. But *Town Without Pity*, *The Man Who Shot Liberty Valance*, *Half Heaven–Half Heartache*, *Just One Smile*, *Nobody Needs Your Love* and things like that, they were the end result of going through hundreds and hundreds of songs. Fortunately — although we didn't know it at the time — if you are going to be doing them in twenty years time, then you'd prefer it that way. But it is the different concept of me going out and doing a full show and saying: 'Here I am, a performer, and I can do this, and I'm capable of doing the whole show for you,' as opposed to me walking out and just singing X amount of hit songs and saying: 'Thank you very much, goodnight.'

No, I don't think that a lot of the artists are being used on such shows. In fact, I think those appearances have been very helpful to them because I don't think a lot of them ended up being very good performers. I don't think that they are capable of doing a full show. That's not meant negatively, but I think it has given a lot of them a chance to do something to earn money.

My own favourite artists? I listen to a lot of people, but I just saw probably the best video show that I have ever seen in my life. It's probably the only video of a concert that I would ever buy and it was Phil Collins' concert in Dallas, Texas of *No Jacket Required*, the last LP. I think that it's incredible and the band is just out of this world: it's the old Earth, Wind & Fire horn section.

I have a Sony Trinitron large-screen set in my sun-room. They've only now come out with stereo and I bought this prior to real stereo. It's got tone and ambience controls on it, and what it does is give you a fake stereo and a fake bass response. When I pumped it up for the two of these things, my wife came out screaming: 'What are you doing?' I had the thing so high 'cause I wanted to hear everybody that was cooking. That thing is just musically incredible and Phil Collins can do it all. Very unusual for a drummer to be that capable in all the other areas; it's usually someone who has a tonal instrument. He is a percussionist as well as being a unique drummer, but to be able to be objective enough to do vocals and production is just unbelievable.

Today, apart from publishing interests, my partner and I have a private membership beach club on a beautiful trout-filled lake. It has 1,000 feet of sandy beach, picnicking facilities, a big giant deck, a four-storey building, and we have slips for powerboats and moorings for large sailboats. It's only about one mile by one mile, but it's just three minutes from my house and makes for a great summer spot.

I cannot ever see myself being a gentleman of leisure, or confined to the business side of things. There is no way in the world that I could do that: I'd wither away and die. I'm involved in business and invest in a lot of different things like real estate through my accountant. However, the business side has made me have an interest, keep an eye on it and watch it: it fascinates me. I'm very involved in the stock market when I'm not on the road. I think that it's one of those things that allows me to generate the same amount of energy in a different direction, and then come back fresh into the music business. If you don't have something like that, and just sat around doing nothing, then I think that would be very, very bad. I don't know whether that's an inbred thing, a work ethic that comes from parents or what. I think that my kids would be more apt to do something like that than I would.

As far as my music goes, I don't own everything, but I own quite a few of them as far as the masters are concerned. Currently, I'm in negotiations for the last part of it. But looking at the future, we are just starting again and I had some talks last week prior to coming in to do the *Little & Large Show* last Sunday. There'll be some new records coming out here in the UK and we were also talking about a release in conjunction with a Canadian tour in March. So, I've got a feeling that I may end up back in the record business, and maybe on the production side of it as well. Again, laterally — not that I intended to — things are just gonna happen that way.

19

RUNNING BEAR
Johnny Preston

Johnny Preston was a protégé of the Big Bopper — Jiles Perry ('Jape') Richardson — who wrote *Running Bear* for him. Sadly, Richardson died with Buddy Holly and Ritchie Valens in the February 1959 plane crash and the record was delayed by several months. When it was finally released, the poignant tale of the two indian lovers, separated by a river and their tribes' animosity, shot to the top of the charts on both sides of the Atlantic. Unfortunately, it was also a hard act to top and, despite several worthy follow-ups like *Cradle Of Love*, *Feel So Fine* and *Charming Billy*, Johnny's hits ran out in 1961. He never left the business, however, and has remained a firm favourite on the club and nostalgia circuit ever since.

My real name is John Preston Courville Jr. and I was born on August 18, 1939 in Port Arthur, Texas. Naturally, dad was John Sr. and my mother's name was Margaret (*née* Schexnayder). Dad was a chemist for Texaco Incorporated. I have a brother, Mike, and sister, Helen. I went to Catholic schools and then to Lamar University in Beaumont, Texas although I didn't graduate from there because the music business took me away. It's hard to say what I would have done had I not gone into showbusiness. For two years at university I was studying to be a geologist for oil exploration; that's what I wanted to do.

I sang in school choirs, was president of the glee club and sang in a state-wide Texas competition called the University Inter-Scholastic League. We were singing songs like *Danny Boy* and an Irish folk tune called *The Kerry Dance*. I was lucky, I guess, as I got a superior rating from the school system. I sang in the church choir and still sing in a church choir, where I am a song leader. I've been singing in church all of my life. Naturally, whenever we got out of school, particularly during my last year of high school, we became interested in starting a band. At Lamar, I met some other musicians that were trying to do some work. We all got together and formed a group — the Shades — and, as they say, the rest is history from there.

When Jape Richardson and his manager, Bill Hall, saw us, we were playing in the Twilight Club, which is actually in Port Neches, Texas and not Beaumont — the towns are connected and you never know when you're in one or the other. There were a number of venues in that area within 30–40 miles. At that time in Texas there was a lot of dance clubs — private and otherwise — but we were playing in clubs that were open to the public. As we started

Johnny "Running Bear" Preston **mono**

JOHNNY 'RUNNING BEAR' PRESTON

MERCURY

playing, we became pretty much a town favourite around there. We played six nights a week, four hours a night. Showbusiness now is fun because you only work twenty, thirty, forty minutes to an hour. I was the only singer in the band, so I was singing on a four-hour dance job for three hours. It was hard work, but I enjoyed it.

I didn't have a personal relationship with Jape, though I had known who he was as he had been a disc jockey in the town for some ten years. Evidently, when he and Bill Hall saw us in the Twilight Club they were looking for talent.

I recorded *Running Bear* in 1958 in two separate sessions. I don't know if I was nervous or anything on the first of those sessions, but the band was having a hard time going into the change for the shuffle beat and the takes really weren't that good. Then we came back and added an old-time saxophone player, Link Davis, and it sounded much better the second time we did it. I think we were there one weekend for just three hours then we went back the next weekend and finished it. That was in Houston at Pappy Daily's Gold Star Studio. Pappy was also a record distributor. Those two sessions for *Running Bear* were my very first recording sessions. I had done some live stuff on the radio before, but nothing recorded or with the intent of being a record.

You ask how the country singer George Jones became involved in singing back-up with Jape Richardson and Bill Hall on *Running Bear*. Well, I'll tell you a little story: Bill Hall had also been George Jones' first manager. Now Bill and George had a relationship, but Bill couldn't handle George. George was unmanageable at the time, but they still remained friends. Bill just didn't want to do business with him or represent him, as George had a habit of sometimes not showing up. Anyway we were in KTRM Studios, Beaumont, and they said that they were going to record me. George wasn't working, so he wanted to come with us because he had recorded for Pappy Daily, who also had the Big D and Starday record labels. That's how George figured in the recording of *Running Bear*.

Jape said he got the idea for *Running Bear* when the White Dove Soap advert came out and he took the maiden's name from the product.

I didn't like the song. It was very different from anything that we were doing, which was mostly R&B. In fact it was *totally* different. The Shades weren't on *Running Bear*; we used all studio musicians from Houston.

Although I recorded *Running Bear* in 1958, I didn't have a contract with Mercury Records at that time. We had a lease agreement with them on the first song, and then they had an option. Well, they picked it up after *Running Bear* became a hit.

The record was ready for release in early 1959, but on February 3, 1959, Jape was killed in the plane crash with Buddy Holly, Ritchie Valens and the pilot Roger Peterson. Now Jape had minor children, and in the state of Texas if you have a minor child and you die, then your estate is settled through probate. They probate the will: the wife gets half of the estate and the rest of it is set aside in trust for the children until they reach the age of twenty-one. There was a hang-up there. It had to go through probate before they could do anything with anything that he stood to make a dime off: that was the reason the release was delayed.

As to whether I thought it was a hit in spite of not liking it, well, I'll give you two thoughts on that. Before he died, Jape tells me: 'This song is a hit!' and, because it was so different from what we were doing, I'm thinking: 'Well, from what I'm hearing, I don't think it is.'

Well they got it out. It jumped into the charts and then fell out. Bill called me a couple of weeks later, when the record had been out of the charts for a couple of weeks, and said: 'We got a hit!' and I said: 'We have a hit, where?'

Bill explained that Mercury's record distributor had just called him from St. Louis to tell him that they had just sold 15,000 copies that day to jukebox operators. So naturally it went on all the Rock-Ola boxes. I don't know how much area that covered, but St. Louis is a big town and there's plenty of outlets. When they sold that 15,000 records, it brought the record back into the charts and it went, like, bam-bam-bam! It just started climbing the charts, and it was in there going up right to No. 1. From the time it started up to the time it came all the way out again, it was in the charts for quite some time.

I was in Port Arthur when it charted the first time, and when it fell out I was on a two week camp, discharging an obligation to the National Guard at Fort Hood in Templeton, Texas. I joined the National Guard when I was seventeen years old and still at high school: you had to join for eight years. When I got back home, it was then that Bill called to say: 'We're back in the charts again and I think we've got a hit.'

Matter of fact, the National Guard called me up about seven years after that to say they needed me in Fort Smith, Arkansas, to teach the M1 rifle. So I had to go up there and teach the M1 rifle for two weeks and finally finish my obligation.

Billboard, January 1960

Jape Richardson was never my manager. Bill managed me, Jape and some guys from Louisiana like Rod Bernard, Johnnie Allan and Jivin' Gene. When I met Jape with Bill at the Twilight Club, he already had *Chantilly Lace*, and was out on the road and busy. Apart from the recording of *Running Bear*, I won't say that we had meetings, but we were together a number of times. He was a wonderful fellow and had a lot of definite ideas about what he wanted to do with his career. He largely left it up to Bill to take care of the business end and he was really writing a lot of songs in those days. I would say that we were friends, and I wish he'd known that *Running Bear* was gonna be a hit before that tragic accident happened.

Did I like *Running Bear* any better when it was a hit? Oh, I'd *love* to have another one just like it right now! *[laughs]* It kind-of grows on you. The story grows on you, you know. So many people like the song, I'm not going to say anything against it. I like to do it now, it's a lot of fun.

Yes, I was concerned with what we were going to follow it up with. Naturally, we had changed recording studios and we were going to Nashville and using an arranger called Cliff Parman. Cliff had written some great songs in his career and in fact he owned the copyright to *Dream*. He was quite an arranger and real hot at that time, arranging for Brenda Lee and all the top acts. Cliff was one of the first to start using strings in Nashville instead of the straight country sound. The Nashville sound I'll have to attribute to Cliff and a few other arrangers who got that sound really going and selling. He told me: 'Johnny, I've got a song I'd like for you to listen to.' Now, the old singing cowboy and western movie star, Tex Ritter, had two fellows — Jack Fautheree and Wayne Gray — who worked for him in his band and they wrote *Cradle Of Love*, which was the song Cliff had. They sold the song, and the actual ownership of it wound up with the country singer Webb Pierce. I think he gave them $15,000 in advance because he wanted that record. He didn't want the song to sing at all, he wanted the publishing and writer's royalties. *Running Bear* sold about three million copies, so he knew that the next single was going to do something and he just gambled on it. Probably a good business move for him and a bad business move for Jack and Wayne because they would have made more money than that. But a bird in the hand, I guess, is worth two in the bush.

When I heard *Cradle Of Love*, I liked it immediately and thought 'this is *good*'... and it was even better when Cliff wrote the arrangement for it. It was all in mono: just two tracks, the band and me. It was recorded in two takes and that was it, done. There was no pressure because, when you find a song like that to follow a hit with, that's not the hard time. The hard time is finding a song when you *don't* have one.

Feel So Fine was a version of Shirley & Lee's *Feel So Good*. I always did it as *Feel So Fine* and, because we didn't have the two voices, I did the falsetto. That's where the song comes from, but if you listen to the two songs you wouldn't know they were related because the other one has an entirely different beat. But that's the way we did it with the Shades.

As a matter of fact, that song was done in the last fifteen minutes of an album session. We'd finished everything we wanted to do and someone asked me: 'Johnny, is there anything you want to do?'

I said: 'Yeah, let's try something here with a few minutes left.'

So, I showed the guitar player what I wanted played, the band just fell right in, and we ripped it off. It ended up being the best thing on the album session and we put it out as a single instead.

The Shades disbanded when I started going out on the road. Now, my guitar player, Johnny Wilson, was in the Shades and he came with me on the road for about five years as a musical director. Johnny was going to school at Huntsville, Texas, and he is now a certified accountant. Mike Aiken lives somewhere in Germany. I haven't seen him in about three years: me and his sister are looking for him. Larry Barbien has a fencing company up in east Texas, and Dale Gothia, who played saxophone with us, was a chemical plant worker and is now retired.

Charming Billy was my next release. It did fairly well, but not so great as the others: I think it got to about No. 40 or something like that. About that time, the music started to change and we really had a hard time finding good songs. But, you know, that really wasn't my job and I didn't have any control over what I was recording because the A&R men for Mercury were choosing the songs for the sessions. I'd give 'em input and say: 'Yeah, I can sing that song' or 'No, I don't think it fits'. However, I'll just be perfectly frank with you and say this: whenever a company trusts one person to take an artist and produce him, if he doesn't have an *outstanding* track record I think they're making a mistake, no matter how well-founded his credentials are.

There's so much politics in the music business it's unreal: 'Oh, we gotta do this song because this company's been good to me',

185

'This publisher here is going to work on the song', 'That's a good song, but I don't think we can get much help from him'. Now, which publisher in the music publishing business would get you one of his songs to record and yet not help on the promotion? What's he gonna do, hurt himself? He's gonna take a hammer and hit himself on the thumb? It doesn't make much sense. So, there's a lot of politics played in recording and in what's recorded — then and now, I'm sure. I think the artists now have much better control over what they record than they did thirty-nine years ago.

My 1960 tour of the UK I remember very well. Conway Twitty and I, and Freddy Cannon was here for a while. Wee Willie Harris was on the bill, Tony Crombie & The Rockets, and also Don Arden who was the promoter. Don was all right. Talking of promoters, Henry Sellers who used to promote these nostalgia tours is now retired, I think, and living in Florida. I don't know if it's true, but I've heard that he's putting on jello wrestling with women: they dress them up in bikinis and they wrestle in a vat of jello!

After 1961, I kept on working and recording. I recorded for Kapp, Imperial with Lou Chudd, and 20th Century Fox. Yes, my hit records were all unusual and in a different vein. I call that 'teenybopper music'. I don't know if 'teenybopper' is correct, but I had a nursery rhyme song, another one with a falsetto gimmick in it, and what have you. But they were successful then. On the other labels, I did some R&B songs and some country songs. Matter of fact, I had a country song get into the charts: I recorded a song written by Jerry Foster and Bill Rice, who are great songwriters with tons and tons of hits. It was called *Kick the Can*, and I think it got to about No. 40 in the country charts at one time. I guess that I recorded for about eleven years from 1959, but never really did get anything big back in the charts. I had some regional hits that kept me working.

I never left the business and have always worked and been really fortunate for that. In the States I did a lot of state and county fairs, although we've lost a venue or two and there aren't that many any more. I used to work at Disney World in Florida at Lil' Darlin's, and later on it was Wolfman Jack's. I'd go down there about four times a year. A lot of private and corporate jobs come my way, and that's *really* a good business. Only two weeks ago I was over here in the UK to do a corporate job for British Aerospace workers in Bristol, and then one in Manchester. After that, I went to do a rockabilly show at a Pontin's holiday camp and I was the only American artist on the bill. That was earlier this month, and now I'm back over here for this tour. Next year, at the end of January, I'm back in England again, and then I'm going to Spain for a couple of weeks. I've been over to Europe a number of times. It's as busy as I want to be.

Yes, I have memories of the big tours. I got involved with one of those when we went to Australia. Gosh, there were so many people on that show like Jerry Lee Lewis, Tommy Sands, Jimmy Clanton and the Diamonds. I didn't work with the Dick Clark *Caravan* as I was working up in the Pacific North-West and Canada. I worked with the Brenda Lee show for about three years, and worked a lot with Jerry Lee out in California and around. I stayed pretty busy.

Bill Hall continued to manage me until 1974–75, and it was an amicable split. He got really involved with his publishing company. He and Jack Clement had Big Bopper Music, which was a *tremendous* publishing house: you name it, they had it. Finally they sold out to Lawrence Welk, and then Bill ran Lawrence Welk Music. He had a five-year contract with them, but died — I think — in his fourth year. They made millions out of the publishing company, and had tremendous writers and tremendous songs: Dickie Lee wrote for Alabama; Bill Rice and Jerry Foster wrote nearly all of Charlie Pride's hits.

I had contacts and was still working. At one point I moved up to Nashville, as I was going to start working for Paul Cohen as an A&R man for Kapp Records. I was on my way up there when Paul died of a heart attack, so they closed that office down. They didn't want to let someone as inexperienced as I was take over the top job there. I wish that we could have worked together, as he made many great records and I really could have learned something from him.

Oh, yeah, I always got paid. I'm one of the lucky ones. I have to say that I'm very fortunate. A lot of guys I've talked to have had big records — I'm not talking about one or two — and they've told me that they've never got a penny. Never. A case in point: Johnny & The Hurricanes had one instrumental smash after another for about a year and a half: *Red River Rock*, *Blue Tail Fly [Beatnik Fly]*, *Rockin' Goose*, all those. We were on tour in Australia and Johnny Paris told me: 'Man, I need some money,' and I said: 'What's the matter, what about royalties?'

He said: 'Hell, I haven't got any. I'm living off the performances that we're doing.'

I told him: 'That's a shame. You need to go to New York and get yourself a music attorney.'

The highest spot in my career? Man, I don't know. I suppose it has to be *Running Bear* going to No. 1 in every English-speaking country, if you're counting that as an achievement. I think the real highest spot in my career though, would be the people that I associate with, the other artists that I work with. I have made some good friends throughout the years. Conway Twitty was a good friend. Also Ray Stevens, Bobby Vee and Chris Montez. Through the years I've had some great players who were good friends — like Billy Carter, who played with Bob Wills. I recorded with Wills on Kapp Records. Mel Tillis did an album with him, and Merle Haggard and I did one with him. That was great fun. He's dead now, but he was a legend from the Forties 'til the day he died in the late Seventies or early Eighties. Texas Swing — I love that kind of music.

Bobby Vee and I have been working for thirty-nine years. That's longer than most marriages last! He's a fine, fine fellow and I've always respected him highly. I like getting to know these guys and finding out how they are. There are some real good ones, and there are some people that have got attitudes. I hope I will never get one, as I never have had one. I just feel fortunate: I was lucky. How lucky can you get? To have someone search you out and *give* you a hit record! Well, I mean, what's the chances of doing that? Not too much.

Coming to terms with not having hits was no problem: Bill had prepared me for that a long time ago. He told me that it was a funny business and — like the old saying — that you're only as good as your last record. And if you don't believe it, just put out a few and see what happens! *[laughs]* It's disheartening when you do the best you can, you find the best material that you can, and nothing comes of it. But, you know, I have a great outlook on life. I have fourteen grandchildren, a beautiful wife — we get along fabulously. In fact, she's here with me now. I mean, it's kind-of hard to make grandmama leave

home and leave the grandbabies there. All of my children and grandchildren are healthy. That's probably the real high spot in my life for me, and I haven't had too many lows. Stardom is a fleeting thing. I love to perform and I love to sing, and even if they didn't pay me I'd probably do it anyway if they asked. It's just a business that gets into you. My wife and I are both religious people. We go to church Wednesday night, Sunday morning, Sunday evening. Yeah, whenever I'm home we're in church.

Even if I'd had my way back then about choosing my material, I don't think that I could have strung my hits out for as long as some people are successful. That really amazes me. Like Conway Twitty, when he changed over from rock and roll to country. Bam! — he hit. And he hit and he hit and he hit. He got with Loretta Lynn and he hit. I think he had something like fifty chart records and, like, thirty-odd No. 1's on the country charts. If I knew the answer to how it's done, I'd be as wealthy as Sir Paul McCartney!

Country fans in the US are the most loyal fans; the rock fans are not. In England, I don't know about the country scene, but I know that the fans who like rock and roll are the most knowledgable. They know more about you than *you* know about you! I've had them quiz me. They'll ask me who the guitarist was on a certain song, and I'll think and try to answer to the best of my ability. And they'll say: 'No, it was Hank Garland, etc.'

I tell them: 'Well, you got me there. I believe that you're right.'

They're *real* fans: they dress it and they love it. They are most enjoyable to perform for, and without a doubt England is my favourite place to perform.

Nostalgia shows? I love 'em and have been to some myself — they're really good. They bring you back to where you were. We've only been out on this UK tour for seven or eight days, and some guy said: 'Man, you don't know what it means to me to come back and see you after thirty-eight years!'

There are a couple of fellows over here that I know fairly well. Every time I'm playing — it could be two hundred miles away — they come to the show and always get an autograph and put the date on it. When they come back, they'll ask me if I remember this or remember that. They'll say: 'Remember the night we got drunk at that football club over there?' And I tell them: 'I remember that too, you know.'

I have no problems with doing *Running Bear, Cradle Of Love* and my other hits night after night. None whatsoever. On my set, I do the songs that were biggest for me, and I think that's what they've come to hear. They don't want me to get up and do a Paul Anka tune. If Paul Anka was singing and I went to the concert, *I* surely wouldn't want to hear him sing *Running Bear*.

Of my own material, my favourite is *Cradle Of Love*. Do I wish that I could have recorded someone else's material? You bet! For me, it would have to be *Stagger Lee* that Lloyd Price did. That's a great song and I do it on some of my shows. I think that it's a real rock and roll song, a R&B song, a great one, and I like to sing it.

Today, I write some songs, and I've recorded. Even among the studios that we have around my hometown, there are some 32-track studios and they're all digital and whatever. But I don't think the records have the same feel that they did when they were mono, where the whole band has to cook at one time, and you're there on the mike and you've got to do it. You've got to perform and get it right, and it's embarrassing when they say: 'Okay, take seventeen.' You start again: waa, waa, waa waa, beep — and then you make a bloop in it. Then it's: 'Whoops, hold it. All right, take eighteen!' That puts a little pressure on you, and I think you're more careful. Now, if we were recording today, I'd probably go in with a piano, bass, drums and guitar — basic rhythm. Each one of them is on a track and I'm singing just dead into a mike somewhere. It's click-track or whatever. You get that done, you get through it, and the arranger plays it and says: 'Yeah, I like that one, I'll put some horns in here.' So, they bring in three or four players and they put it down. They get some brass and they do it, then some tympani, and this and that, etc. After a while, the thing becomes so *big* — depending on what you're trying to achieve — that when you hear it back and you go to sing with it, you say: 'Is that the song we were doing?' You hardly even recognize it! It just changes that way. But I'm sure that with today's techniques you have a lot better recordings: they're clearer, they're crisper. If you sing flat, they can speed it up; if you're singing sharp, they can slow it down. There are just so many tricks.

Looking back, I don't think I would have done anything differently, I really don't. I think that you're right about my hits categorizing me — which happened early in my career — because when I finally signed with Mercury, they didn't know what to do with me, they really didn't. Believe it or not, I had a fellow look at me from their classical department, and he was dead serious about it. I don't know how to say this, it's not that I'm bragging — I'm not — and I'm not trying to say one thing and another, but I am a legitimate singer. I can be a stand-up singer like Frank Sinatra and Tony Bennett and do the cabaret thing, I can do the rock, and I can sing country. I did some big production numbers and they loved them. It was up to them to do it, but I don't know exactly how much control Bill had over that. They wanted to do me like Eddie Fisher and make a pop singer, a crooner, or whatever, out of me. So, who knows?

20

DIZZY
Tommy Roe

Initially heavily influenced by Buddy Holly, Tommy Roe first hit the charts in 1962 with the driving *Sheila* before switching to a softer sound for finely-crafted follow-ups like *The Folk Singer* and *Everybody*. After a relatively barren time in 1964 and 1965, he re-established his career with a string of huge 'bubblegum' hits including *Heather Honey*, *Jam Up Jelly Tight* and the million-selling *Dizzy*. Drifting in and out of the public eye, he remains a vastly under-appreciated talent.

We'll just start with my date of birth: May 9, 1942 — that looks good to me. I was born Thomas David Roe in Atlanta, Georgia. My parents are Mr. and Mrs. Thomas H. Roe. Father's in the construction business, mother is a 'home technician' *[laughs]*, and I have a brother three years younger than myself.

My whole family is musical. Mom plays the piano a little bit. My dad taught me to play a few chords on the guitar when I was thirteen or fourteen, and I wrote *Sheila* straightaway in 1956–57 — my first year in high school. Dad plays quite well as a rhythm guitarist, and still plays in a bluegrass country band in North Georgia. I am the only one in the family that took up music, though. My brother works in construction with my dad, so I kind-of followed my dad's footsteps, musically. I think that if my dad had the opportunities that I had as a youngster, he could have been a bigger star than myself. *[laughs]* I always thought he was very good and still do.

I started to sing in the Baptist Church in Atlanta when I was twelve or thirteen years old. Of course, my parents and my grandparents gave me a lot of encouragement, as well as cousins, aunts and uncles. My father's family is a very big family — like, fourteen brothers and sisters — and my mom's family was also large with eleven or twelve brothers and sisters. So, they both come from big families, and I almost had a built-in audience right there! *[laughs]*

Influences came from all the early rock stars like Carl Perkins, Elvis of course, Chuck Berry and Buddy Holly. In the Fifties, Ed Sullivan's TV show was a great influence on me as it always featured a contemporary artist, and at that time it was very hard to see rock and roll on television.

Guitar is the only instrument I play, but I don't consider myself a guitarist. Chet Atkins is a *guitarist*, whereas I use the instrument more as a tool to write songs with, structuring chords and stuff. However, I *do* use the guitar in my performance, and play what limited amount of guitar I use in my show.

My first amateur performance was in Atlanta, Georgia on the *Georgia*

Jubilee Talent Contest. They ran it for a month — if you won the first week, you came back the second week, etc. Well, I won through to the fourth week, but lost to Marvin Benefield. He later did the double session with me when I recorded *Sheila* in 1961. Marvin, who sounded just like Elvis Presley and recorded under the name of an Elvis film character — Vince Everett from *Jailhouse Rock* — cut an Elvis song, *Such A Night*.

So, I landed in second place to Marvin, but when we did the split session I've just mentioned, *Sheila* was the hit and although Marvin's record charted I think, it didn't get real big.

Just so you will know what I'm talking about when I say a 'double session', let me explain: for instance, they would take two artists at a time and hire a Nashville studio for three hours. Normally, you did one artist in three hours but, because they were gambling, these independent producers would cover their backs — so to speak — by cutting two guys at once. This was done in the hope that they'd get four sides instead of three sides, and a winner out of one or both artists.

I formed a band when I was still in Brown High School, Atlanta. We would work locally after basketball games, playing the music for what we used to call 'sock hops', which were dances in the gymnasium. Then this disc jockey, Paul Drew, opened up Paul Drew's Hop in Atlanta every Friday or Saturday night. He hired us to perform there and through that I met Felton Jarvis, a producer with ABC-Paramount Records, and got in touch with Bill Lowery, and the whole thing. They asked me if I wrote songs and I said: 'I think I do, I'm not sure.'

We went from songwriting to making records. Then, from a hit record, I became a performer. I had never really thought about being a performer — I wanted to be a songwriter for other people. Having always been a rather introverted person, I was never really comfortable in front of other people. Gradually, after thirty-one years in the business, I feel pretty good about it now, but it took me a long time to get comfortable with performing.

The Satins was the group that I put together in high school and we just more-or-less came up with that name. I don't know where the name came from — probably because we used to wear these silky things. The group was formed in my sophomore year, so I was probably about fourteen or fifteen. Originally we just had the line-up of drums and guitar — I played rhythm guitar — no bass. Then a friend of ours, Drolé Bush, who had dropped out of high school and lied about his age to join the navy, became our bass-player when he had served his time. As Drolé could also play harmonica, we used to do a lot of blues stuff like John Lee Hooker and Jimmy Reed which was an added dimension to our band.

We played a lot of college fraternity parties at Georgia Tech and the Universities of Georgia and Alabama. They loved the blues to dance to, so when Drolé joined the band that really helped us cover a bigger medium of music. I did mostly Elvis, Carl Perkins and some blues — I used to love doing Jimmy Reed songs. Then I would do hit songs like Bobby Darin's *Splish Splash*, and of course material by Buddy Holly, Eddie Cochran and the early rockers. Sometimes I would do my own material, but I was always very unsure about doing that live until after I got some hit records.

The other members of the Satins were Bobby West, a guitar-player, who now works for Delta Airlines. He should have stayed in the business, but I think he just got burned out on the travelling, and he was married and had his family and all. Mike Clark was the drummer and he now runs Southern Tracks

Recording Studio in Atlanta. I still work with Mike quite often. Then there was Drolé Bush and myself. We had another guitarist who joined us occasionally. His name was Dickie Richardson and we called him 'the ice man'. He was a big guy weighing about 280 pounds and he also played a lot of blues. Of course, in the South, if you could play rhythm & blues, then you were really 'in' because you couldn't hardly hear it on the radio then; you had to tune in late at night to hear R&B. So, when you went out to any of the dates you played — fraternity parties especially — and you started playing some R&B, all the kids would know it as they stayed up all night listening to the radio stations. Besides that, it was great music to play.

Our first payment for the Satins was $15 for the whole group. We really didn't worry about money back then as we had a whole lotta fun with what we were doing. It also made you popular in school and you had a lot of friends, and that's all we were really interested in. The money started to come gradually when we were working the fraternity parties, with fees of $100 and $200 a night.

In the first place, the Satins recorded for a local guy in Atlanta who had a little label — Mark IV Records — which was sold to Judd Records. Jud was Sam Phillips's brother out of Memphis, Tennessee and he started that label. We had a record out on Mark IV called *Foreman* — which had a real Jimmy Reed bluesy sound — with Drolé on the harmonica. It got a lot of play out of Nashville on WLAC, which was a 50,000-watt station that could broadcast everywhere. *I Gotta Girl* was on Judd Records, and the *original* cut of *Sheila* — which was not the hit version. Also, songs like *Pretty Girl*, *Caveman* and maybe one or two more were released on Judd while I was still at high school. They got me recognition in the South-East, as they were played in that area. *I Gotta Girl*

and *Sheila* were hit records in the South-East of America, but never made it nationally. I wrote all those songs. The first recording of *Sheila* wasn't a big hit because Judd Records didn't have a national distribution network.

Originally, *Sheila* was written as a poem called *Sweet Little Freda*. I wrote it about a little girl I met in high school. Freda was my first girlfriend: we had a little crush on one another and chased each other round the playground — nonsense really, you know. *[laughs]* I don't know where she is now. Later on, when my dad taught me to play guitar, I took several of these little poems that I'd written — *I Gotta Girl* was a poem, they were all poems — and tried to put them to music. That's how that all happened.

I know that I get a lot of flak over here in England for *Sheila* being in the style of *Peggy Sue*, but it wasn't deliberate. In fact, I was very upset when I read the programme notes for tonight's concert because it states that it's a bald rewrite of *Peggy Sue*. Actually, if I'm not mistaken, I wrote *Sheila* before *Peggy Sue* was a hit. Certainly the poem part of it; the music came later. On the first cut, the drums were just straight-sounding drums, not *Peggy Sue*-sounding drums.

The reason why the *Peggy Sue*-style drums were on the second version of *Sheila* was because my producer, Felton Jarvis, thought that would be a clever way to get airplay — and he was right. What can I say? *[laughs]* His idea was that, after Buddy's death, there was a void of original-sounding Buddy Holly records. He thought that we could fill the void with that raw sound of three pieces — no strings — and get attention from radio stations, and we did! Jerry Allison, apart from writing *Peggy Sue* with Buddy Holly, was *the* drummer to copy, and my drummer on the hit version of *Sheila* was Buddy Harmon out of Nashville.

We always felt that *Sheila* was a hit song, and Felton thought the same thing. All we needed was something different and more exciting about it, and that's what we were striving to do with the drums. The original 1960 Judd recording was much slower.

I got the chance to sign with ABC-Paramount through Felton Jarvis, who I met in Atlanta through Paul Drew. Felton got involved with Bill Lowery, and then they put the deal together to go to Nashville and cut *Sheila* on that split session with Marvin Benefield *aka* Vince Everett, that I was telling you about. They produced it for ABC, who liked it and put it out. Felton, by the way, ended up producing Elvis four or five years before he died. He went to Nashville, and I moved on to Los Angeles.

Leaving the Satins to go solo just kind-of happened when we cut *Sheila* for the second time in 1962. We went to Nashville and they didn't want to use the Satins on record, as they wanted to use studio guys. So, obviously, the Satins were a little upset, and from that point on the group just dissolved and we never worked together after that.

When I was fortunate enough to get a hit with the second version of *Sheila* in 1962, I was working at General Electric as a card technician making electrical cards. Today it's computer chips, but back then they were big bulky cards and I used to solder those things together. After high school, I started the University of Georgia on an arts scholarship for a few months, then I dropped out. I lost interest in that right away because of the music, and I was also married at a very young age. So, I worked at General Electric to support my wife and my child, then I did my music at the weekend. Apart from the music business, that's the only job I

Eager Music
Nitetime Music
(BMI)
Time: 2:02

Produced by
FELTON JARVIS

45-10329

AMP 45-10787

SHEILA
(Tommy Roe)

TOMMY ROE

A PRODUCT OF ABC-PARAMOUNT RECORDS, INC.

ABC-PARAMOUNT

194

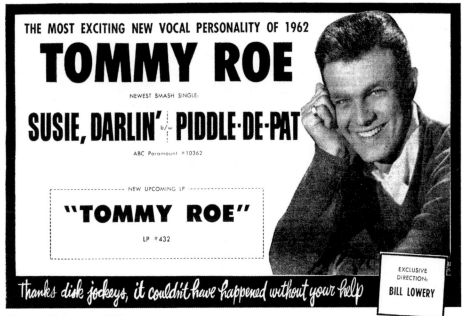

THE MOST EXCITING NEW VOCAL PERSONALITY OF 1962

TOMMY ROE

NEWEST SMASH SINGLE:

SUSIE, DARLIN' b/w PIDDLE-DE-PAT

ABC Paramount #10362

------ NEW UPCOMING LP ------

"TOMMY ROE"

LP #432

Thanks disk jockeys, it couldn't have happened without your help

EXCLUSIVE DIRECTION:
BILL LOWERY

Billboard, September 1962

ever had.

My agent, Bill Lowery, called me at work one day. I already knew *Sheila* was a hit in Georgia: it had received a lot of airplay and was something like a No. 5 record in Atlanta. Bill called to tell me that it was a worldwide Top Ten record. I didn't know what to think about that as I didn't know what it meant. He asked me if I would consider leaving my job at General Electric. This scared me, as I had a family to support and rent to pay, so I refused to quit my job. He invited me to his office, had a big chuckle about that and advanced me $5,000. Of course, I didn't make $5,000 in a *year*! When he wrote out that cheque for $5,000, I immediately turned in my resignation at General Electric and was off on the road, and I never looked back. General Electric now owns RCA Records — maybe if I'd stayed there I'd have been in the record business anyway. *[laughs]*

It was a great feeling to hear *Sheila* broadcast for the first time, and it still is. One of the highs we get as artists is when you hear your records on the radio. Once the record was a hit, it really happened fast. I wasn't a professional and still amateurish, but I had the No. 1 record in the States, in England and in the world. The next thing I knew, I was on the road performing. I didn't know a whole lot about it and had to learn as I went along.

Susie Darlin' — the Robin Luke hit — was the follow-up to *Sheila*, and *Piddle-De-Pat* was the other side. Felton Jarvis wanted to record that song even though it had been a big hit for Robin Luke. I didn't want to record it, but he loved it and thought that, as a new producer with a hit record, he could do everything he liked. I more-or-less just copied Robin Luke's version. They never really decided which side to play, and so it got split airplay and the record never did a whole lot. I think *Susie Darlin'* charted in the thirties.

After that, *Everybody* was a big record for me. There were other records in between like *Gonna Take A Chance*, which I think charted in the US. *Town Crier* was another, but it didn't do anything.

There wasn't a whole lot of TV to do in the US for rock artists. I didn't make the *Ed Sullivan Show* until 1969 when I had *Dizzy*. It was right before his show went off the air and I'm glad I made it, as it was very difficult to get on.

Of course, I toured a lot and came over to England for my first tour in March 1963 with Chris Montez and the Beatles — that famous tour.

I never really *moved* to Britain, but when I came back in November of the same year for another tour I got an apartment there for a while. People thought I'd moved to England as a resident, but I hadn't. I think I stayed there for a three- or four-month spell at one time while I was working.

During the Sixties, I was able to sustain myself and wasn't affected by the 'English Invasion'. I think the reason for that was my style was so different to everything else. In that time you had it all: folk-rock, acid rock, hard rock, British Invasion, and then you had Tommy Roe who did the soft rock — 'bubblegum' they called it at one time. So, I had my own style and there was definitely an audience there for that. I got a lot of airplay and the records were successful.

Last week, I did the Empire Theatre, Liverpool. It was really magic when I walked through the theatre, as it was the last venue on the 1963 tour with Chris Montez and the Beatles. It was such an exciting time for music and I realized that at the time, but looking back on the history of it, it is even more so. I remember after the show we couldn't get out of the theatre as there were crowds in the street outside and they were going bananas.

Every day of that tour the Beatles were getting bigger and bigger, and then their records actually started breaking. In essence, they were actually the headliners of the tour in the long run, although it was originally booked as Chris Montez and myself. The Beatles turned that around. They were so huge and on the upswing that there was no denying them. And they *deserved* it: they were really great! I really enjoyed watching them perform. Last week at Liverpool Empire, I just stood on the stage at the side because I remembered standing there in 1963 to watch the Beatles perform. You get a lot of chill bumps in that theatre — it was great.

Yes, *The Folk Singer* in 1963 *was* unusual. I think that in those days the record companies were so naïve, but the good side of that was they were prepared to try things. Their thinking about *The Folk Singer* was that they wanted to cut a record just for England.

When I was over here in 1963, doing the first tour, I found the song in London. It was a national song, but it was pitched to me in London. I just thought it would be a great song for England, so when I went back to the States we cut it — thinking just to release it in the UK. It got to be a big record in England, so the record company thought they would also release it in the States. However, it did *nothing* in the US: got into eighties or the nineties and dropped right out. It's still one of my biggest numbers when I visit the UK.

In 1963, *Everybody* was a Top Ten hit on both sides of the Atlantic. After that record, I had other hits in the US right up until 1972 including Top Ten records like *Sweet Pea* — which Manfred Mann recorded as an instrumental, *Hooray For Hazel* and *Jam Up Jelly Tight*. In 1969, I had a No. 1 in America and Britain with *Dizzy*. Funnily enough, in England it replaced *Get Back* by the Beatles at No. 1. That record marked the end of a six-year spell of dryness for me in the UK.

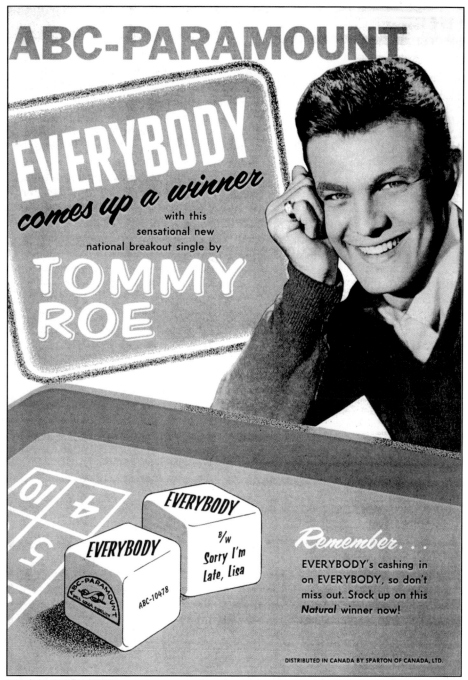

Billboard, October 1963

Looking back, if I could — and I don't even know that I could — I would like to have taken charge, or be more in control of my recording sessions and choice of material. You really lost that in the early days. The record companies would come in and tell you: 'This is what we want you to do, and in this style.

And if you can't come up with a song in this style, then we're going to get a song brought over here.' So, I always tried to write what they wanted me to write. It worked, but I think it could have been better if I'd had a little bit more control. Hey, I could be wrong, but I feel that anyway.

You always had that pressure to follow up a hit. The record companies would tell you that they wanted something sounding just like your last hit, so you had to come up with something similar. For instance, *Piddle-De-Pat* — the follow-up to *Sheila* — had the same drums going and it was the same type of song as *Sheila*. They wanted everything to sound the same. You'd run that course, milk it out, and then they'd change their minds and say: 'Right, now we want everything to sound like *this*!' So, it was kind-of frustrating.

My own favourites are *Heather Honey*, which is a nice one, and *It's Now Winter's Day* which did nothing in England, but was a pretty good record in the States. It's one of my favourite songs that I've written. Regarding other artists' material, I liked *Under My Thumb* by the Rolling Stones — which I *did* record, but it didn't do anything. I *love* that song.

Having joined the US Army Reserves, I did ten months active duty and got out in 1964, although I continued to be in the Reserves until 1970. Following my army service, I moved from Atlanta to New York and studied acting for a while. After that, I moved out to California and appeared on Dick Clark's *Where The Action Is*. This was a networked show which was on every afternoon and followed *Bandstand*. It was about teenagers romping on the beach and doing their songs — an Annette-type thing — and I was there as a regular for three years. I was pretty busy with that, so I didn't have to tour a whole lot, although I did do some Dick Clark tours.

How much would I get paid from doing a Dick Clark package tour? Well, he didn't pay very much — sorry, Dick. *[laughs]* The idea was, because you were on his show, you were kind-of obliged to do his tours for him as he was helping so much with your career. It kind-of paid in the long run.

Yes, most of the time I got paid by promoters. Usually the ones who would stiff you would be club owners. Their clubs just weren't doing well and you got stiffed. You didn't argue with them or they would meet you in a back alley and break your legs. When I toured the UK with Chris Montez and the Beatles in 1963 I got about $3,500 a week, which I think was the going rate at that time. I was probably making more than the Beatles! *[laughter]*

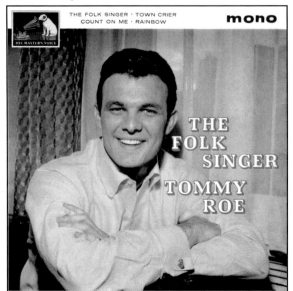

The Seventies were a dead decade for me. In the early Seventies, I had a number of hits of which *Jam Up Jelly Tight* and *Stagger Lee* were the biggest. However, from 1974 on it was just nothing for me in the record business. I worked with my publisher and stayed in the business, but didn't perform again until a few dates at the end of the Seventies. I just stayed busy with my songwriting, producing records and working with young kids in Atlanta, passing along my experience so that — hopefully — they didn't make the mistakes I had made. Disco was just the thing in the Seventies, and it hurt a lot of live music. I remember the unions were up in arms because they had stopped hiring live musicians and were just playing disco music.

I was probably managed as well as you could expect. The one good thing about the people I was involved with — from *Sheila* being a hit onwards — was that there was honesty there. I didn't get ripped off financially: I usually made pretty good money. Most of the young kids from that time didn't — they just ended up with not very much — but I was very fortunate in that respect.

As far as being paid record royalties — on a scale of one to ten — I'd have to give my treatment about a seven. There was a lot of things I had complaints about. You never get every penny that you're owed, but I think I got the majority of money that was due to me. If I didn't, I'm getting it now because I'm still in the business after thirty-one years — and having a ball.

Maybe I haven't reached the highest point of my career yet, I don't know. I just keep chugging along. My career has been like a long-distance horse that's just good year after year. He never wins the big races, but wins enough to sustain and keep a name for himself. That's how I look at myself, and occasionally I'll come through with a big record or success. Maybe that's my destiny.

The lowest point has to be in the Seventies: I was very depressed in the Seventies. Music was depressing, my personal life was depressing — I was going through a divorce. 1974 on to the end of the Seventies was the lowest point.

I feel great about the new interest in our music, which for me started in the early Eighties. Then, it was mainly people who grew up with our music and fans from that era. Now I'm finding in the Nineties that these people are bringing their *children* to the shows. That's exciting! I do a lot of fairs in the States, and they are family-oriented entertainment. You see moms and dads out there with their kids, and they aren't afraid to bring them 'cause they know they won't be offended by that entertainment. If that's the way it goes, then it's great, because I'm having a lot of fun and it's really a wider audience for me. The kids are also exposed to our music through television, commercials and nostalgia radio stations.

Vic Reeves re-recorded *Dizzy*, which went to No. 1 in England. I know a lot of people aren't crazy about his version, but, being the songwriter, I'm happy about it and it's good for the bank account.

Singing hits over and over again from nearly thirty years ago isn't as hard as it may seem. When I go on stage and sing *Sheila*, *Dizzy*, *Sweet Pea*, *Heather Honey* and all those songs, every time it's different, it's never the same — to me. It may sound the same to the audience, but you are using different bands, you're in different venues and it'll sound different because of different sound systems. So, it's always different to me. Strangely enough, I never get tired of the hits, they're always fun to sing — *Sheila* and *Dizzy* especially. I've never gotten tired of them, and hopefully that's the way it will stay. Once I start getting tired, it's probably time for me to back off 'cause then it won't be fun.

You mention Del Shannon's views on artists performing their hits and what audiences expect when they pay their money. Del, God bless his soul, was a different guy. I always say he had a lot of demons working in him, and a lot of things tugging at him that he couldn't quite sort out in his mind. He used to hate performing sometimes, and we'd be on tours and he'd say: 'Man, I wish I wasn't here. What am I doing here?' He just really *hated* being there. He hated facing the audience. He hated signing autographs. Yet

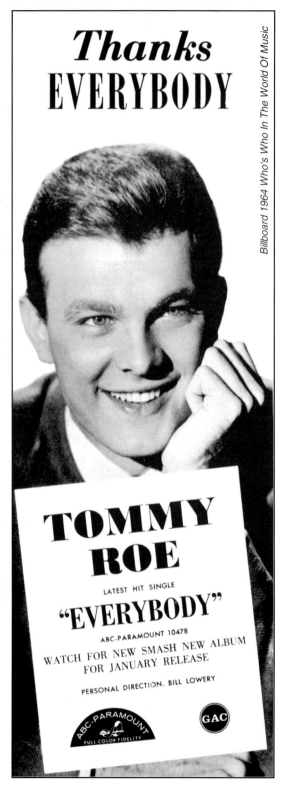

the people loved him and they loved his songs. You see, he had come to the point where he just didn't like it. I don't know if I could perform like that. If it gets to the point where I'm miserable, then I gotta find out why I feel like that and why I'm still trying to do it. I gotta figure out what's wrong here, you know. Del had some problems. I loved the guy, and his music was terrific, but he did have some tugs and pulls in his life.

In the endless years of touring I've never had any drug problems, but I enjoy my drink. *[laughs]* God forbid that it ever becomes a problem. When I come over to England, I love drinking the bitter and other English beer. I love wine with my meals, but I've never had a drinking problem. We were talking about Del for instance — well, Del was admittedly an alcoholic. We'd go off on tour together sometimes, and as soon as he'd get off the plane he'd go to AA meetings, you know. God forbid that ever happens to me. I certainly hope not, and I don't think I'm even near that.

Over the years I've formed some good friendships. Bobby Vee is a real good friend, and of course a lot of great musicians like Hal Blaine in California, who was the drummer on *Dizzy*, Joe Osborne the bass-player, and the guys in Nashville — Larry Knetchel, David Corrigan and David Briggs. A lot of great musicians have played on my music.

Before last year's tour with Duane Eddy *[1991]*, the last time that I was over in the UK was 1973–74. After that, I wasn't performing and had backed off completely, so there was nothing to bring over. In the early Eighties I started back, but never really got any requests to tour as, without any hits, there was no reason to ask me. Then, when the nostalgia thing started to happen over here a little bit, they started to play my records again and then there was an interest in bringing me over. I have been over twice in two years, so who knows?

My spot is a little longer this time, but not much. *[laughs]* That was one of my frustrations the last time, and that's one thing I've really haggled about this time and it *still* hasn't worked out! I still haven't gotten to do the tour exactly the way I want to do it — but it's fun. I get a lot of comments from the audience about doing a short set, and it's terrible billing. I'm very frustrated about that and I don't know really know why that happened, but maybe it'll work out — it's business stuff.

Away from touring, I enjoy my recording studio and my farm in Georgia — I enjoy them a lot. Yes, I did produce for other artists, but none that you'd know! *[laughs]* I liked the old simple ways of making records, but I also like today's technology too. They are totally different mediums. I think that it's hard to beat the spontaneity of having live musicians in the studio and laying it all down at the same time on the tracks. Today, a lot of stuff is done with the technology — drum machines and all this — and you just have to look at it differently. A lot of the younger musicians today, particularly in California, are now turning their backs on technology: they are going into the studio with their instruments, playing live, and making some great records. Who knows, it may revert right back to that. As they say, 'everything that goes around comes around', and I see that happening with the young musicians now, so it could be an indication.

Looking ahead, I'm just gonna keep on rockin' and doing my thing. I still love writing songs and I love making demos in my studio. There's always a possibility of having another hit record — you never know. There's always on the road, travelling and touring, and I love that too.

21

RUNAWAY SUCCESS
Del Shannon

A self-contained talent, Del Shannon not only played guitar and sang, but also wrote and produced his own material. The intensity and drive of his personality were reflected in his recordings, with dramatic arrangements, shrill pipe organ and falsetto vocals all adding to the excitement. In later years, Del turned his hand to production, scoring successes with Smith's *Baby It's You* (1969) and Brian Hyland's *Gypsy Woman* (1970), and briefly returned to the US charts himself in 1981 with the Tom Petty-produced album, *Drop Down And Get Me*.

I was born Charles Westover on December 30, 1939 in Grand Rapids, Michigan. The family moved to Coopersville, Michigan when I was three years old, and I remained there until I was eighteen.

My father isn't living any more, but mother is and I have two sisters. They were not a musical family. My mother taught me the first song that I ever played; it was *Doodle-Doo*. She taught me how to play the ukelele a little bit and that one song — that was it. Following my introduction to the ukelele, I quickly graduated to the guitar and used to sing and play guitar at school, and was allowed to practise in the school gym. Mom encouraged my interest in music, but my dad didn't, he thought that I was *crazy*.

If I hadn't followed a musical career, I don't know what else I would have done — all I wanted to do was play music. Growing up in the mid-Fifties, I was influenced by Fats Domino, Hank Williams, Lefty Frizzell, Carl Smith, Roy Orbison, Jerry Lee and Paul Anka, who was a great songwriter. I liked Bill Haley's guitar player, Franny Beecher, but didn't appreciate some of the other rock and roll artists until later on. The Ink Spots appealed to me because they had the falsetto. I always liked the falsetto, and that's why I used to sing one or two of their songs.

I guess that my decision to become an entertainer was probably because I realized that you got attention that way. When I was a kid, I thought that if you could sing, you attracted girls and stuff like that. Later on, I wanted to be on the radio and *Grand Ole Opry*.

I was in the army around 1957 — I can't remember the years — and spent some time in Germany. In the army *Get Up And Go* shows I didn't sing, just played guitar for a Spanish dancer — it was a minor thing and kind-of silly.

After I got out of the army, I moved to Battle Creek, Michigan and formed a band — Charlie Johnson & The Big Little Show Band — at the Hi-Lo

Club, which used to seat about four hundred people. They just tore it down last year and gave me a brick from it. We played country & western, Paul Anka, Elvis, Jerry Lee and material by just about anybody who was out then.

A disc jockey, Ollie McLaughlin from WGRV in Ann Arbor heard me play and took me to Detroit where I met Irving Micahnik and Harry Balk of Twirl Records. Through them, I was signed to Bigtop Records in New York and went there to record a couple of songs, but Ollie thought that they were too slow and suggested that I come up with a faster tune. Shortly afterwards, Max Crook and I came up with *Runaway*.

It was at the Hi-Lo that I met Max Crook. He joined my band to replace another musician and played the musitron, which was an electronic organ and a kind of early synthesizer. The two of us created *Runaway* in two days on the stage of the Hi-Lo Club, Battle Creek — the lyrics, melody, everything.

I wasn't aware that we were cutting any new ground with the sounds in *Runaway*, I was just trying to cut records. Having said that, it *was* unusual to me too when I found Max Crook and he played that solo on his little musitron. I thought that he was great and hired him for the band right on the spot. These days, Max has a studio out in the middle of the desert and does religious music.

Runaway was aimed at the rock market, but there is no story behind the lyrics. The tune came first — out of a chord change improvisation on the musitron by Max while we were playing onstage at the Hi-Lo. That's why it was put together and completed right there.

My day job was selling carpets. The owner of the store had a Cadillac Coupe de Ville car and I took the name 'Del' from that, and 'Shannon' from a Hi-Lo customer who wanted to be a wrestler called Mark Shannon.

We sold *Runaway* to Bigtop Records by means of a lease deal arranged through Twirl Records of Detroit. They cut it and then sold it to Bigtop. At this point, Irving Micahnik was guiding my career, but after five years I got rid of him. Then, Dan Bourgeoise took over and we got our publishing rights back and all the old masters.

I can still remember when *Runaway* got to No. 1. It was great. I was in Battle Creek, Michigan in the Hi-Lo Club. I called up and said: 'How is *Runaway* doing?' They said that it was selling about 80,000 records a day! I said I couldn't even count that far, but did it mean that I could quit the Hi-Lo Club. They said that it did, and that I was opening on Broadway — the Brooklyn Paramount, New York — for $600 a week. That was more money than I could make in nearly two years in that dump.

As I have told you, *Runaway* wasn't the first record I cut. In New York, one of the slow songs I recorded was *I'll Always Love You*, but it was never released until it was included in my first album. After *Runaway*, I had a

say in my material, but had to fight for it. *Hats Off To Larry* — I had to fight for that as they were going to make *Don't Gild The Lily, Lily* the main side, and I didn't think that was too smart.

No-one dictated my image — whether I was simply standing singing and playing guitar or in an evening suit, without guitar, on my knees singing the final lines of Roy Orbison's *Cryin'*, which is a song I still do.

You mention the risk and originality of *The Swiss Maid* with its Bavarian-style backing, and the fact that I managed to find new sounds. Well, Harry Balk — my old producer — and I went to Nashville, as I had always wanted to record there. We got down there and found Roger Miller and his publisher who had a couple of songs. One of them was *The Swiss Maid*. The other we liked even better, and he was going to finish it the next day. We were supposed to meet him at ten o'clock in the morning, but he never showed up — he went to California! That's where Roger is *[laughs]* — he is amazing and a very talented guy.

So, we did *The Swiss Maid*. Yes, it is very unusual. I thought that it would be a hit in the States, too, but it only made the Top Forty. In England it was big record: I

Billboard, June 1961

think *Disc* magazine made it 'Record of the Year'. Looking back, it was a risk for me at the time. Dion told me that I must be crazy bringing a record like that out and thinking it would sell. But it *did* sell well in the European countries.

You say that many people regarded *Runaway* and some of my other records as original and ask me if it's possible for any artist to be original. Well, I don't think that anybody in this business is original: we steal from everybody. If a man says he is original, maybe he is — I can't argue with that. He could be the *only* original, I don't know. The Beatles got from somebody, and *they* got from somebody.

I left Bigtop in 1964 when I was having a little confusion, and my manager took me over to Amy–Mala. My contract at Bigtop ran out and then I went into litigation with them, which took a couple of years. The time you can waste in this business is amazing, but this wasn't wasted time as I got my contract straightened out. However, it took a long time, and it took its toll too. The legal stuff kept me out of the recording business for two years. My old manager said that I was still under contract to him and that it was all legal. No-one will touch you while you are in litigation.

In 1963, I formed my own record label, Berlee Records, named after my father and mother — Bert and Lee Ann —- and put out a few releases in between leaving Bigtop and joining Amy.

Just released . . . the **NEW** sound of

DEL SHANNON
MOVE IT
ON OVER

AMY 937

Billboard, August 1965

The 'English Invasion' led by the Beatles didn't hurt me too much, although I thought that it might. *Keep Searchin' (We'll Follow The Sun)* and *Stranger In Town*, they did all right for me and then I went into production with Smith, who were very successful in America, and Brian Hyland: I produced his version of *Gypsy Woman*. I haven't seen Brian for seven or eight years — he just stopped working. Last I heard, he was up in Oregon. So, I kept going in that way, and those times certainly weren't lean for me: it was a good time. I had some guarantees from record companies and was pretty well set up, so not being prominent with my own hit records didn't bother me.

Runaway was re-cut in 1967 — not because Bigtop had the master, but because Andrew Loog Oldham, the Rolling Stones producer, wanted to and I wanted to. Andrew was having some problems with the Stones and wanted to do some outside things, so we did that and a whole album. I also had a hit in the States around this time with the Stones' *Under My Thumb*. In 1968, I released an album, *The Further Adventures Of Charles Westover*.

I loved California and its weather when I visited, so it was natural to make records there, but there was no conscious decision to go from the East Coast to the West Coast for recording purposes. Phil Spector I only met once and we never worked together. I don't know what he is doing now — not much.

Movies? I made two: *It's Trad, Dad* and *Daytona Beach Weekend* — a *horrible* movie that was! *It's Trad, Dad* was a funny movie. My part in it was filmed in New York, and it was hard work, too. Four to five hours of strenuous camera shots — it was weird.

You mention the question of motivation, and the fact that I take my public performances very seriously and work hard to produce the original sounds of my hit records. Well, its fun from up there when the band is rocking and the audience is getting off — then it's all right — but I do it for the money a lot. I suppose I could quit, but I just had a divorce a year and a half ago, so it makes it difficult. *[laughs]* Even so, I could still quit and, in fact, keep saying that I want to quit and do something else. However, if I did, I don't know what else I would do. There can be nothing to replace this business once you're hooked into it, I think. How could I go to an office for eight hours a day? I think that I would go bananas, even it was only for four hours. I am so used to being so free — you're very free when you're like this — yet it's lonely and has got its drawbacks. You're in different places and you sleep in different beds, but you

Billboard, October 1963

get used to it. I notice that a lot of artists who weren't working for the last five, seven, eight years are now coming out and working, so what does that tell me? It tells me that they must not be too happy doing something else. So why bother? I will just keep doing it until I want to stop, and someday I *will* probably want to stop.

When things were bad in my career and I was down, I would drink like a fish. I haven't drank in eight years. I don't take drugs at all, but I had to stop the drink or it was going to kill me. Since I stopped, things have been a lot better. No matter how bad you feel today, drink will only make it worse — it's *horrible*! For me, drink is bad.

As far as religion goes, I guess you would say that I am spiritual. I've just visited Durham Cathedral — I always visit it when I come up here. It drives me to it in some way: a beautiful old place. Some power greater than myself helped me to get sober. If I let it, it helps me do other nice things too, but I get in there and try to stop it all — that's the way I am.

Even when I was out of the limelight from 1970 to 1980, I was always busy. I would go to Australia, come to England, go to Canada, work in America. You never stop working in this business. Last year I worked *all* the time, it just never stops. February and March are quiet, and I usually go overseas.

Something wants me to quit, but something else tells me not to — I don't know why. I don't do a lot for recreation except ride my motorcycle when I am home.

The Richard Nader *Rock'n'Blues Reunion* show that toured England last year *[1985]* was one of the best tours I have ever done. It was also extremely professional — which is the way things are *meant* to be done — and I enjoyed it. I felt a comradeship, as I know Bobby Vee and Rick Nelson... well, nobody ever gets close to Rick much as he is very shy and he used to hide out, but his band were always there. I've worked with Rick a lot, but I've never seen very much of him — maybe for five or ten minutes before he'd go on, just to talk a little bit. The last time I saw Rick alive was at Heathrow Airport when he said: 'I am not going to Canada with you, I'm going home.' That followed a little spat he had with Richard Nader. A lot of people have spats with Richard, but I seem to get along with him. I find something inside of him that's okay.

When it comes to my business dealings, I do business with certain people and we seem to get on all right. I just settle a thing and that's it, that's what I want — and if I don't get it, I won't work with them anymore. It works.

You mention that on that tour Rick Nelson was the only artist who performed his hits and then presented new stuff. Well, as far as my own act is concerned, unless you have a hit record out with something that's current, then who wants to hear that new material? Go home and do it, or put a record out and *then* go for it. I don't think that the vast majority of people who are paying their money to come and see an artist want to hear anything new unless it's a current hit, and then you would be a fool not to do it and maybe even throw in a couple more — but you need that strength to do it. If you don't have that strength, then to me it's a throwaway, just wasting your time. Do artists who do that think that people hearing new material will say: 'I must go out and buy it!' or

something? It's silly, and I wouldn't do it. But maybe I *would* do it, because I've done it before. Sometimes you get off as an artist just doing it, so why not?

You can look at it anyway that you want, it depends on why you are doing it. If you're doing it to get yourself off, and you need that to keep going, or if you're doing six, seven, eight hits a night and you want to throw in an extra song, fine. I think that it's a waste of time for myself to do it. I don't get off on doing something new for my audience, because they don't want to hear it. Just give them the hits and get on with it.

I go to see Frank Sinatra and he does all his old hits — I love it. I just love to

hear his old beautiful hits, and when he does a new song I say: 'Why is he doing *that*? How boring!' It's so boring for me to hear him sing *[sings]* 'America is...' Come on Frank, give me a romantic beautiful ballad! If you want to do all of those other songs, then say: 'Frank isn't doing any of his hits. Come and see him do all this new stuff.' And I'll say: 'Fine,' and won't go. I wouldn't want to go and see Roy Orbison do five new songs. Who wants to see and hear that? I want to hear his old hits. Now, if they're on the radio and they're hits and I get to like them that way, then fine.

Yes, it was ironic for Rick, after his statement about nostalgia and playing his old hits which he summed up in *Garden Party*, to go out and do them on a revival show. He had to eat his words! I think that he was very sad over that, to have to go out and do things that he didn't want to do after he had told people in that song that he didn't want to do them. But he went through a very big divorce, too. Also, people change. There was a time when I did that *Charles Westover* album when I didn't want to do anything old anymore either: 'That's it! I'm going to do what *I* want to do!' Well, that's not an entertainer. An *entertainer* goes out and entertains people; he doesn't go out and get himself off. If you want to get yourself off, there's a lot of clubs you can work that don't pay the big money and you can do all your new stuff there forever — but you don't get big money. I've tried that before, and when you go and finish your tour and you're $15,000 in the hole, you say: 'Why did I do those clubs?' Forget it! It's a joke.

Sometimes I find it sterile playing my hits, sometimes I don't. I can sing *Runaway* over and over because I like the song. Bobby Vee may not like singing *Rubber Ball* because it's 'bouncy-bouncy' and he doesn't like that song and, therefore, he is just satisfying the audience — so you give him five for that. But if you really *hate* a song, then don't do it. They like *Kelly* over here, so I do

210

Kelly almost every show I go to over here in England because they want to hear it.

If I could have had my pick of other artists' hit records, I would like to have had *Cryin'*, *Oh Pretty Woman*, *Black Is Black* — those songs don't age. I like *The Wanderer*... there's just so many great songs over the years. Sting had a great record I would love to have had, *Every Breath You Take*.

You know, life is amazing. You get money and you get all this other stuff, and all of a sudden you find that this isn't it either. When you're a kid, you say: 'Oh, if I only had that... if I only had that car... if I only had two hit records... God!' Then you get two and you want three. You get three and then you want four. I think that every artist is that way, and it grabs you and eats you up. A lot of people go to drugs and booze for that, because then they find that this ain't it. How sad that is. But yet, it's only life. It's partly the same with a plumber. He plumbs and plumbs. All of a sudden, he says: 'Shit, I've plumbed all my life! What am I doing, what is it all about?'

So, I am in that area of my life again — what is it all about? You get cars that you always wanted as a kid, and you can get all these toys. I used to love electric trains and I could never afford one as a kid. We used to have to get real cheap ones. Now, I can afford any of the trains I want and I don't even want them. I say it makes me mad, you know, I can have all the trains I want that I couldn't have when I was a kid. But it's getting something that you *can't* have — always after something you *can't* have — when enough isn't enough.

Most people get to a stage where enough is never enough. No matter if you live in a small-scale situation or a big-scale one, it's the same thing. The majority of humans get to that point, and I think that is why there is a searching back into yourself to find your spirituality. Really, I think that's it, and I don't care what people say about this religion or that. I'm not religious. I'm just searching for something to make me feel good inside. I used to get it off booze and pills. When you get everything and lose it – like wives *[laughs]* and things like that — mainly it's your own fault. Then you look back and think: 'Yes, I spent too much time on my music, thinking of myself rather than the other person.' That is truly love, spending time with the one that you love. But it's *hard* when they want this or that and you have to go out and get it. This is a crazy business!

Yes, I have worked for Dick Clark's package tours many times and still do — as recently as last year. I just thought of him this morning. In March last year I was wandering around some place in California for an hour, trying to find Dick and the rehearsal hall, and got a spur in my foot as a result. Now I can't run any more and have to get an operation. It wasn't Dick's fault of course — I was carrying my guitar and kept pounding the pavement. I couldn't find the rehearsal hall! So, whenever I think of Dick Clark, I think of my spur. I did a lot of bus tours for Dick, they were just fun and party — that is all you ever did. But a lot of this stuff gets old after a while — how many times can you party?

My memories from the Dick Clark package tours are of the fun and good times we had. I was young, it was exciting, fresh and new — and it was scary. I was close to Brian Hyland, Bobby Vee, Dion — I was close to Dion a lot. He wasn't easy to get close to, but we had a nice friendship. I've heard that he is coming out now to do more of his rock music. He is a great artist — one of the best rock and roll artists ever. If you listen to Mick Jagger, you'll hear a bit of Dion in there — a lot of his little hooks. Not that Mick isn't great too, you know. Dion's original old records are just so teenage, so rock and roll — just pure beauty. An *amazing* artist.

Today, I hardly do any cabaret, I only do concerts. I do one club in Canada which seats four thousand people for three days, twice a year. Other than that, I may do a hotel which will open up their big ballroom to maybe one thousand or two thousand people. But as for club cabaret, no, there's no need to do it anymore. It's a lot of work, and there's something about the venues and their facilities. The dressing-rooms aren't great and neither is the smoky atmosphere or layout. You miss the closeness of a concert audience and the auditorium environment which makes it easier to perform. The PA systems are better in concert halls, the sound is better, everything is much more music-professional. When you come down and do the clubs again, you miss all that.

The smoke in clubs does affect your throat, but today just about everyone is on an anti-smoking kick. I despise smoking now, and I used to smoke three packs a day! There is probably nothing worse to a smoker than a self-righteous *ex*-smoker. I bitch at smokers now! If I am sitting next to them on an airplane, and they ain't supposed to smoke, I bitch and tell the stewardess: 'Please...' I had to do it on the way over when somebody tried to stoke up by lighting up two — and nine years ago, when I smoked, I would have done the same damn thing! I would have died without a cig. That's the way it is.

Yeah, after being in this business for over twenty-five years, I do regard myself as a survivor — very much. I don't know whether it's this business or any business, but when you're drinking and you're in this business it's really a tough one. You've got so much *time* to drink. You get to a club and you're there for an hour and a half. A half-hour to get ready, an hour for the show and maybe another half-hour to do autographs or such. Then you get dried off and go back to your hotel and drink, drink, drink, drink, until you're drunk.

So, I am a survivor — but I nearly didn't make it. And all the cars I have been in, and all the miles I have travelled, it's unbelievable that I'm still alive. I have never even been injured, except for last March when I got the spur in my foot while walking with my guitar trying to find Dick Clark and that rehearsal hall. That's about the only injury that I have suffered, and it amazes me when I look back and think of doing 110 mph down the freeway. I drove up here today that fast.

The constant 'one night stand' touring is part of the job. Country & western artists do it — Willie Nelson does it all of the time. I don't think that I could do what he does, but then again maybe I do. I guess I do. Last year, I toured like that for over one hundred days at least, but I do it differently. In the States, I get an airplane and fly four hours from the West Coast to the East Coast; I'm picked up at the airport, taken to my room and I'm usually working with a band that I've worked with before.

It's very easy. I do my twenty-five or thirty minutes with three or four other acts, get on the plane the next day, and either go home or go on to another state. If it's another state, I then travel maybe another two hours in an airplane, land, get picked up, do the same thing again and then go home on the Sunday or Monday. I do that all of the time, and get three to four days off a week — not bad.

I pick up thousands of dollars doing this. Sometimes I think, what if I were a crook and I robbed banks? Just flying in every weekend to rob a bank somewhere, then flying out again. It wouldn't be such a bad living for the money that you make. Plus, I've got my publishing and my record company — it's nice. I got all my old masters and my publishing rights back about eight or ten years ago: once they were returned, things weren't so bad. NBC-TV has a series, *Crime Story*, coming out and I did the music for that, and I've just had a Juice Newton single that's a hit on the country charts.

Once you get it together you think 'Oh well, it ain't so bad... so what's next?' It isn't mind-blowing like it used to be. I don't get the mind-blowing anymore and I miss that. Getting a hit would blow your mind. If I had a hit *now*, it would be nice, but I don't think that it would blow my mind like it used to do. The spark goes away, I think. It has to. I mean, a human being after twenty-five years in the business...

There *are* sparks on stage with a show. I can get right into doing that, as it's such an act. It's like a guy who acts and does Broadway or London for seven or eight years, he does the same scenes every night because he is an actor. Well, I think that singers are actors, too.

**After suffering bouts of depression throughout his career,
Del tragically took his own life on February 8, 1990.
Amazingly, at the time of his death he had still not been
elected to the Rock & Roll Hall Of Fame.**

22

SOUL AGENT
Edwin Starr

In 1965, a hitherto unknown vocalist with Bill Doggett's combo called Charles Hatcher renamed himself 'Edwin Starr' and signed up with Detroit's tiny Golden World/Ric-Tic Records. The result was instant success, with giant crossover hits like *Agent Double-O Soul* and *Stop Her On Sight (SOS)* quickly making him a household name. However, what puzzled Motown's Berry Gordy Jr. was Ric-Tic's uncanny ability to replicate his label's distinctive sound. When Gordy discovered that his studio musicians had been moonlighting, his response was to buy out his competitor. Never given the attention his talent deserved, Starr's eight-year tenure at Motown was comparatively disappointing, though he did win a Grammy for his hard-hitting 1970 chart-topper, *War* — the biggest hit of his career and the song with which he will forever be associated.

I was born on January 21, 1942 in Nashville, Tennessee. Mom is deceased, my father is still alive, and I've got two brothers and one sister. My father was a career soldier for over twenty-one years and from there he went into governmental work, postal services and banking.

I don't have the typical ghetto influence or church background story, 'cause that's not the way I was raised. My father had a very, very, good position in what he did and we, as children, grew up in a real good, healthy environment. In fact, I grew up in an integrated neighbourhood, so I never did face any segregated situations.

In my immediate family, I don't think that that anyone was musical unless it came from the basis of maybe my grandparents or something. But having said that, travelling in my organization is my brother who is very, very musical, and my sister is an absolutely incredible singer. My brother has pursued a career, but my sister hasn't.

We moved to Cleveland when I was about twelve years old and it was there, as a member of the Tiger Fan Boys' Club, that I started to sing. At first I used to play drums and from that I went on to try my hand at singing. I realized rapidly that I had the ability to sing, so I just furthered that and dropped the drumming. Most definitely I was encouraged.

From about the age of fifteen on, I was very, very influenced by the media — which was the radio at the time. This is before music became a chartable entity. It was when all music was rock and roll. There was no pop

charts, soul charts and country & western charts because it was all purely and simply just rock and roll. Being from the city of Cleveland — which is the home of Alan Freed, the person who coined the phrase 'rock and roll' — the influence of music was very, very prevalent, because Cleveland was the hub of the entertainment industry for years.

It was the era of the groups like the Drifters, the Cadillacs, the O'Jays, the Penguins and the Flamingos. I quite liked the El Dorados and the seriousness of the Flamingos, but I liked the comedy aspect of the Coasters. They were the comedy relief, so to speak, of the music industry. The Drifters were more of your romantic aspects, and the Moonglows were the singers.

I had a formal education, went to high school and graduated. I did all the normal things and didn't drop out or anything like that. I had good influence in the army, where I served from 1960 until 1962. There, I worked as a translator for the American government but on a German concern. I worked only with Germans, so consequently I had to learn to speak German quite quickly. This has been beneficial as far as my career is concerned, because I've travelled a great deal to Germany and other foreign countries since then.

The army took care of my first job, but after that, before I got a chance to record and travel on the road, I was a chef. I worked initially for the Theatrical Grill, and from there I transferred to the Sirloin & Saddle which was a restaurant chain. Possibly, if I hadn't got a break, I would still be at the Sirloin & Saddle.

It wasn't a great decision to go professional. You have to remember that at sixteen or seventeen I was already being paid for my performing, so the minute that you start to become a paid performer you are a professional. This is away from the boys' club: I was doing nightclub things at this stage. At that point they had what they called in Ohio 'cabaret parties', and we used to do a great many of those. There wasn't any liquor on the premises, but people could bring their own if they so desired. Consequently, we were able to work in those places because they didn't actually sell liquor.

I was the first singer in Ohio with a combined singing group and band and we were called the Futuretones. We had everything self-contained including the MC, so when people bought my show they got everything together. A couple of musicians have gone on to make quite a name for themselves backing people like the O'Jays. For the most part though, the singers — we were all lucky enough that they met really fine people — got married and stopped singing for one reason or another. It was a good time for all of us and, yes, that was down to my business acumen.

Regarding my distinctive style, I was lucky enough to come up in an era of such profound musical stars that I had a chance to pull a little bit from everybody. So, when you do that, and make the nucleus of your career off of several different people, you can always come up with your own identity. Basically, I worked off the mistakes of other people: I took the mistakes, turned them round and made them positive things. My role models were Jackie Wilson, Chuck Jackson, James Brown, Jesse Belvin and Little Willie John; Jackie Wilson was smooth and agile; Chuck Jackson a mover; James Brown commanded respect; Jesse Belvin was very articulate; and Little Willie John had a great range.

Yes, I had to work at trying to be a good communicator. All those things you have to work on. You have to try and build and develop what your strengths are based on, work on your weaknesses, and capitalize on the best that you have to offer as an artist.

You're talking about an era of time when musicians weren't afraid to tackle music. It was music that they were formidably dealing with, not political aspirations or anything else. They did this because they had everything to gain. No matter what their roots were, they had a chance to pull themselves out with their music and become whatever it was that they wanted to become. If they had the stamina and fortitude to fight and to keep working at it, then it could happen for them. But if they were going to lay down and accept what circumstances had to give them, then they had nothing to gain.

When *Agent Double-O Soul* became the powerful record that it actually was and charted, I was staying in a hotel in Detroit, Michigan, as at that point I didn't have a place to stay. I had moved on the pretext — or whim — of signing with Golden World's Ric-Tic Records. Not knowing whether the record was going to be a good record or a flop, I was in a state of limbo and was staying at the hotel for a kind-of 'wait and see' period. I was driving in the car that I had when I heard my voice coming back over the radio. It was probably the greatest thrill that I ever had in my life!

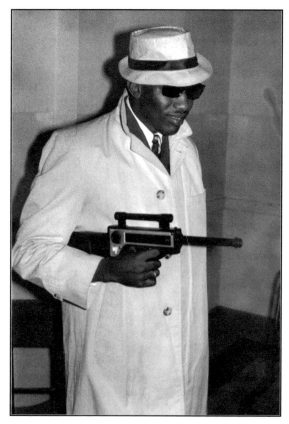

Agent Double-O Soul was my very first recording as a single artist, but I had made a record before then *[in 1957]* with the Futuretones. We did it on a small label in New Jersey *[Tress]* and it was called *I Know*, backed with *Roll On*. It received a lot of play in Cleveland and I would *love* to be able to find a copy of it. At the time of *Agent Double-O Soul*, I was managed by Bill Doggett — who recorded *Honky Tonk* — and Laban Taylor.

I didn't have any option over going to Motown. They bought me from one company, so I didn't have any say-so whatsoever. *War* was written by Norman Whitfield and Barrett Strong, and with a very powerful message intended. Although Norman Whitfield also produced the track, the interpretation of the song was all mine as it was impossible for Norman to produce my performance. Given a track that powerful to sing against gave me lots of room for scope and vision to do whatever I wanted as far as the singing was concerned. Everybody was satisfied with it. Norman said it wasn't a comment against the war in Vietnam, but that it was a comment of the times. What he was trying to say was that there was a war on a day-to-day basis, just trying to survive.

There was no choice at Motown, you took what was given to you. They had an in-house built-in situation and you worked around the premise of that situation. What was assigned to you as a personage, or what was assigned to you as a piece of material, was what you dealt with. Oh yes, it was definitely an interference with me as an artist. It was an interference on my behalf; it was an interference with the Isley Brothers, the Jackson 5, Gladys Knight & The Pips... that's the reason we all left during that time-period when artists were leaving Motown. We left because we had no creative control or creative say-so whatsoever.

AGENT 00 SOUL

Edwin Starr

Ric-Tic 103

So, the amount of hits that I'd had with Golden World, I was never going to be able to duplicate at Motown. I mean, I had four hit records in a row at Golden World, and I barely got out of the box with two or three records *period* at Motown in an eight-year spell. I wasn't on a long-term contract.

From the best of my knowledge, Motown only rode out the contract that I had with Golden World when they bought the company. I don't know how long the upper end of the contract would have extended because I was lucky enough to get out of the contract by forfeiting a great deal of money. My choice was between being signed with them and having nothing to happen as far as my career was concerned, or to be able to leave the company without any rows, arguments or upheavals, and I chose the latter.

I don't really know whether Motown, because of its size, opened the door for black artists, even though the music was aimed at middle class whites. I wasn't there at the early stages to know whether they were responsible or not. From what I can gather, although they were publicly the first black company, there were companies other than Tamla that were doing as much, if not more, for black artists. There was Brunswick, King, Roulette and Atlantic. Atlantic was probably the forerunner for non-exploitative development of black artists.

My relationship with Berry Gordy, the Motown boss, was never more than a passing one. I wasn't in the first echelon of artists, so consequently I didn't go to no garden parties. *[laughs]*

The nostalgia thing doesn't bother me as I don't think of myself as an 'oldie but goodie', and I won't allow anybody to put me in that niche.

There are a lot of artists that I like, but no-one in particular. I'm still of the old school and like the old artists with their values of *entertaining* an audience as opposed to trying to razzle-dazzle them with lights and gadgets.

I have many good friends in the business: Chuck Jackson, James Brown, Demis Roussos, the Supremes, Michael Jackson and other members of the Jackson 5. I know and have met a lot of people, and have been lucky that I've got a great deal of respect from the likes of Bruce Springsteen and others.

My own favourite recording is *Stop Her On Sight (SOS)*, and if I could have recorded any song at all it would have to be Jackie Wilson's *Whispers (Gettin' Louder)*.

There are all kinds of things — highs and lows — that happen in a person's career, but you don't dwell on those. Your highest points are the ones that you haven't achieved yet.

My funniest recollection is of falling off a stage at a major London concert. I was backing up, bowing to the audience and fell off the back of the stage! Most of the funny things that have happened to me are related to a performance. One time I was counting — I used to count with my foot like 'one, two, three' — and my foot went through the floor!

23

POETRY IN MOTION
Johnny Tillotson

Johnny Tillotson spanned rock, pop and country with consummate ease, the light vocals and punchy arrangements on his records appealing to both kids and parents. Between 1958 and 1965, he clocked up no fewer than twenty-six US hits including *It Keeps Right On A-Hurtin'*, **Talk Back** *Trembling Lips* **and** *Poetry In Motion* **— the 1960 worldwide smash that secured his international touring passport for a lifetime.**

I was born Johnny Tillotson on April 20, 1938 in Jacksonville, Florida. My parents' names were Jack and Doris Tillotson and I have two brothers, Danny and Tom. I kept my name because my dad had a petrol station and I figured that if we sold a lot of records in Jacksonville, then we'd probably sell some gasoline, too.

My childhood was great and I graduated from the University of Florida with a BSc degree in Journalism and Communication, which I enjoyed. I was sent to Palatka, Florida to take care of my grandmother when her husband passed away. I was the oldest child in the family and they asked me to go down there. This was very helpful as it was a small town and both she and my mother encouraged my singing. My mother always wanted to be a singer and a dancer and my father used to sing at certain charities, so they thought it was nice that I had this natural interest in it.

My earliest musical influences were Hank Williams, Johnnie Ray and Elvis Presley. I played a little bit of guitar — meaning that I know about four chords — and I've written most of my songs around those four chords. I try to write very simply with words that people can relate to, and a song — musically — that people can retain in their memory. That's why I have been successful with *It Keeps Right On A-Hurtin'*. I just received an award for the song being played over one million times on the radio. That was a big honour for me, and it has been recorded by 112 other artists. *Without You* is another one I wrote; also *Dreamy Eyes* and *Princess, Princess*.

Sometimes, I would write songs for other people and wind up doing them myself because the other artist had something that they had written or they had already recorded. My producer at Cadence Records, Archie Bleyer, would say: 'Since you wrote it, you sing it really well — so why don't *you* do it?'

When I was a little boy, I used to listen to Hank Williams on the *Grand Ole Opry* radio show. My mother took me to see Eddy Arnold and, as a small boy, I looked up at him and bought some records and pictures which he signed.

I said: 'Mr. Arnold, I want to be just like you,' and he reached down, kind-of patted me on the head, and said: 'That's very nice m'boy. I want to wish you the very best, Johnny.' He had a real easy Southern accent — 'This is Eddy Arnold' — and I just thought it was great. He took time to write my name when he signed his autograph.

Elvis Presley was another person who was very nice to his fans and exceptionally nice to me. No matter how often I saw him, if I brought friends or family in he would always take a lot of time with them. Elvis would always sign his name and always sign it to the person who asked, and I think that's very important.

My first public performance happened when my dad was being installed as an officer at the Lions Club and wanted to know if I would go over there and sing. I was so short I had to stand up on a chair to sing! I liked it and haven't stopped.

There was no direct church music influence, but I like gospel music and the Lord is really my rock, so to speak. You need that, especially in this kind of business, keeping you level and taking away some of the stress. Also, when my daughter was killed nineteen months ago — that's a lot to carry. The various religious leaders were helpful to me, my wife and to her brother. I think that I am religious in a very balanced way.

A ukelele was the first instrument I played and I don't know where that came from. I played that, then graduated up to the guitar — from four to six strings, but still the same old four chords!

There was a local radio show called *The Young Folks' Revue* — Herb Young was the piano-player. It was for free and it was on the radio every Saturday. I used to walk down to the radio station, do it, and walk back on Main Street, and everybody would say that they'd heard me that morning. That increased my confidence.

There was a television show in Jacksonville and, of course, I didn't have a car, but I would get on a Greyhound bus and go up to Jacksonville to appear on the Toby Dowdy television show. After that went off the air, I wanted to get my own show at about seventeen or so. The TV company told me that I could have a show if I got a sponsor. I still didn't have a car, but I got a milk company to sponsor me and got my show.

During this time, I wrote *Dreamy Eyes* and *Well, I'm Your Man* and entered the Pet Milk talent contests. Although I didn't win, I brought some of my songs along and Lee Rosenberg took them to Archie Bleyer who happened to be in town recording the Everly Brothers. He heard the tape, took it back to New York, contacted us, and we signed a one-year contract with Cadence Records. They liked what they heard and we just went from there.

When I went to Archie Bleyer, he told me: 'If you believe in my ability, I have a small label, I will send you a ticket the minute you get your diploma.' He sent me a ticket, picked me up at the airport, and I lived at his home as a family member with his wife and daughter because I don't think that I had $50 to my name. Why Archie Bleyer? I just thought that he was the right man. He knew songs and was the most ethical man that I ever met. He knew a hit song and you never went into the studio unless you had a hit song. If you got two songs recorded that was a big deal, and you never had anything in the can.

My first recording was *Dreamy Eyes [1959]* and that was also my first US hit. I loved that song. I was doing an outdoor concert and there was a girl in the front row who had the most beautiful big brown eyes. We had to leave immediately after the concert and the next morning I wrote the song in about ten minutes. This was long before I got on Cadence Records or anything like that. It was just something that I felt, so I wrote *Dreamy Eyes* about this young lady in the front row.

I always liked Roy Orbison's work and I wrote *Without You* in 1962 on a Sunday. The person I was going with had to say goodbye on that day. It was a sad day and I wrote that pretty quick too, except I couldn't come up with anything for the middle. I had the verses, but I didn't have the bridge. So when Archie asked me what I'd written lately, I showed him this and told him that it wasn't finished. He told me to show him what I had in the chorus. I told him that that I didn't have anything except 'dum-dum-dum-dum maybe tomorrow' — a talking thing like Elvis might have done. Actually, the Fleetwoods had something similar in *Come Softly To Me* — 'ooby-doo-dum-dum' — and I guess some of that was in my mind. He told me that he liked the sound of it and that it was very different. Archie said that I wasn't to write a tune for it, but I would speak it and the vocal group would go 'dum-dum-dum-dum'. That's how we did it, and I got my first songwriting award for that song!

Poetry In Motion had been heard by Archie Bleyer, and he called me in to listen to it and told me that he thought we should do it. We cut it first in New York, and it didn't quite have the right feel: it was too stiff-sounding. Archie told me that he thought I performed better in Nashville, so we re-cut it in Nashville with Boots Randolph, who worked on all the Presley things. We did it at ten o'clock in the morning and we kind-of felt that we had it there. Our opinion was that it had universal appeal because the subject matter was about ladies and the charm and grace ladies possess.

Archie was a perfectionist, so we didn't stop and start. Boots and I were talking about this the other day. We did twenty-three takes on this. He would just keep going until he got it. Inevitably, when he said: 'That's it!' the artist will say: 'I can do one better!' You don't do one better, because you're *trying* now, whereas he's captured the *feeling*. So, I always listened to him from that point on. Whenever he said: 'That's it, you've got it', then that was it.

I knew that *Poetry In Motion* was timeless when I heard it. It was not only No. 1 in America and England, but also Thailand, Indonesia, Malaysia, Singapore and South America, so we work all those places. I think that ladies knew that I was singing about them. And you know it's a true song — it's not some prefabricated thing.

The two guys who wrote it, Mike Anthony and Paul Kaufman, couldn't write anything one day. They took a break and looked out of the window of

Billboard, May 1962

their writing studio which was right next to a girls school. So they said: 'Well, we haven't done anything else today, why don't we just relax and watch the girls?' The girls were enthusiastic — it was after school and they were heading home and moving around. The writers said: 'Gee, youth is so exciting, it's just poetry in motion. Why don't we write about what we are looking at?' And that's how it happened.

I do remember when they said that they were going to try and release *Poetry In Motion* in England, and I thought 'Wow!'. I can also remember when they told me it was in the Top Twenty there, and I said: 'I can't believe it!' I was so euphoric that at last I had a song that finally broke through. We had been praying and hoping for a Top Ten record, and finally when *Poetry In Motion* went to No. 1, we were going crazy. But it was such an exciting time that I cannot pinpoint a day in my mind when they said: 'Hey, it's gone to No.1!'

When *Poetry In Motion* went to No. 1 in the UK — England was the first country out of the States where we had a major hit record — I thought that was pretty exciting. Since I am of English descent, it also made me very proud. However, I wasn't sure how they'd accept someone from another country, so I was really pleased when it went to No. 1. Of course, that song made it possible for me to tour the UK in 1963 with my good friend Del Shannon. We were friends before then, and we were friends all during his life. That tour was good fun. You had Kenny Lynch and the Springfields. Dusty, who was just talking about going out on her own, was my bus riding-partner.

For the follow up, Archie hadn't found a hit and decided on re-releasing *Dreamy Eyes*, which he still believed in. That went in to the Top Thirty in the

US, as people then knew me through *Poetry*.

I let Archie run my recording career and I was constantly bringing him songs. However, if he didn't feel the songs himself, then there was no way that you went into the studio. He was the producer; he owned the company; he mixed the records; he distributed them. So it was all him, and I trusted him completely. At that time, he had an 89% success rate for hit records with people like the Everly Brothers and Andy Williams. He had a lot of experience and always taught me that it was the song, the song. If we didn't have a hit song then we didn't have a hit record.

Send Me The Pillow That You Dream On charted in 1962 when I was in the army. I was in the army reserves for six months and based at Fort Jackson, North Carolina. We had done this album on Saturdays and Sundays and completed it in two weekends. Archie called me and said: 'Pick your favourite country songs, call me, tell me what they are and give me the keys.' So I gave him sixteen songs. We kept talking on the phone and he said: 'Now, how does this sound for twelve titles?' *Send Me The Pillow That You Dream On* was one of the twelve songs.

Archie had an ability to arrange them so that I, as an artist, could be myself, but he would frame them in a way that I would perform them a little bit differently, without even knowing that I was doing it. He just put in little subtle things. In *It Keeps Right On A-Hurtin'*, he put those little breaks in — it wasn't written that way. So I definitely trusted him musically all the way. My own favourite song from my own work would have to be *It Keeps Right On A-Hurtin'*.

When I came out of the service I had all these hit records and the only change was my crew-cut. As soon as I got out I was at Palisades Park performing, so there was total continuity.

At Cadence I was treated fairly for royalties, etc. They were an honest company, but Archie decided to sell the record company and the masters when the Beatles came out, as he wanted to do other things. We have most of our early hits on Ace Records in the UK, which has been great to us. In Singapore it's Warner Brothers, so we've got good representation.

I stayed with Cadence from 1959 through to 1966. Then I went to M-G-M Records with a production deal of my own and I picked a song called *Talk Back Trembling Lips* which did about 900,000. There was a guarantee with that contract. We made the money back for them right on the first song and the first album, so M-G-M was *very* happy. With M-G-M we did *She Understands Me, Worried Guy, I Rise, I Fall* and *Gidget*, from the television series starring Sally Field.

My manager during this period *[1961–76]* was Mel Shayne — who died at a very young age — and Jim Wagner has been my manager for the past fourteen years.

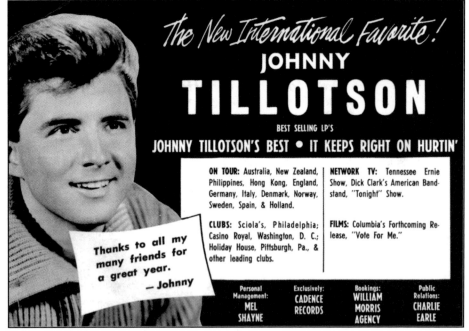

Billboard 1963 Who's Who In The World Of Music

The last thing we did was two years ago *[1991]* on Atlantic Records called *Bim Bam Boo,* and it was country rock. Country music is the hottest music in America, and there are short playlists of thirty songs on each list, and maybe they'll add one song per week. The places where it got played it made Top Ten and sometimes even No.1 and 2, but we weren't able to follow quickly into a major market like New York or Dallas. It's like television series in America: they only give them a short run and if they don't happen, then that's it.

After the mid-Sixties, I just kept on working right to Las Vegas, Tahoe and Reno. We did the Copacabana and fair dates just as we do now. I'm lucky to have hits all over the world and get the chance to do different kinds of venues: clubs, fairs, rock and roll shows, country shows and television shows. It never gets boring, it never gets old.

Yes, I did a lot of Dick Clark tours. He was my next-door neighbour about seven houses away and we had *a lot* of fun. We headlined numerous tours for Dick with Gene Pitney and the Supremes. Being one of a number of different acts didn't bother me. I already possessed the discipline of delivering my act to a tight time on my television show.

Those tours taught me how to relate to an audience by being courteous and taking your time with them because they are very kind to you. You owe them your very best.

If you're really honest and open yourself up to an audience they will relate to you no matter what. You should never be afraid of an audience as you have something to give them. When each artist comes out onto the stage, it's up to them to be themselves and sing and perform the best they can. If they do a good job, people will respond accordingly.

I have lots of high spots in my career. This tour is one, and we've been blessed with so many of them. We don't think of these tours as nostalgia tours in the States. We just love to work when people love our songs, whether they are people who bought the songs originally or whether it's their children who hear them on *Dirty Dancing* or commercials. The nice thing is that you get to work with people you've known all your life and not having to quit at twenty-eight or something.

I never get frustrated or have any conflict about singing my hits every night. Hits are a big deal and I'm proud of them — so, if you get a hit you're lucky, and I thank people for giving them to me. I try to make the songs fresh as if I'm doing them for the first time. Also, I try to colour them. By that I mean putting a lot of feeling into a song — without overdoing it — and trying to paint a picture with it.

My wife, Nancy, is very helpful because she is very honest with me. If some night I do it really well she tells me, and if there's one night when I miss it ever so slightly she mentions that too. I think that's good because you need someone with you who tells you the truth.

When we get to do a regular show — like in Thailand we do an hour and fifteen minutes — or even on a tour like this one, we do other songs so that there is a show there. The only difference would be if we had more time to do more hits.

Recording was simpler in the days of Cadence because it was live and you had all these musicians around. You'd walk into a studio and basically the same people who worked with Elvis — he was always the artist I admired the most — were working with you. You thought of it as a great team. You thought that if you had a hit song and could sing relatively well that day — and your mentor was there with you and he was telling you that you were doing this good — then you could feel pretty secure.

But the exciting part was hearing the song come together immediately, almost like a live performance, and getting the pay-off right there. The other day I was talking to Don Williams and Mickey Newbury about the same thing. In one night, you would go in, record it, mix it and leave the studios with the hit under your arm, and you knew that you had it. You weren't doing it in pieces and waiting to put it all together. I don't have any problem with the way it's done now, it's just that it was quicker and a different way earlier.

Looking back, there are probably a lot of things that I'd do differently, but I can't think of one. *[laughs]*

Breaking Big On All The National Charts!

JOHNNY TILLOTSON

Talk Back Trembling Lips

MGM K-13181

his first MGM record!
his biggest single smash!

Billboard, November 1963

24

SINCERELY YOURS
Bobby Vee

Bobby Vee may have got his big chance as a result of his idol Buddy Holly's death, but this one-time pop pin-up had the talent, tenacity and acumen to survive in the music business for over forty years. A constant chart presence from 1959 until 1970, he racked up a massive thirty-eight US hits including such classics as *Rubber Ball*, *Take Good Care Of My Baby*, *Run To Him* and *The Night Has A Thousand Eyes*. A greatly respected work-till-you-drop performer, Bobby still headlines shows throughout the world, often touring with his sons' group, the Vees.

I was born Robert Thomas Velline on April 30, 1943 in Fargo, North Dakota. My earliest musical influences would be the country acts of Hank Williams and Ernie Tubb, then popular singers like Johnnie Ray and Frankie Laine. There was always a lot of music in the house and my father, a chef, played violin and piano, and mother sang, but not professionally. I had an uncle who did play professionally.

My brother Bill, Jim Stillman, Bob Korum and I formed a group called the Shadows while I was at Central High School in Fargo. We played the popular music of the time: Eddie Cochran, Gene Vincent, Ronnie Hawkins, Everly Brothers, Elvis Presley and Carl Perkins — all those early rockers — plus instrumentals.

Without a doubt my biggest influence was Buddy Holly. He was *so* popular when he died and he was huge in my home town. I was a big fan and had all of his records. To this day I still believe that he was one of the most authentic rockers and, of course, that is why the legend has developed around him because his music was so original. In my opinion, Buddy Holly never made a bad record — even the ones he didn't intend to release. The early Elvis Presley Sun records are wonderful, as are the Carl Perkins recordings — they are just so well done. The whole Sun catalogue is incredible.

My first amateur performance is hard to remember as I got into this business so quickly. I just backed into it — one of those crazy things. We used to go to the college and rehearse, and would end up doing dances in Moorhead, Minnesota — so there weren't too many amateur shows, just lots of practising in our houses. I've been singing since I was six years old, and I started playing guitar at an early age helped by my older brother, so we were always doing music. My mother and father were supportive. Like any parents, they were happy to see me involved in something that kept me off the streets.

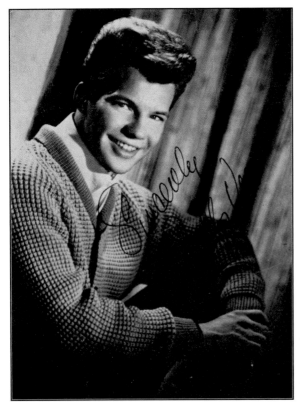

It's crazy, but our real break was simply due to a deejay on our local KFGO radio station asking for a group to come forward and fill in on the *Winter Dance Party* one-nighter due to visit Moorhead on February 3, 1959. This request was made due to the death of Buddy Holly, Big Bopper and Ritchie Valens in the early hours of that same day. We answered the call, got ourselves matching outfits, and sang *Bye Bye Love* and *Long Tall Sally*.

I agree that it seems odd that the show should still go ahead, but I didn't think about it that night. When you're fifteen years old you don't ask those kind of questions. It never even occurred to me. In the years since then, however, I have asked that question several times of myself. How can you put on a rock and roll show when the three main stars are dead? It was a bizarre thing to do. Obviously, there was money involved, but I honestly think that nobody knew what to do. What do you do — cancel the show? I don't know, it just happened.

There was a guy in the audience that night called Bing Bingstrom who filmed the show. Backstage, we were told by somebody that he was the local booking agent and so we contacted him sometime after that about getting us some bookings. In fact, he did start booking us and kind-of directed our career for the first year.

In June 1959, we paid $500 for our own recording session at the Soma Records studios in Minneapolis. We cut *Suzie Baby*, which I had written, plus an instrumental called *Flyin' High*. *Suzie Baby* became a regional hit in the three-state area in which it was released. It went to No. 1 in Minneapolis and then record companies started to contact us wanting to buy the master for national release.

During the summer of the same year, we experimented with amplifying the group's sound and tried out a piano player calling himself 'Elston Gunnn' — yes, three n's, he had his own way of spelling — who was visiting Fargo. He played a couple of live dates with us, but his style of playing didn't fit in with the group, so he left with a payment of $30. The pianist was Bob Zimmerman who later became Bob Dylan!

Somebody advised us that Liberty Records was a young company and that they only had a few acts like Eddie Cochran, Julie London and the Chipmunks. Plus, Snuff Garrett — who had been a friend of Buddy Holly's —

contacted us and told us that *Suzie Baby* sounded like a Buddy Holly record. Joining Liberty just seemed like a natural thing to do. *Suzie Baby* came out under 'Bobby Vee & The Shadows', but Liberty signed the Shadows and myself under separate contracts. That was the beginning of the split. I am sure that their intent was not to do anything with the Shadows, but just to develop me.

The band stayed with me for three more years and we worked together until 1963. It was very covert the way the whole thing happened. Not so much on my part, I don't think, because I always wanted them to record and it seemed fair to me that they were signed to a separate contract, and that Liberty was going to develop them as a separate group. Unfortunately, the reality was that Liberty wasn't very interested in doing that. After I signed a separate contract, we brought in another singer into the Shadows who sang when I wasn't onstage, and he was very good. Then, the other extreme was that they weren't really interested in another instrumental band because by then they had the Ventures.

My name was changed to 'Vee' by the guy who was managing me. He thought that my legal name of Velline was just too complicated, and at that time it was Brenda Lee, Peggy Lee, and all that stuff. I didn't like the name change at all, and it took me a long time to get used to it. To this day, I have never legally changed it.

When Liberty took us on they bought the master of *Suzie Baby* and released it nationally, which gave us a Top 100 hit. My first solo recording with Liberty and Snuffy Garrett was a cover of the Adam Faith recording of *What Do You Want?* — wasn't *that* something! That was the first session that I did for Liberty Records. I flew out to California and split the session with Johnny Burnette. My next record was *One Last Kiss*. During 1960, I had my first big hit in the States with *Devil Or Angel*.

We were still a local band working around Minneapolis when *Devil Or Angel* went into the US charts. When it was presented to me I had never heard the song before. It had been an American R&B hit in the mid-Fifties for the Clovers and was a favourite of my producer, Snuffy Garrett. Although I didn't particularly care for the song, I gave Snuffy's choice the benefit of the doubt and did it. *Devil Or Angel* was my fourth record and my first Top Ten hit.

It was amazing when the thing started climbing up the charts, it was just so *solid.* It was getting airplay and it stayed in the charts *forever.* I remember working a club in Minneapolis at the time. Really, I was too young to be working there as I think that I was only seventeen and the legal minimum age was twenty-one. However, I just sneaked in. That week, the song was No. 1 in Minneapolis. That was really the launching-pad for my entire career. After that first major hit record then it became much easier.

In between *Devil Or Angel* and my follow-up, *Rubber Ball* — which was

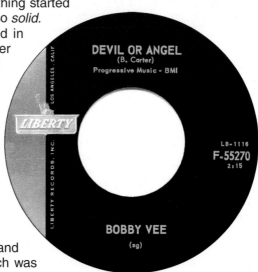

231

written by Gene Pitney — there was a lot of recording and a lot of looking for songs. I think that *Rubber Ball* was originally written for Jimmy Jones, who did *Handy Man,* and I'm not really sure how we ended up with it. It's kind-of a *Catch 22* situation: if you *don't* have a hit you can't get any songs, and once you have a hit *everybody* sends you their songs. We were flooded with all kinds of material.

I think that the toughest thing is that second hit song. That's why we were so excited by *Rubber Ball* because it was so completely different to *Devil Or Angel*. In America, *Devil Or Angel* was such a huge hit for me and it was on the charts for something like twenty weeks. This gave us time to experiment with a few other things. *Rubber Ball* was probably the most important record of my career because it did go into the Top Ten again. Incidentally, *Rubber Ball* was the first hit I had in England.

My third hit record, *Stayin' In*, wasn't such a big hit in America. However, the flip-side, *More Than I Can Say*, was a big follow-up hit to *Rubber Ball* in Britain, and that's when I started coming over here.

The UK was interesting back in the early Sixties because there were so few radio shows that played pop music and there were so few television shows. If you were lucky enough to get on *Thank Your Lucky Stars* or *Top Of The Pops*, everybody in the entire country heard you and saw you. It was amazing the coverage that you could get, and I was very fortunate to be a product of that time-period.

Regarding my clean 'boy-next-door' image — no, it wasn't any more 'packaged' than anything else around that time. We didn't sit down and have brainstorming sessions about what the market place was looking for. I don't think anyone is so smart as to know exactly what the public wants. You do what you need to do and the public will discover you. You don't discover your audience, your audience discovers you. It would be easier for me to look back and give you all kinds of baloney about how we planned it, but we didn't. My success has been due to the songs that I recorded.

Primarily, Snuffy would get songs, but I would also find them and we would bring them in, record them and put out what we wanted to put out. We didn't employ any market researches for our record releases. It was like the Wild West: we just shot from the hip, and it was great. Although Snuffy, as producer, always had the final say in what was being released, nobody else had any influence. So, he wasn't talking with merchandisers or considering demographics and all that baloney.

Take Good Care Of My Baby was presented to me on an album session when I was doing a Carole King song called *How Many Tears*. She flew out to California to be at the session and presented me with *Take Good Care Of My Baby* and also another song that she had written with Gerry Goffin called *In My Baby's Eyes*. They both just sounded like great songs and later Snuffy apparently had her write the ad-lib introduction to *Take Good Care Of My Baby* which became a significant part of the arrangement. I don't remember any of this, but that's the way he tells the story.

My hit songs by Goffin & King were probably songs that would normally have gone the rounds that *didn't* go the rounds. After *How Many Tears* — which was the first Carole King song that I recorded — we pretty much had the pick of their material for the next year and a half, and there were a lot of good songs in that time period like *Take Good Care Of My Baby*, *Walkin' With My Angel* and *Sharing You.*

In actual fact, there weren't that many songs that were tailor-made for me. I recorded a song called *Bobby Tomorrow* that was written for me, as was *A Letter From Betty*. Although it wasn't put out right away, Dion did the original version of *Take Good Care Of My Baby*. *Run To Him* was written for the Everly Brothers and I just happened to get it. Snuffy used to go out and audition the material and he'd come back with folders full of demos. The material was all up for grabs — you had publishers coming in to present songs to whoever would listen to them.

The *I Remember Buddy Holly* album wasn't commercially motivated; it was something that I'd always wanted to do. As I mentioned earlier, Snuffy had been a friend of Buddy Holly and there was very little deciding about that album as we both felt the same way. As a matter of fact, it was different here in England than it was in America. In America, once an artist was deceased, they no longer played his records. The attention that Buddy Holly got in the UK after he died was therefore a real surprise to Americans. So, if we had considered the album from a commercial point of view it would never have been done, because there was just no commercial value to it in America. It was just a project that we did out of love, as was the *Bobby Vee Meets The Crickets* album. The Holly album of 1963 was very successful in Great Britain and it was reissued a couple of years back. The *Bobby Vee Meets The Crickets* album made in 1962 was also popular and is reissued around the world — including Japan — from time to time. However, neither one of them was successful in America.

People have often criticized the early Sixties music as being sandwiched in between the rocking Fifties and the 'English Invasion', but I think that a lot of great songs came out of the early Sixties — some *wonderful* records — most of which were done live in the studio. I like pop music — no matter how I do a song it always comes up sounding like pop — but I'm really very eclectic in musical tastes and like classical music as well.

I tend to gravitate towards earthy kinds of music. That's why I like Buddy Holly stuff and the early Elvis material. I like Bob Dylan and the Band, and I *love* Dire Straits *[laughs]* — 'That ain't workin', that's the way to do it' — classic stuff! At the same time I think that Elton John is amazing, and Paul McCartney — that whole Beatle thing is crazy. In America, Billy Joel is an amazing talent and keeps cranking out the hits.

Talking of artists who I liked, but never made it big, look at Cliff Richard. He is so successful in Great Britain and the rest of the world, yet in America he has never achieved the same level of fame. I can't give you an explanation for that, as a record sounds just as good in America as it sounds in England, but he hasn't had the attention that he might have had. It is those kind of things that happen. Why does a record like *A Forever Kind Of Love*, which I recorded in England with Norrie Paramor in 1962, get into the UK Top Twenty but isn't even released in America? That is marketing and business which has got in the way there somehow, and those kinds of things happen all the time.

When Cliff Richard toured the States with his group, the Shadows, in a package tour headlined by Frankie Avalon early in 1960, we went to see him as our group had the same name. I didn't even know who he was until he hit the States, but he was brilliant and his performance was very well received. I really admire Cliff Richard for doing gospel and pop shows and living his life the way that he wants to live it.

I would like to have recorded *Summertime Blues* in the Fifties and Rick Nelson's *Believe What You Say*, which I think is a great record. I love all Del Shannon's records. We're good friends, I'm always rootin' for him and he is always rootin' for me. I did record *Bo Diddley* on an album, but certainly not in the same style as Bo, as everything I ever did comes out real 'pop and country with a little rock and roll'.

I'm not a great singer, but see myself as a stylist. I have a style of delivering a song, and I learn songs and put them through my machinery. Bob Dylan has a style, Buddy Holly had a style. Certainly, I don't have a voice like Elvis Presley or Cliff Richard, but I *do* have a style of delivering a song without strain.

Billboard, November 1961

When it comes to interpreting and performing their songs, songwriters are the hardest people in the world to please. After I cut *The Night Has A Thousand Eyes*, Ben Weisman, who wrote a lot of songs for Elvis Presley and was one of this song's writers, came up to me and said: 'Cat, you know you sang a wrong word in this song. It sounds good, but I'm afraid it's going to kill the song because you sang a word that doesn't rhyme.' And you know, it was true. In the third verse I sang a wrong word and nobody caught it until after the session, but Ben caught it of course because he wrote the song. They have an idea in their heads about how things should sound. The best thing to do when you're recording is not to let the songwriter in! Sometimes they've spent months working on a piece of material. I might get the song and learn it in a day — I've done that. I've learned a song in an hour and gone in and recorded it — it's just the way it is.

With the song *Come Back When You Grow Up*, I got a call from my producer at the studio who wanted me to record the song. I told him that I would come down and listen to it, and if I liked it then we would record it. Well, I liked the song, learned it in about an hour, and then we went into the studio for another hour to record it and that was it. We didn't spend months, weeks or hours labouring over it. I can carry out a quick study on a song, listen to it a couple of times and learn it.

All of music — not just that of American artists — was affected by the Beatles and English music, and the industry has never been the same. I don't mean that in the negative sense as I think it was very positive thing. The only negative aspect for me was that I was doing music that was no longer as popular as the current thing, but realistically I had a very good run through those first three years. As a fan of music, I was very excited about the new English music and in 1964 I did an album, *Bobby Vee Sings The New Sound From England*. I got raked over the coals for that, but it was a sincere project and I have no regrets about it.

In 1967, I had a hit in the States with *Come Back When You Grow Up* which reached No. 3 in the charts. That song was my most successful in terms of record sales, as I think that record sales in the late Sixties were better than they were in the early Sixties. After that, until December 1970, I had seven records that went into the US national charts: *Beautiful People*, *Maybe Just Today*, the *My Girl/Hey Girl* medley, *Do What You Gotta Do*, *I'm Into Lookin' For Someone To Love Me*, *Let's Call It A Day Girl* and *Sweet Sweetheart*.

At the end of the Sixties, I was working but had become disenchanted. I had gotten to a point in my career when I wasn't really enjoying what I was doing or the kind of places that I was working. I was questioning my own musical values and even thinking about packing it all in. At that point, I was working big hotels and in Sydney, Australia I was working in huge hotels with big bands and arrangements, but that is not rock and roll and I *hated* it.

My idea of rock and roll is not to hear *Take Good Care Of My Baby* with three trumpets, five saxes, trombones and that whole thing, because that isn't what the record is all about. The record is about a rhythm section, some background vocals, some orchestra, and it's pop music. So, from that point on, I kind-of just packed it in from a performance standpoint. I went back into the studio and recorded an album under my real name of Robert Thomas Velline, and called it *Nothin' Like A Sunny Day*.

It wasn't a protest; it was a very positive and very personal album which helped me to get things in a better perspective. Even though it may have been a self-centred thing, it allowed me to get in touch with liking music again. As a result, I passed through that stage, moved back into the Bobby Vee thing and learned how to integrate my old songs with the reality of my life, my family and my career.

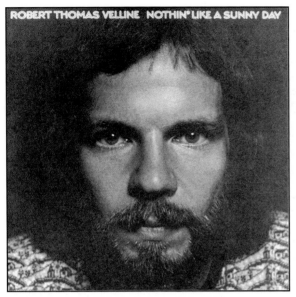

ROBERT THOMAS VELLINE   NOTHIN' LIKE A SUNNY DAY

The toughest time to get work was really during the late Sixties and early Seventies when the sentiment in America had changed over the Vietnam War. All the kinds of things I had done up to that point were considered part of the establishment and it was an anti-establishment time-period. I absolutely feel that, if there was ever a low point of acceptance for Fifties and Sixties rock and roll then it was during that time. I still went out and toured, visiting England to do some nightclubs and that sort of thing. The dates that we are doing now are really like the old days — we're playing theatres and doing thirty-night tours.

Yes, I tried to change my image in the early Seventies. I think that anyone with any sensitivities did. It was a very difficult time in America and that whole Vietnam thing hadn't yet been sorted out, so we had a whole lot of emotional chaos going on. However, for me, it was a time of enrichment as I was able to look at my career and my own writing and creativity. I put out what I thought was some very good product in the early Seventies — like *Nothin' Like A Sunny Day*. It didn't sell, that's all.

Even at that time I never got depressed. I'm not the type to get into heavy sulks or those kind of moods. I've always been able to work, although I miss recording as I've spent so many years doing it. Next year *[1989]* will be my 30th anniversary as an entertainer, so I'm working on an album to bring out.

As I've said, *Nothin' Like A Sunny Day* was something I needed to do and was part of that time, but I've made amends with that. I say 'amends' because I went through a period with an identity thing when I wanted to be called Robert Thomas Velline. I didn't take the fact that *Nothin' Like A Sunny Day* didn't sell as the second rejection of my music. We got great reviews on the album, and the fact that it didn't sell didn't make me think less of it. The tendency is to say: 'Well, it has sold, it's No. 1 — that means that it's good.' That's not necessarily the case. There's a lot of great product which never gets any attention at all, but that doesn't lessen it.

What I realized after I did that album is that being in the record business is a team effort, and if the team is disjointed you have problems. The record company was also going through a bad patch: it was a transitional time for them too, and they weren't really geared up. They fell down on the promotion and distribution of the product. There's a lot more to the industry than meets the eye.

After that album came out, it was a high point for me in the sense that I had done something that I had wanted to do. It didn't need a commercial success as I felt that it had been a success artistically.

The title *Nothin' Like A Sunny Day* may sound a bitter title, but it wasn't meant to be. Actually, it's a line in one of the songs, called *Hayes*. He was an old grandfather-type of guy who lived down the block from me in Fargo. He'd walk by my house every day and go fishing. When I got to an age where I could leave the house on my own with my rod and reel, that's when I discovered where he was going. He was going down to fish by the river, and I'd go down and fish with him. He was a very nice old man and it seemed to me that all that mattered to him was that the sun was shining so that he didn't get rained on while he was fishing. I met his daughter by chance last year when I was playing Iowa. This woman came up to me, introduced herself, and said that her father used to live in Fargo. We got talking, and he was the guy! I sent her a copy of that record and it knocked her out to think that someone had written a song about her father.

Yes, it was a real weird thing putting out a record under my real name as I never really stopped being Bobby Vee. If I had to do it over again, I wouldn't put the album out under 'Robert Thomas Velline'. That aspect of the name was something that we really gave a lot of thought to, and we were on the fence with it. It almost appeared as if I wanted to deny a part of who I was, and that really wasn't what I wanted to do. The material was so different from the kinds of things that I had been putting out that we thought maybe by just using my real name on it people could be objective about listening to it.

I don't really have a personal favourite among my own records. I was just so excited about all the material that we were doing. Over the years, I have never really got tired of singing *The Night Has A Thousand Eyes*, but although I loved the novelty of *Rubber Ball* when I first heard it, I *have* gotten tired of singing it at times. You say that I made it sound fresh tonight — well that's good. It's like acting in a sense: first of all you have to enjoy the role. It's finding a way to make them live, and I think that is what actors do — they find ways to make their parts live so that they can do them night after night and keep it fresh. So, I guess that is what we all have to do.

In reconciling myself to doing the same songs over and over again, I have gone through a lot of different changes with them. From initially when the songs were hits, and it was a lot of fun to sing them, to the late Sixties and early Seventies when there was very little acceptance for Fifties and Sixties rock and roll. At this point in my life, they are good friends of mine. They are like members of the family and it's fun to be able to come back and share them, and the memories, with the people.

If ever I get to a point where I really get desperately tired of singing something, I just stop singing it for a while. When that happens it's only for a

night or two, then I'll bring it back in again. The bottom line is that I *do* enjoy my songs. They are good, very well-constructed songs by great and talented writers like Carole King, Gerry Goffin and Ben Weisman. I'm fortunate in that respect that I don't have to go out and sing *Alley-Oop* or something like that.

When I got into this business, I was so shy I could hardly talk to people. In fact, in the first band that we had I never did any mike work at all: the bass player used to do all the announcing of our songs. Over the years, it has been like a mental therapy for me to be able to stand up in front of an audience and communicate with them. There is a joy in performing that goes beyond any particular song that you might be singing. Yes *[laughs]*, I make the audience *pay* for me singing *Rubber Ball*: if I have to sing it, then *they* have to sing it along with me!

I learn from every performance that I do and I have a way that I love to perform. It's like you when you write your book: you'll put it down when you feel like you're done with it. If someone makes you put it down before you're done, then you're not going to feel comfortable because it doesn't require any more effort to do it right. It might require a couple more pages, but that's only paper. For me, it might require another song, but it's only *one* more song —only two and a half more minutes. So I need a certain amount of time to do what I do, and that's my pressure on package shows like this one.

I don't like to just go out and sing songs — it's a living thing to communicate with people in the audience. You are dealing with people, their emotions, and all sorts of images that they bring in with them. I like to be able to communicate with people when I'm out there. The venue doesn't matter. All I need is time — and I need more than twenty minutes to do what I do. It's crazy, years ago it was *hard* to do an hour's show: now, it's hard *not* to do an hour! In being true to the music, I don't want to go out and do a bunch of medleys — I don't want to do half a show. When I sit out in the audience and listen to Del Shannon, Gene Pitney or Neil Sedaka, I want to hear the *whole* song.

You've got to get to know your audience and not just exchange a song for hand-claps. I'm really not very good in front of a group of people, but I'm better on a one-on-one. Therefore, I have to think of the audience as one person so I can create a rapport with them. I've had some audiences that look like paintings out there.

Another thing that I've learned in performing is that you can't jam things down people's throats. We all have different rhythms going through us and you have to be respectful of that. If an audience is laid-back, then you work with that mood or they may just shut off completely. So, you have to meet people where they're at and you can go from there — and that's true of an audience, too. Sometimes I never know what I'm going to do. I may go down into the audience, or might run up the aisle or do whatever I want to do. If there is someone sitting out there who strikes a chord or something, I'll take it from there. That is really the fun of performing and communicating — being present to what is going on. For me, it's no good simply giving them what they've come to hear and performing by rote.

No, I never consider that I work an audience or get them going by involving them in a singalong. *Rubber Ball* is a fun piece of material and it's easy to have people get involved with that during the show. On this tour, people have joined in the refrain of *More Than I Can Say* without any coaxing. Listening to an audience and responding to them is what performing is all about. I've got an hour's-worth of songs that I can stand up there and sing — in fact, I can do *two* hours'-worth of material with my band, who have been with me for six and a half years. So, I can sing songs all night, and I can talk to them, and I think that is how we tell people who we are.

The precision and discipline which struck you about the *Rock'n'Blues Reunion* show *[1985]* was down to the fact that everyone has passed through their problem times. Del doesn't drink, Bo doesn't drink — I like to have a couple of beers at the end of the night, but no-one really gets carried away with it because you can't do that.

As long as nostalgia is taken in the right context, I think that it's fine — these are *fun* shows. Again, you don't want to eat the same meal forever. I can go out and have fun with these shows if they are well presented and the artists are presented with the proper attitude, and the band is good. I know that I'm biased because they're my band, but the Ricochettes are a great band. When I'm on, they're giving it their best shot for me, and when Del's on they're giving it their best shot for him, and that's what I like.

The only compromise to artists doing any modern material on the *Rock'n'Blues Reunion* show was with Rick Nelson, and I agree that it was ironic that he should be singing *Garden Party* — a protest about nostalgia package shows — out there: '*A simple twist of fate*' as Bob Dylan would say. Rick really came full circle on that tour and made amends with his past. That night, he was really representing who he was. I hope to do more new material also, but I would never stop doing my old songs as they are part of who I am.

Long tours are tiring and I don't do very many. This is the curse of the business: the tour. In America, I go out and do three or four days at a time and then go home. It's the travelling that's tiring, not the actual working.

Those early US package shows were terrible and probably the toughest shows that we had to do. A typical day would be just riding all day on the bus; getting to the hotel; cleaning up; going to do the show; going back to the hotel and getting up the next day! On one of the Dick Clark *Caravan Of Stars* tours, we travelled every other night on the bus. You got to a point where you never really knew where you were. You just showed up when they told you to be there. One of the good things that came from those tours was that as it was a very young business — we were all in our late teens and early twenties — and many lasting friendships were formed. I did a lot of tours with Brian Hyland, Del Shannon and people like that.

The package tours were good promotionally, although the money was on a much smaller scale than it is today. It was important to be on a Dick Clark package because his television show was so important in America. If you had a hit record and did an appearance on his TV show, that could mean up to 250,000 record sales and that is nothing to turn your back on. Alan Freed always seemed to have his fingers in the pie, but I never had a sense of Dick Clark using his show as bribery or anything like that. Dick was straight-ahead in his dealings and still is. He is a multi-multi-millionaire and probably the greatest advocate of that time-period. He's done it honestly, and he has had such a wonderful platform in *American Bandstand* to do it from.

I was on a Dick Clark tour when Kennedy was killed. We had arrived in Dallas, Texas about eleven o'clock in the morning, having been awake on the bus all night. Brian Hyland was with me and said that he was going to see Kennedy — I didn't even know he was in town. I was already in bed at that point — about 11:15–11:30 am — and I said: 'Well, take my camera and get a picture of him when he comes down the parade.' He did take the camera and he did take a picture, but he forgot to take the lens cap off! Believe it or not, the promoter that night wanted to go on with the show, but we didn't. Of course, we couldn't leave Dallas for a couple of days as they closed the town to look for the killer.

Yes, most of the time I did get paid, but you don't have to in this

business. You have contracts, but contracts can mean nothing. You can book anybody you want, sign the contract, bring them in, do the show and then *not* pay them — so what are they going to do? They might *kill* you, but if you escape with your life you *still* don't have to pay them! Thankfully that didn't happen often.

In the early days, I was lucky with my management as I had a very honest guy who was really a professional manager. He managed some television people, a comedian and a writer, and all of a sudden he became my manager for nine years. Then it got to a point where I really needed to take it over on my own, and that was fine. We're still good friends.

I have really enjoyed the different career phases that I have gone through — from the early years of recording through the Sixties and the Seventies. I have always been a very private person and I've enjoyed that. I like being able to walk down the street and not be recognized. It's phenomenal to me that we can come over to work, pull in the crowds and do well. People say good things about our shows and we get to come over and do it again, yet I can still walk down the street and nobody knows who I am. I don't mind the 'attention from the fans' thing, and I do appreciate fans who buy my songs dropping back after a show to say 'hello' and have me sign their records — that is wonderful. However, most artists get to the point where, although they appreciate and respect it, they don't need adulation, and it's not what gets my motor running.

You raised the point about the ups and downs of careers and artists seeking religion. This is such an egocentric business and that works to our advantage, I think, at some point in our career when we are young. But also, it is our best friend and our worst enemy. It can kill — and has killed — many people in our business and in all kinds of businesses. The common denominator in a lot of people's lives is religion, as it allows you to find a greater power — I've always believed that.

I *am* a religious man and I have just produced a children's Christian album called *Take Out Your Crayons* which is really nice. We've just issued it on our regional label out of Minneapolis and it looks like we're going to be able to sell it to a bigger label. They are great reflective songs — not songs about Jesus or God *per se*, but they talk of feelings and self-esteem and feeling good about ourselves. The album was made with my own family: in other words, 'walking the walk rather than just talking the talk'.

Family is the most important thing in my life. I met my wife, Karen, when we were both about sixteen and she lived in a town about fifty miles away from me. It was my first summer playing with the band and I was introduced to her by a mutual friend. We started dating and got married on December 28, 1963. Karen and I have three sons and a daughter. My wife is probably my best mentor. She has vision that I don't have and we complement each other in that way.

We live a very normal life in a country town of 60,000 people outside of Minneapolis. When I'm home, it's the Velline family, and when I'm working it's Bobby Vee. It isn't rock and roll twenty-four hours a day. Our big family activity is skiing, and we've spent our Christmas holidays doing that in Germany and Austria. Other than that, most of the things that I do revolve around music — like producing. My three boys are playing now and they have taken the small winter quarter off of college as they decided to work, so I'm doing some producing with them. I wouldn't discourage my children from going into the business. I don't think that you should have that sort of power to direct their lives. We would encourage them to do what they need to do and to develop the necessary skills, and that is what we have stood by in our parental duties.

Looking to the future, I will continue to perform as Bobby Vee as I've already got the history to do that. As I think I've mentioned, I would love to make more records and will do so, but the cold reality is that if I never come out with another new record I can always go out and sing my old hits. From a creative standpoint that isn't very satisfying, and I still want to create. Today, I also get involved in the promotional side. I don't think that you can be involved in the business completely and not pay attention to what is happening on the promotional front.

I am sure that I would have done lots of things differently, but I won't ever get that opportunity so it doesn't matter. Had I not gone into showbusiness, I don't know what I would have done. Apart from this business, the only other job I ever had was delivering a paper in Fargo — and I knew that I didn't want to make a career out of *that*!

The Interviews

1   Gary 'U.S.' Bonds
17 November 1986, City Hall, Newcastle-Upon-Tyne.

2   Pat Boone
By correspondence, 1992.

3   Freddy Cannon
4 November 2000, Empire Theatre, Sunderland.

4   Crickets: Jerry Allison
16 September 1988, County Hotel, Carlisle.
18 September 1988, Empire Theatre, Sunderland.

Crickets: Sonny Curtis
11 June 1987, Ambassador Hotel, South Shields.

Crickets: Joe B. Mauldin
18 September 1988, Empire Theatre, Sunderland.

5   Bo Diddley
8 November 1985, Holiday Inn, Newcastle-Upon-Tyne.

6   Dion
By correspondence, 1990.

7   Fats Domino
17 March 1986, Royal Albert Hall, London.

8   Duane Eddy
17 April 1990, City Hall, Newcastle-Upon-Tyne.

9   Frankie Ford
16 July 1988, New Crown Hotel, South Shields.

10   Charlie Gracie
By telephone, 1981.

11   Brian Hyland
17 October 1987, Beamish Park Hotel, Beamish, County Durham.

12   Marv Johnson
8 October 1988, Empire Theatre, Sunderland.

13 Ben E. King
26 April 1985, Post House Hotel, Washington, Tyne & Wear.

14 Brenda Lee
16 March 1993, Empire Theatre, Sunderland.

15 Little Eva
30 October 1998, Empire Theatre, Sunderland.

16 Chris Montez
8 March 1989, Empire Theatre, Sunderland.
30 October 1998, Empire Theatre, Sunderland.

17 Johnny Moore
1 December 1988, Beamish Park Hotel, Beamish, County Durham.

18 Gene Pitney
By telephone, 1985.

19 Johnny Preston
30 October 1998, Empire Theatre, Sunderland.

20 Tommy Roe
2 April 1992, Empire Theatre, Sunderland.

21 Del Shannon
27 September 1986, Lumley Castle, County Durham.

22 Edwin Starr
30 September 1989, City Hall, Newcastle-Upon-Tyne.

23 Johnny Tillotson
16 March 1993, Empire Theatre, Sunderland.

24 Bobby Vee
8 November 1985, City Hall, Newcastle-Upon-Tyne.
16 September 1988, Sands Centre, Carlisle.
18 September 1988, Empire Theatre, Sunderland.

Index

ILLUSTRATIONS AND PHOTO CREDITS

Ads on pages 14, 16, 33, 35, 37, 39, 40, 81-83, 113, 128, 139, 142, 164, 166, 173, 176, 200, 205, 218, 224, 226 and 235 courtesy of *Billboard*/George R. White; ads on pages 22, 73, 108, 114, 125, 129, 152, 158, 168, 195, 197, 206, 207, 227 and 238 courtesy of *Billboard*/Tony Wilkinson; ads on pages 41 and 59 courtesy of *New Musical Express*/Terry Kay; ad on page 44 courtesy of *Cash Box*/Alan Clark; ads on pages 48 and 183 courtesy of *Billboard*/Alan Clark; ad on page 47 courtesy of Alan Clark; ad on page 63 courtesy of Showtime Archives (Toronto); ads on pages 93 and 99 courtesy of *Billboard*/Showtime Archives (Toronto); ad on page 103 courtesy of *Billboard*/Alan Mann.

Back cover illustrations from author's collection.

Book cover on page 21 from author's collection (courtesy of Prentice-Hall Inc. © 1958).

Front cover illustrations from author's collection and courtesy of Steve Armitage, Terry Kay and George R. White.

EP sleeve shots on pages 26 and 29 from author's collection; EP sleeve shot on page 95 courtesy of Victor Pearlin; EP sleeve shots on pages 182 and 198 courtesy of Terry Kay.

Label shots on pages 15, 45, 70, 107, 123, 144, 185 and 204 courtesy of Paul Sandford; labels shots on pages 24, 32, 34, 157 and 194 courtesy of Tony Wilkinson; label shots on pages 65, 150, 167, 225 and 231 courtesy of George R. White; label shot on page 86 courtesy of Arthur J. Moir/Duane Eddy Circle; label shot on page 92 courtesy of Victor Pearlin; label shot on page 112 courtesy of Peter Grendysa; label shot on page 135 courtesy of Keith Tillman.

LP sleeve shots on pages 17, 219 and 237 courtesy of George R. White; LP sleeve shot on page 94 courtesy of Tony Wilkinson.

Photographs on pages 3, 12, 18, 30, 42, 50, 56, 60, 77, 78, 80, 84, 90, 100, 104, 110, 116, 148, 154, 180, 190, 202, 214, 220 and 228 by Dave Nicolson © 2002; photographs on pages 15, 115, 130, 153 and 232 courtesy of *Melody Maker*/Bill Millar); photographs on pages 20, 87 and 210 from author's collection (courtesy of London Records); photograph on page 27 courtesy of Dot Records/George R. White; photograph on page 53 courtesy of Viva Records/Tony Wilkinson; photographs on pages 58, 106, 134, 136 and 213 courtesy of Terry Kay; photograph on page 66 by George R. White (© George R. White); photograph on page 68 from author's collection (courtesy of Arista Records); photograph on page 71 courtesy of Trevor Cajiao/*Now Dig This*; photographs on pages 72, 76, 146, 184, 216 and 222 courtesy of Bill Millar; photographs on pages 75, 89, 119 and 193 courtesy of George R. White; photograph on page 97 courtesy of Ace Records/Steve Armitage; photographs on pages 98 and 140 by Brian Smith (© Brian Smith); photograph on page 102 from author's collection; photograph on page 113 courtesy of United Artists Records/Bill Millar; photograph on page 120 courtesy of Marv Goldberg; photograph on page 122 from author's collection (courtesy of Atco Records); photograph on page 132 courtesy of Brenda Lee; photograph on page 138 courtesy of Decca Records/George R. White; photograph on page 156 by James J. Kriegsmann (courtesy of George R. White); photograph on page 159 courtesy of Bell Records/Bill Millar; photograph on page 160 courtesy of Gene Pitney; photographs on pages 170, 208 and 241 courtesy of ABC-TV/Terry Kay; photograph on page 179 courtesy of Musicor Records/Tony Wilkinson; photograph on page 188 from author's collection (courtesy of Mercury Records); photograph on page 218 by Steve Richards (© Steve Richards); photograph on page 230 from author's collection (courtesy of Liberty Records).

Poster on page 64 courtesy of *Rhythm & Blues*/George R. White; poster on page 151 courtesy of Terry Kay.

Programmes on back cover from author's collection.

Sheet music covers on pages 25, 57, 107, 199 and 209 from author's collection; sheet music cover on page 137 courtesy of Terry Kay; sheet music cover on page 143 courtesy of George R. White.

OTHER TITLES FROM MUSIC MENTOR BOOKS

The Complete Bo Diddley Sessions
George R. White
ISBN 0-9519888-0-8 *(paperback, 92 pages)* **1993**

Complete US/UK discography of this legendary American guitarist by the man who knows him best — his biographer. Includes band history, session details, list of all US/UK releases from 1955 to 1992, selected foreign rarities, BBC radio recordings, film and video performances, guest appearances on other artists' sessions, label shots, vintage ads, etc.

(35 Years of) British Hit EPs
George R. White
ISBN 0-9519888-1-6 *(paperback, 256 pages)* **2001**

At last, a chart book dedicated to British hit EPs! Includes a history of the format, an artist-by-artist listing of every 7-inch EP hit from 1955 to 1989 (with full track details for each record), analyses of chart performance, and — for the first time ever — the official UK EP charts reproduced in their entirety. Profusely illustrated with *over 600* sleeve shots. A collector's dream!

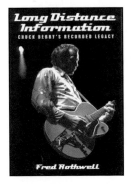

Long Distance Information: Chuck Berry's Recorded Legacy
Fred Rothwell
ISBN 0-9519888-2-4 *(paperback, 352 pages)* **2001**

Detailed analysis of every recording Chuck Berry has ever made. Includes an overview of his life and career, his influences, the stories behind his most famous compositions, full session details, listings of all his key US/UK vinyl and CD releases (including track details), TV and film appearances, and much, much more. Over 100 illustrations including label shots, vintage ads and previously unpublished photos.

Elvis & Buddy — Linked Lives
Alan Mann
ISBN 0-9519888-5-9 *(paperback, 160 pages)* **2002**

The achievements of Elvis Presley and Buddy Holly have been extensively documented, but until now little if anything has been known about the many ways in which their lives were interconnected. For the first time anywhere, rock & roll expert Alan Mann, author of *The A–Z Of Buddy Holly*, takes a detailed look at each artist's early years, comparing their backgrounds and influences, chronicling all their meetings and examining the many amazing parallels in their lives, careers and tragic deaths. Over 50 illustrations including many rare/previously unpublished.

**Music Mentor books
are available from all good bookshops
or by mail order from:**

Music Mentor Books
69 Station Road
Upper Poppleton
YORK YO26 6PZ
England

Telephone/Fax: 01904 330308
International Telephone/Fax: +44 1904 330308
email: music.mentor@lineone.net
website: http://musicmentor0.tripod.com